BREAKING THE GRASS CEILING
A Woman's Guide to Golf for Business

Cheryl A. Leonhardt

© 1998 Triumph Books, Inc. All rights reserved.

No part of this publication may be reproduced, stored in a retrieval system, or transmitted, in any form by any means, electronic, mechanical, photocopying, or otherwise, without the prior written permission of the publisher, Triumph Books, 644 South Clark Street, Chicago, Illinois 60605.

Printed in the United States of America.

Library of Congress Cataloging-in-Publication Data

Leonhardt, Cheryl A.
    Breaking the Grass Ceiling : A Woman's Guide to Golf for Business / Cheryl Leonhardt.
        p.   cm.
        ISBN 1-57243-276-4 (pbk)
        1. Golf for Women.   2. Businesswomen—Recreation I. Title.
GV966.L46   1998
796.352'082—dc21   98-4466
                                                                   CIP

This book is available in quantity at special discounts for your group or organization. For more information, contact:

Triumph Books
644 South Clark Street
Chicago, IL 60605
(312) 939-3330   Fax (312) 663-3557

Book design by Sue Knopf.
Cover design by Salvatore Concialdi.

ISBN 1-57243-276-4

The text appearing on pages 107-109 and 112 is reprinted with the permission of Simon & Schuster from *The Unplayable Lie* by Marcia Chambers. Copyright © 1995 by Marcia Chambers.

*This book is dedicated
to all the women
who are standing on the first tee,
trying to keep the butterflies down,
as they tee it up for the first time
with a colleague or client.*

Welcome to the Club!

Contents

Preface vii

Acknowledgements ix

Introduction 1
Why Golf?:
It's the Best Business Tool in Your Briefcase

Chapter 1 15
Getting Started:
Selecting an Instructor, Buying Equipment,
and Dressing for Success

Chapter 2 31
Rules and Etiquette:
Act Like a Pro Even If You're a Novice

Chapter 3 57
The Handicap:
Golf Is an Equal Opportunity Sport

Chapter 4 65
Games Within the Game:
From Friendly Wagers to Outing Formats

Chapter 5 73
Plugging into the Business Golf Network:
Identifying Clients Who Play and Hosting a Round

Chapter 6 87
Charity Outings:
Springboards for Your Success

Chapter 7 95
Mentoring:
Helping Other Women to Use Golf as a Business Tool

Chapter 8 101
Presenting Yourself for Membership in a Private Club:
What You Should Know Before You Apply

Chapter 9 115
Exercises for the Body and Stretches for the Mind:
There's More to Your Game Than You Think

Appendix I 127
Recommended Courses:
Where to Play for Business and Leisure

Appendix II 147
Golf Courses and Resorts:
Out-of-Town Destinations to Fit Every Budget
and Ability Level

    United States 152

    Bermuda and the Caribbean 186

    Canada 190

    Mexico 195

Appendix III 197
Golf Schools:
Choosing a Program That's Right for You

Appendix IV 211
Golf On-Line:
Web Sites to Visit for Course Information,
Shopping, Playing Tips, Discounts, and Conversation

Appendix V 217
Golf Groups and Organizations:
Getting Involved with Other Women Golfers in Your Area

Glossary 267
Golf Terms and Definitions:
How to Walk the Walk and Talk the Talk

Bibliography 281

Main Index 283

Golf Courses and Resorts 292

Preface

When I decided in the early 90s to take a sabbatical from the daily commute into Boston, I turned my full attention to golf while I was trying to decide what I wanted to do about my so-called midlife crisis. I went to golf camp, took lessons, practiced, and played several times a week. Clearly, I was hooked.

As the holiday season approached, my sister-in-law, Mary Leonhardt, gave me a subscription to *Golf for Women* magazine. In addition to offering terrific advice about the mechanics of the game, *Golf for Women* also showed me that career-minded women all across the country were faced with the same issues: finding good instructors, making time to play, meeting other executive women who play, and wanting to gain confidence to host clients at the course. So while I was considering my next career move, I decided to put my association management skills to work and created a local businesswomen's golf association. In the early spring of 1993, the Business and Professional Women's Golf Association was launched with a dinner meeting at my golf club featuring a prominent local businesswoman as our guest speaker.

It didn't take long for the BPWGA to grow to several hundred members. I provided them with four evening leagues, golf clinics with my PGA friend, Susan Bond, who was the Assistant Pro at Wellesley Country Club in Wellesley, Massachusetts, several charity outings, and dozens of networking luncheons and dinner programs each year. What also grew was the list of questions I was getting daily about golf. Members needed instructors, wanted information on what equipment to buy, and asked questions about what to wear. They wanted to learn the rules and they were particularly worried about not playing well with clients and colleagues.

I started making a list of their questions and created a quarterly newsletter called *CONTACT*, which addressed many of their concerns and needs. Still the questions flowed in on a daily basis.

When I told my sister-in-law, Mary, how things were progressing with the association, she shared my amazement at the number of questions the women had about golf. She said I should write a book, from the point of view of a businesswoman who has learned how to use golf as a business tool. Since Mary is an author of four books, I took her comments seriously and began to work on an outline for *Breaking the Grass Ceiling*.

In November of 1996, my longtime family friend, Tom Wallace, asked me if I would consider joining his sales team at Wallace Associates. An avid golfer, Tom was keen on having a female sales executive who could play golf with clients. Having accomplished my goal of helping Boston-area women executives to combine golf and business, it was time for me to move on to another challenge, knowing that they would continue with their leagues and lessons.

I hope that the information, advice, suggestions, and ideas presented here will help to make golf "the game for a lifetime" for you, too.

Cheryl A. Leonhardt
Sudbury, Massachusetts
November, 1997

Acknowledgements

A cast of hundreds should be properly thanked for their help in creating this book. Starting with my sister-in-law, Mary Leonhardt, who urged me to write it. To the women who shared their stories for the book. To my mother, who has said enough "Aves" on my behalf that I probably won't have to check in at the Pearly Gates—I can just head directly to the first tee.

To my boss, friend, and mentor, Tom Wallace, for recognizing that professional women who golf are good for business.

To all the dynamic women I met through the Business and Professional Women's Golf Association, especially Bonnie Rafuse, Gail Ferreira, Ginny Rivenburg, Dorothy Granger, Pat Gangemi, Patti McQuillan, Janice Drake, Sue Macdonald, Joan Tonra, Hallie Quirk, Pam Galgay, Amalie George, Joan Preston, Joan Zilch, Deb Cuzziere, and Marie Brumme: thanks for your friendship and support. Didn't we have fun!

To Susan Bond, outstanding golf teacher and dear friend: thanks for making learning fun and for sharing your boundless enthusiasm for the game.

To my wonderful Woodland Golf Club buddies who patiently listened to countless reports of how the book was or was not going: Leslie McQuillan (my best pal in the world), Gerry Letoile (my Woodland "Godmother"), Janet Fitzgerald, Ellie Zenis (who commanded me to start using fairway woods years ago), Joan Kilcoyne (who makes the coolest earrings from golf tees), Jeannie Murphy, the zaniest, most adventuresome woman I know, Terry "The Rider" Hansberry, and Joan Sawyer.

A very special thank you to Triumph Books Publisher Mitch Rogatz, who saw the potential in the book, and to Laura Moeller, my editor, who has smoothed the rough edges, kept me on schedule, and helped in countless ways. Also thanks to Sarah Burgundy, Chris Smith, Peter Balis, Eric Bogner, and Sunny Byers.

And finally a heartfelt thank you to my husband, Larry, for enduring life with a woman trying to give birth to a book. A lesser man might well have moved back with his mother. Thanks for listening, not listening, being there, not being there, understanding, trying to understand, admitting you may never understand me, laughing with me, making me laugh, and always being the center of my universe. Vous et nul autre.

A big hug and cookies for our golden retrievers, Buckley and Beau, who spent countless afternoons snoozing in my office when they really wanted to be out walking and who occasionally helped me with the big words. Good boys.

Introduction

You Are Not Alone

There are 7.7 million women business owners in the United States today. We account for $1.4 trillion in sales. We employ 35% more people in the United States than the Fortune 500 companies employ worldwide.* Women own 28% of all American companies and are expected to own half of all businesses by the year 2000. We are starting businesses at two to five times the rate of men. It is estimated that 75% of women-owned businesses succeed—an impressive success rate when compared to the 20% success rate for all businesses. There are some fifty million women working for corporate America today. The projection for women entering the work force between now and the year 2000 is 61%.**

If you hold aspirations for a successful career, golf will help you—whether you own your own business, work for a Fortune 500 corporation, or at a small company. Currently, more than five million women play golf; the National Golf Foundation estimates that this number will double by the year 2000. Since the beginning of this decade, we represent nearly 47% of all new golfers and 25% of the current total market. While I realize that not every working woman in America is going to take up golf, I thought you'd like to know that should you decide to, you will not be alone.

Many corporate cultures in America today are golf-oriented. In fact, nearly 90% of all Fortune 500 CEOs play golf. I would venture

---

* U.S. Small Business Administration, August 1995
** LPGA Demographics, August 1995

to say that if the other 10% were pressed, they would admit to having a golf bag somewhere among their possessions! If most of the senior executives from your company play and your company sponsors local or national golf events, you can rest assured that the road to the corner office is over the fairway. Sales incentive trips, executive retreats, conferences and conventions have taken scores of executives (and their spouses) to exclusive golf resorts all around the world. Golf is the operative word in this scenario—not tennis, swimming, shopping, snorkeling, shuffleboard, or bridge. Just golf.

The Importance of Generating Revenue

If you haven't had a chance to read the book *Members of the Club: The Coming of Age of Executive Women*, by Carol R. Goldberg and Dawn-Marie Driscoll, you may want to borrow it from your local library. The stories of senior executive women who were passed up for promotion because they were not "making rain" are particularly poignant. Making rain means that you are bringing in new accounts—generating revenue—for your firm, rather than merely keeping current clients happy. The truth is, you can't make rain at your desk, but you can get soaked by sitting at it too much. If you are generating revenue by playing golf with current and prospective clients, you may rest assured there will be no repercussions when you head for the links on a Wednesday afternoon with a customer in tow.

Women have traditionally been concerned with appearances: "How will it look if I'm out of the office?" But you might ask yourself, how will it look if everyone else is out of the office bringing in new business and taking care of current clients, and you're the only one in your office trying to generate leads and close deals over the phone?

Tom Peters will tell you in his book *The Pursuit of Wow* that if you aren't taking the time to visit your customers personally, then you may not have them very long. He writes that 70% of lost customers hit the road not because of price or quality issues, but because they didn't like the human side of doing business with the provider of the product or service. Loosely translated, we are being told that no matter how good our products are, how quickly we deliver those products to our customers, or how often we call them to "touch base," there is nothing that will replace, or even come near to personalized attention. The golf course is the perfect way to accomplish that goal. For women who own their own businesses, golf is a particularly great vehicle to meet potential clients, as well as entertain current clients. As the CEO of your business, you want to deal directly with the decision-makers in the firms you are trying to acquire or maintain as customers. If your prospective clients play golf, the best way to cultivate a long-term business relationship begins at the first tee.

Golf Opens Doors

If I still haven't convinced you of the power of golf, read on. According to a survey conducted in 1994 by the Hyatt Hotels, executive women who hold a 10-handicap or lower (average score 82) tend to earn 30% more than their male colleagues who hold similar positions.

Imagine yourself walking down a long corridor. At the end of the corridor is a large glass door and all the people you would like to meet and do business with are on the other side. You can see them talking, laughing, and enjoying each other's company. They are introducing themselves to other people and you can sense there's an air of collegiality among them. The sign on the door reads "Welcome Golfers." What side of the door do you want to be on?

Are you left sitting poolside, playing tennis, or going on the spouses' shopping or sight-seeing excursion at your company's golf outing because you don't know how to play—or worse—because you don't think you play well enough? Are you the only female professional left in the office when your male colleagues head off for a day of golf sponsored by an industry-related vendor? If you are not on the golf course, then you are on the outside looking in.

For decades, our male colleagues have been using golf as a business tool. When they are out on the golf course with clients or prospects they are not shirking their office responsibilities. They are selling. They are "making rain" and thus building economic power bases within their companies. Courting prospects or entertaining clients on the golf course is viewed as an extension of their business activities. The social interaction between these people during a round prepares a foundation upon which they build long-term business relationships anchored in trust and mutual admiration. It doesn't matter who hits the longest drive, sinks the toughest putt, or tells the best joke, although those are all admirable skills.

What does matter when you play is whether you know how to accept both victory and defeat graciously, brush off a day of poor play without complaint, or quietly pull a foursome to victory during friendly competition. It definitely matters that you know the rules, observe the etiquette, are familiar with the games within the game, and that you show up dressed properly . . . all of which are covered in this book.

Imagine spending four or five *uninterrupted* hours with someone whose trust and respect you want to earn. To those women who have mastered the art of business golf come not only the desired sales, but more referrals and more introductions. The golf course is the ultimate resource for networking that not only pays off, but pays dividends: the banker knows the lawyer who knows the accountant who knows the CEO who runs the company to which you wish to sell your product or service.

Learning the Hard Way

I have a dear friend at my club who has two daughters. My friend is a superb athlete and enjoys not only golf, but skiing, softball, and tennis. She had always encouraged her daughters to take up golf, but they were not interested and she did not push the issue. Then, when her second daughter graduated from Boston University about two years ago with an outstanding academic record, she was quickly hired by one of the Big 6 accounting firms in Boston. They were so impressed with this young woman that they decided to send her for an MBA, which she would earn while working for the firm.

Introduction

Arriving for her first day on the job and sitting in the orientation room with a few other new hires, one of the partners came in and explained that he was taking a couple of clients out the next day for a round of golf and the other fellow from the firm had to cancel. Would someone from this new group like to play?

Oh, too bad. My friend's daughter did not know how to play golf. But the young man who was sitting next to her certainly did, and the very next day, he was out on the links with a partner and two clients. Assuming that he conducted himself properly, and I hasten to add that he did not have to be a terrific player, all he needed was a knowledge of the etiquette and a handful of good shots, he gained a mentor within the firm—someone who would take an interest in his career. What did my friend's daughter have? A job. She is now learning how to play golf and I'm certain she will develop into a fine player.

Golf Builds Bridges

Have you ever noticed how much easier a first meeting goes when you have something in common? Having a mutual interest deflects the immediate need to talk about ourselves in terms of our company, products, and services. Asking someone what he or she does with leisure time casts everything in the warm light of chatting about things that we enjoy doing when we're not being "captains of industry." Whenever I go to a business meeting, a networking event, or even to dinner with new people, I almost always wear a golf pin. Both men and women see it, ask if I play, and we are immediately magically transported from where we are standing to the first tee of our favorite course. We can discuss golf trips, places we've played, tournaments we've been to, equipment preferences, people we've played with, and hopefully set a date to play together. We have built a bridge between us through our interest in golf. Suddenly, a stranger is no longer a stranger, but a fellow golfer.

Golf Offers a Level Playing Field

Golf is a game that we always play against the course, usually against ourselves, and occasionally, against an opponent. It is a game which requires a high degree of self-knowledge and self-control. Golf is, for example, the only game I know of where an individual player is responsible for penalizing herself for her errors. It is, above all, a game of honor. If you are honest on the golf course, people will trust that you will be honest in your business dealings. If you are calm and patient on the golf course, it is more likely you will be level-headed in demanding business situations. If you are encouraging to others in your foursome, you are more likely to be a dependable leader in the office environment; one who will motivate others and create an esprit de corps. In short, golf reveals many aspects of a person's nature.

Furthermore, golf offers complete equality between the sexes because it is more a game of skill than strength. The course architect takes into account the strength differential between men and women and designs the tees accordingly. In other words, if two women and two men are playing in a foursome and the men hit from the blue tees while the women hit from the red tees, all four balls should land around the same spot on the fairway. This is assuming all four players hit their balls reasonably well and reasonably straight. The game offers an additional "equalizer" with the Handicap System (see Chapter 3).

So right from the start, women have an equal chance of achieving a significant measure of success at this game. There are no 250-pound football players charging at us, no padded hockey players looking to send us into the boards, no pitcher hurling a baseball toward us at ninety-eight miles per hour.

All we have to do to be safe on the golf course is be mindful of errant shots from players on other fairways and tees and to head for shelter in the event of electrical storms.

Intimidation: Your Largest Mental Hurdle

Back in 1994, I was in a pro shop and overheard a woman inquiring about lessons. She was dressed in a tailored suit and had mentioned something about her travel schedule, so I safely assumed she was involved in the business world. When she had finished her dis-

Introduction

cussion with the pro, I approached her to introduce myself and to offer her my business card. I wanted to tell her about my golf association and see if I might be of some help in introducing her to other women who were also starting out with the game. The woman's mouth dropped, she put up her hands in a "stop right there" gesture, and took a step backwards.

"I'm just a beginner," she said, the tension mounting in her voice.

"That's OK," I told her with a smile. "We were all beginners once. Besides, we have lots of beginners in the association. They've joined to meet *other* women who are beginners."

Still the woman refused the card and walked away. She had decided for herself that as a new golfer she wasn't good enough to talk to another woman who played, or to attempt to associate with other business women who played—even though it meant giving up a chance to meet potential customers or to make some new golfing friends. Interestingly enough, a man who was trying out a new club overheard the conversation and said he'd like to give the card to his wife.

Ask yourself a question. If you were new to a company and were invited to a meeting, would you decline the invitation just because you were new? Of course not! You would go to the meeting to meet the people, listen to the discussion, learn as much as you can and hopefully participate enough to contribute.

Having spoken with many professional women about mixing golf and business, the one issue that seems to trouble women most is that they feel they are not good enough to play with men. Let me share a little secret: half of all male golfers don't break 100! Furthermore, only four million of the country's twenty million male golfers have handicaps, with 17 being the average handicap, according to the USGA.

If you have ever seen a new male golfer out on the course, I hope you noticed that he doesn't look much different from a new female golfer. Men whiff, they go into the water, they hit out-of-bounds—just like we do. But there is something about their nature that does not cause them to feel inferior or inadequate. I believe the differ-

9

ences in the way men and women look at golf, at least in my generation, is a function of how we were raised. Even though I began skiing as a toddler, played team sports in high school, and took up golf and tennis as a young adult, there was always the voice of the concerned mother saying, "Don't get hurt, dear. Be careful. Be nice. Don't get dirty. Don't break any bones or knock your teeth out." This, I am quite certain, is the universal mother's voice that many girls are raised hearing.

Boys, on the other hand, have a different experience playing team sports. They learn how it feels to strike out at the plate, get sacked as the star quarterback, endure a hip check into the boards, and have the soccer ball scream into the net behind them. And what is the universal father's voice? "Go ahead, you can do it! Don't worry, it's just a scratch. Take it like a man."

No wonder women have a hard time taking divots, because the very act of digging up a clump of earth as the result of a good swing seems violent and unnatural to many of us. Well, I just want to say that it's OK to take a divot—a great big divot. And it's OK to get wet when it starts to rain, and you're having a grand old time with your pals out on the course, so you decide to finish the game anyway. And it's OK to take the risk of hitting over the water instead of playing around it if you think you can get to the green sooner by doing so. We have learned to take risks in our businesses, now we must learn to take risks in golf.

So if you have a 28-handicap (average score 100), and you invite a prospective client who holds a 10-handicap (average score 82) out for a round, you are hitting just one more shot per hole on average. Maybe you'll hit a second fairway shot, or need an extra putt. Not to worry. You're still very much in the game and I can assure you that your guest won't even notice because he's concentrating on his own game.

Betsy Ann Duval, former Chairman of the Boston area hi-tech advertising firm, Duval Woglom and Brueckner, shared this observation with me over coffee one morning, "Men don't want to play with *other men* who aren't good golfers. So it's not so much that

Introduction

you're a woman on the golf course, it's more a matter of whether you are a woman who can hold her own on the golf course."

She adds that beginning golfers should stay away from the really hard courses. "They just put too much pressure on you to play well, and the added stress will most likely have a negative impact on your game."

Finding a course with a rating and slope (see Chapter 3) that are commensurate with your game, knowing the rules, practicing the etiquette, and being mindful of pace of play are all the tools you need to feel in control and secure with any group.

Your one true goal should be to get out and play as much as you can. Have fun. Be yourself. Laugh, curse under your breath if you wish, but stay with it. Finding people who are fun to play with will make a huge difference on how you feel about your game.

The "Sins of the Father" and Other Unnecessary Baggage

At a networking evening, I was talking with a group of women business owners about golf and was surprised by one woman's response.

"I'll never play," she said through clenched teeth. "My father played and was gone all day on Saturday and Sunday from morning till night."

At first, I just filed it away, thinking it was a single incident. As I spent more time talking to women about golf, I heard this same complaint several more times.

It is possible to play 18 holes in under four hours. Weekend golf takes a little longer, especially on public courses. (If it takes over five hours, the course management isn't sending rangers out to monitor or speed play, they are overbooking the course to make more money, and you just might want to vote with your feet and find another course.) Even with allowing time for post-round chitchat and refreshments, if someone really wanted to be somewhere else after the round, it could easily be done.

It's not that I'm unsympathetic to golf widows, widowers, and golf orphans, but the reality is golf isn't entirely the culprit. Enough said.

11

Make the Time

Another reason women give for not wanting to take up golf is they claim they don't have the time. They just couldn't possibly be away from their offices that long and their weekends are filled with domestic affairs. With nearly three decades of experience in corporate life to reflect on, I think I can say, without hesitation, that while you are at your desk "being visible," there is a man in your office or from your competitor's office who is putting a deal together outside of his office—at a golf course, a basketball game, or even at his son's Little League game or daughter's soccer practice. The point is the most successful people in any given industry are the ones who get out of the office, get involved in community events, take their clients out, and keep an ear to the ground.

Taking up golf should be viewed just as you would look upon maintaining a fitness program. Just as we are told vigorous exercise is best when done three times a week, try to make a commitment to do something for your golf game three times a week. Take a half-hour lesson on Saturday, go to the driving range for half an hour on Tuesday, and play in an evening league on Thursday.

I asked Cathy Von Klemperer, who holds a Ph.D. in Human Movement from Boston University and owns MOVE, a personal fitness training company in Chestnut Hill, Massachusetts, about how we can learn to make time for ourselves and the activities we want to pursue. An accomplished athlete herself, she has coached Olympic athletes as well as people who are discovering a desire to follow a more active regime, especially as some of us approach midlife. Here is what she shared with me:

"Women's lives seem to have a large 'responsibility umbrella' in that we run businesses, raise children, care for aging parents, volunteer our time for community services, and often look after more of the details of running a home. As a result, we end up feeling as though we have no time 'left over' for ourselves."

Cathy suggests keeping a record book so that we can track what we are doing to pursue our "outside interests" over a long period of time. By keeping a record book of how many times we have

Introduction

practiced, played, or taken a lesson, we begin to see something which we can measure rather quickly.

"Record books," Cathy maintains, "provide a foundation—a proof positive—that we performed certain tasks to accomplish our goals over an extended period of time. Occasionally, we are all going to have a busy week or extended events that interfere with the time we would otherwise be dedicating to golf. It's easy for someone to feel that she has performed poorly or even failed at this point. But when she sits down and reviews her record book, examining what she has done, say over a three-month period, suddenly, a different perspective is gained. Keeping records helps us to build consistency over time."

In one of the newsletters I received from the North Shore Women in Business, an association for businesswomen North of Boston, there was a paragraph sent in by a member which she borrowed from Nancy O'Hara's *A Quiet Corner:*

"Schedule a meeting with yourself. Try to fit YOURSELF into your day. Consider this appointment with yourself as your most critical one, and change it only in a dire emergency. Write it in your datebook. Be careful, though, not to choose the most difficult time for yourself. Setting yourself up to miss this most important appointment will only lead to discouragement and delay. Taking time for yourself is life-affirming. It will teach you that anything is possible if you continue the practice."

In summary, golf is not for women who are not willing to make an investment of both time and money. Equipment, attire, tee times, participating in charity outings, and ongoing lessons can be expensive. The toughest hurdle, though, is getting over the mental roadblocks and telling yourself that you are worth it. You can—in fact, you must—use golf as a business tool if you want to succeed. If you want access to the inner sanctum of American business, golf can be the key to many doors.

Golf's Evolving Policies

The golf industry is rapidly changing to accommodate women golfers, largely by placing more women in executive positions in its leading

BREAKING THE GRASS CEILING

companies. We can expect to see more advances in equipment that better suit our needs and swings. Today's golf attire, designed by women, is more stylish and tailored—less like the "costumes" of previous years.

As each state passes legislation that makes discrimination on the part of private clubs against women and minorities more and more difficult, our opportunities to play and to become more involved with the game will increase.

Even golf course architects are becoming increasingly sensitive to the needs of the woman golfer as more new courses are constructed with up to seven sets of tees, which make the game more user-friendly and speeds play.

Along these same lines, we can expect to see more junior golf camps, for girls and boys, as the golf industry seeks to capitalize on the popularity of so many of the dynamic young players in both the LPGA and the PGA. Smart courses and clubs know that the future success of their establishments rests with the next generation of golfers.

The future of golf for women, I believe, is a bright one, but only if we stay the course and continue to work for equality in what I think is the last great male bastion. Only through working together will we be able to break the grass ceiling.

1

What Constitutes a Good Instructor?

The very first thing a new golfer wants to do is find a qualified instructor. Husbands, boyfriends, brothers, sisters, best friends are all hereby disqualified! The late Harvey Penick summed it up best in his delightful *Little Red Book* when he commented that husbands have done more harm to women in golf than any other entity. For example, no matter where I play, I will inevitably hear a husband telling his wife, at varying decibel levels, "Keep your head down!" Phyllis Diller once quipped that they tell us that so we won't see them laughing at us.

Any golf instructor worth his or her salt will tell you that at address you will want to keep your head still; better yet, keep your *eye* on the ball. From the one piece "take away" that begins the slow back swing, then down through impact and to the follow-through with a nice, balanced finish, your head is going to have to move—not a lot, but some movement will take place.

If it doesn't, I can guarantee that you'll hate the results. It pains me to see a new golfer finishing her swing with her chin on her chest—still "keeping her head down."

Thank goodness Mr. Penick finally told other men to keep their own counsel when it comes to women and golf. Sadly, while we no longer have him to keep us entertained with his musings about the great game, we have the benefit of his writings, which cover some fifty years of incisive observation.

There are as many teaching methods used as there are instructors. How do you find the pro who is right for you? Ask around. See if the people you know who play, and whose opinions you value, can recommend some local pros. If not, call your state golf association, check the yellow pages, or call a few courses to see if they offer instruction. Establish that the people you are calling have PGA or LPGA credentials, meaning they have specialized training to teach golf. Set up appointments to meet with the ones you like (ten or fifteen minutes should suffice) and interview until you find the person who is right for the job. Don't schedule a lesson until you feel you have established a rapport with someone.

Many private clubs allow their pros to instruct non-members. The advantage to taking lessons at a private club is the near certainty that there will be a driving range with real grass (rather than the green plastic mats with white rubber hoses for tees so common at roadside driving ranges), a sand trap for bunker practice, as well as a chipping and putting area.

Some years ago, I attended a weekend golf school at a local course with a good reputation for both play and instruction. An instructor was trying to emphasize the wrist cock I should have at the top of my back swing. He put his hand over mine (I was holding the club at the top of my swing) and bent it back so firmly I thought my wrist was about to break! I also have sport-length fingernails and they bent, too. So while he had credentials, I certainly didn't feel sufficient chemistry to make me want to spend an additional amount of time—or money—with him in the future.

You may want someone who is soft-spoken, someone with a good sense of humor, or someone who will not mind showing a point over and over until you get it down. Good instructors know we are not all natural athletes. When the golf grip, stance, alignment, swing and follow-through are combined, you may end up feeling like a pretzel until you've hung in there long enough that holding and swinging a club begins to feel a bit natural.

Hire someone who will hang in there with you and not make you feel like the world's most hopeless case. Like any other service you buy, it's your money, so make sure you are a satisfied customer. You have a right to ask about your instructor's philosophy: Will you receive written material? Will the rules and etiquette be covered? Can you arrange for a playing lesson when appropriate? All of these little details will determine the kind of relationship you will have with your pro.

The most important thing you need to establish with your pro is trust. If you trust your teacher, then you will relax and absorb the lessons. The second most important thing to establish is a realistic goal. Not too many people go from beginner to a 15-handicap in one season. It takes time—there's a lot to learn. Be patient with yourself and take everything one step at a time.

At the Driving Range

Whether you are at the range to take a lesson or there on your own to practice, here are a few tips to help you use the time at the range to your best advantage.

If you are taking a lesson, arrive about fifteen minutes early so you can get your shoes on, stretch your leg, back, and arm muscles as well as hit a few balls to warm up (see Chapter 9). Lessons usually impart a good deal of mechanical information, so make sure your body is as ready as your mind to absorb the information. Teach yourself to focus just on the lesson and not the traffic jam you got caught in on your way over or what you have to do later that day.

The pro shop sells small and large buckets or "shag bags" of golf balls to use while you practice. Once you have your bag out of the trunk and golf shoes on, pick up your balls and head for a station on the range. (If you are taking a lesson, your pro will provide you with golf balls. Hitting a small bucket before, however, will have you warmed up in time for your lesson.)

Start with a few stretches and gentle practice swings, and then begin with your sand wedge, pitching wedge, or 9-iron. I like to begin with my "short irons" because I am able to take a few short swings to get into the groove and let my muscles warm up. (By a short swing, I mean taking the club back about waist-high and then coming down on the ball with a short follow-through.) After a dozen or so short iron shots, pull out your 5-, 6-, or 7-iron to work on the mid-range targets. Once you are completely warmed up, take out the woods for some full swings until you are ready to hit some shots using your driver.

You will notice several flags out on the range and you should look for signs posted around the range that tell you what the distance is from the driving area to each flag. Generally, the closest flag will be about 100 yards away, the second flag about 150 yards away, and the third flag will represent 200 yards. These are good targets to use while working with the different clubs in your bag and will help you to gauge your distance with each club as well.

If there is a practice putting green nearby, I would urge you to spend some time there, too. Developing pitching skills with a sand wedge, 7-iron for chip shots, and gaining confidence with your putter are the best investments you can make in your game. We use our drivers between fourteen and sixteen times during a round, depending on the number of par-3 holes. Once you consider that a golfer putts at least thirty-six times during a round (two putts per hole), it's not such a bad idea to work on developing some finesse around the greens.

Practice Makes a Difference

I might take a moment here to emphasize the need to practice. If I could insert a subliminal message on every page in this book, it would be to get you to commit to practice regularly. Many women who take up golf drop out because they become frustrated with their lack of progress, saying that "the pros don't teach them anything."

But in fact, they are not making the time to practice or play, and therefore are not building the muscle memory so critical to sound mechanics and eventual improvement. The pro is there to teach you the mechanics, but only you can master them—through practice.

I'm not saying you have to spend hours at the driving range each day—that would just be unrealistic. If you adopt the routine I suggested earlier, which is to do something for your game three times a week, you quickly will be on your way to becoming a proficient golfer. The most important aspect of the game to work on is the short game. You can develop a very good putting stroke by practicing at home on the carpet. Put a quarter down on the rug and try to stop your ball on the quarter from various distances. By the time you get to the course, that 4½–inch hole should look pretty big. I've even gone to the local soccer field and worked on chipping. The best thing you can do for your golf game is to work on developing accuracy from 100 yards in. It's where we give up the most strokes and it's the part of the game most amateurs work on the least.

Here is a good practice routine to try on a day you do not plan to play golf. After your warm-up stretches, work for forty-five minutes with your short irons, then spend forty-five minutes with your woods and irons. Head to the putting green for half an hour, and start with short putts so you can hear the ball go into the hole a few times. If chipping is allowed on the practice green, work on that for about twenty minutes.

Don't be a robot at the practice range, hitting ball after ball with no particular swing thought or target. Practice your set-up routine. Work on alignment. Learn what distance you get from each club. Try gripping down, opening and closing the clubhead to see the changes in the flight of the ball. For added variety, pretend you are playing an actual hole. Begin with a drive to a specific target, then hit a fairway wood or long iron, followed by an approach shot with a short iron. Ask your pro to give you some drills to work on while you're there.

If you follow this routine, combined with instruction and regular play, you'll see improvement very soon.

For the days you plan to play, a forty-minute warm-up routine dividing time between the range and green will loosen you up and have you in top mental shape for a great round. An easy forty-minute warm-up routine to follow is one that begins with a few wedge shots, follows with a few 7-iron shots, then some shots using a 5- or 7-wood, and finishes up with ten to twelve drives. Spend the next fifteen minutes on the practice putting green, sinking a few short putts and then adding distance. Finally, hit a few pitch shots to the green and you're ready to head for the first tee.

Clinic vs. Private Lesson

I have often heard women who sign up for clinics (groups of around ten individuals with one pro) complain that the pro "didn't spend enough time with them during the hour." That's because there is a big difference between a clinic and a private lesson.

The Clinic

The first factor is the price. Clinics are less expensive than private lessons. The second factor is size. Clinics have four to ten students and are ideal for someone who has some skill and needs a few pointers from a pro to put an aspect of her game back on track. Then she has the rest of the time to work on that particular aspect by herself. It is essentially a structured practice session. The pro will verbally explain the mechanics of a shot, and then she will demonstrate the shot to the group. While each student practices the shot, the pro will work her way up and down the line of students, amplifying a point here, making an adjustment there. Each student should expect a total of about ten to fifteen minutes of one-on-one with the pro over the one-hour period of the clinic.

The Private Lesson

A private lesson will be two to three times more expensive because the pro will spend thirty or sixty minutes with you alone. If you are a beginner, I recommend thirty-minute lessons to keep your frustration level in check. If you're an advanced player, consider asking for a one-hour playing lesson.

The woman who commits to taking a thirty-minute one-on-one lesson each week, visits the driving range once (or twice) that same week (it takes twenty to thirty minutes to go through a small bucket of balls) and plays in a 9-hole evening league (allow two to two and a half hours—plus time for post-round networking) will become a proficient golfer more quickly than the woman who takes a lesson, doesn't practice or play, and then shows up the next week for her lesson.

Golf Schools

Going to golf camp or golf school for two or three days or a week can be great fun, especially if you go with a group of friends. Some golf schools are particularly good for people who are completely new to the game and have not been out on a course yet, while other golf schools are more appropriate for intermediate and advanced players who want to lower their handicaps. The ratio is usually one teacher to four or five students, and it's a wonderful way to acquire a large amount of information in a very short period of time. Bring along a small notebook to keep with you during the lessons to jot down tips and ideas, because you will be exposed to a good deal of information each day and it is easy to forget it after a week or so. Being able to refer to notes when you return home will make it easier to recall certain points made during the lessons.

A day of lessons and practice can be exhausting, so make sure you allow time to relax, do some sightseeing, or just take a long, hot soak to ease those newly-found golf muscles.

Don't be surprised if nothing seems to be going quite right in the mechanics department the first time you play after golf school. Your brain is still assimilating all of the good information you were given and hasn't quite delivered the details to your muscles. Be patient. Stay with it and rest assured that it will all click back into place for a better, stronger game once you develop the "muscle memory" after a few practice rounds.

When you return from golf school, try to put into practice what you have learned, but don't give up on your regular lessons with your local pro.

For a list of golf schools around the country, please refer to Appendix III.

Equipment

If you're going to be a serious golfer, you need to have your own equipment. But before you make a purchase, it might be useful for you to know some terminology associated with club construction.

Centuries ago, when the game was in its infancy, clubs were made of wood and had odd names like spoons and mashies. Today, research and technology have given us graphite shafts and titanium clubheads.

In the simplest terms, here is how a club is put together and how it works. A golf club is a long, thin shaft with a rubber or leather *grip* at one end and a clubhead at the other. The clubhead has a *heel*, which is the part that connects to the shaft via the *hosel;* a *clubface*, with a "sweet spot" in the center for striking the ball; a *toe*, which is the outer part of the clubface; and a *sole*, which is the bottom of the clubhead.

Each club we carry has a different shaft length, with the driver being the longest, and a different clubhead angle, because each one performs a different function. Our "woods" have the longest shafts and the largest clubhead sizes because they are designed to send the ball the farthest. Our "irons" get shorter as the number goes up (1 through 9 and wedges). The clubface has more "loft" to lift the ball as the numbers go up as well.

Take your 4-iron in your right hand and your 9-iron in your left. With the clubheads on the ground, look at the difference in the way the clubfaces are tilted. The face of the 4-iron is more vertical in design while the 9-iron is tilted back quite a bit more. It is because of these design differences that your ball will go farther and roll more when struck with a 4-iron, while the 9-iron will loft the ball over a shorter distance with much less roll.

When you are buying your first set of clubs, all you really need are the 3-, 5-, 7-, and 9-irons plus a 3- or a 5-wood, a pitching wedge, a sand wedge, and a putter. Since the goal is to 1) learn to hit the ball, 2) to get the ball into the air, and 3) to develop a swing, these nine basic clubs will keep you busy until you begin to see some changes in your ability. Once you are able to hit the ball a different distance with each club and are looking for more distance or control, it's time to expand your repertoire.

Good equipment is important to the game, but you don't have to buy top-of-the-line when you're starting out. What you do want to avoid, however, is buying equipment at the closest department store and getting the wrong clubs for your particular height, weight, and ability.

Let your pro help you with club advice and selection. He or she can fit you with clubs that will help both your swing and your budget.

Getting Started

Some people trade their clubs in to the pro shop when they upgrade, and you might be able to get a great deal on some used clubs (one or two years old).

Women who are under five feet tall may need to have clubs altered; women who are over six feet tall might need to have something special as well. Today's clubs are designed with more flexible shafts to increase clubhead speed, resulting in longer drives, and with larger clubheads, which offer a larger "sweet spot" for increased distance and accuracy. Your pro will let you try clubs from the pro shop so you can see how different brands perform on the driving range or on the course. Buy with confidence from the pro shop or from a local golf retailer who specializes in golf equipment and attire.

If you are planning to invest in an expensive set of clubs, you should talk to your insurance agent and find out how to "schedule" them on your homeowner's policy for just a few dollars a year. The sales slip will be required, but that's all you need to keep your investment safe in the event of theft, loss, or fire. Naturally, the policy will not help to prevent damage from use (or abuse), but if you have a tendency to take your sticks with you wherever you go, knowing they are covered will make travel just a bit easier.

I know some women who travel a great deal for their businesses and a few of them have come up with the idea of shipping their clubs out to their destination ahead of their arrival. It frees them from having to lift bags in and out of taxis and through airports. If you don't mind taking your clubs with you, a hard cover travel case (available at most pro shops) is sturdy, lightweight, and ensures that your equipment will get there in one piece. I've even tucked dirty laundry into them for the return trip home!

When buying golf shoes, your first priority is that they are comfortable. Just as with clubs, there are dozens of brands on the market today. You may want to invest in two pairs of shoes: a sneaker-style golf shoe which is light, flexible, and inexpensive, and a second pair made of leather and, perhaps, waterproof. Nothing spoils a round faster than shoes that hurt, or wet, cold feet.

No doubt you have been hearing about the soft spikes that are on the market today. You may even be using them. Many clubs agree that soft spikes do less damage to the greens, thus leaving them in better condition. Yet some players do not care for them at all, because they believe soft spikes do not offer the sense of having secure footing, particularly on wet, unlevel surfaces. Still, many private clubs and public courses have embraced soft spikes and require their players to use them. It's a good idea to find out what the individual club policy is with regard to soft spikes before you arrive to play. (One of the soft spikes I like is called "metal lite." There is just a tiny bit of metal protruding from the plastic spike, which results in a comfortable feeling with the sense of added traction.)

We don't buy cars without a test drive or clothing without trying it on. Your golf clubs and shoes need to feel right and fit properly, too. Don't hesitate to ask questions and shop around.

Equipment Maintenance

Once you have decided on clubs, you will want to maintain them properly. It's a good idea to have a club separator in your golf bag. This keeps your clubs from banging into each other during transport in your car or on the golf cart. Most bags come with separators built right in. Put head covers on your metal woods to protect them while not in use. These days, some people are using covers for their irons and putter head as well. I suppose it can't hurt, but it does look a bit unusual to have a "bonnet" on every club in the bag.

Be sure to take your clubs out of the trunk of your car and store them in a safe place. The heat fluctuations in the trunk, especially during hot and humid weather, will do more to ruin your grips than any amount of play. In addition, expensive clubs bouncing around in the trunk do not stay in top condition.

After each round, wipe down your grips with a clean, dry towel. Once a month, scrub your grips with a small brush and mild detergent, then rub some fine sandpaper over them. This will help to remove the sweat and oil left by your hands, as well as dirt and grime, and also keeps the grips tacky, which improves your control over the club.

Buy a club cleaning kit and use a brush with some mild detergent and water to wash away the mud and grass stains from the clubheads. Dry them thoroughly with a soft towel. Finally, have your clubs regripped every year if you are playing twice a week or more during the season. It's a small investment for added control over each shot. Make sure the grip fits the size of your hands—another area where your pro can be helpful.

To keep your shoes in shape, use cedar shoe trees. A regular cleaning and polishing will keep them looking sharp. When your shoes get wet do not dry them on a radiator or in direct sun as that will damage the leather. Just put them somewhere warm and dry and let nature take its course. Be sure to clean your shoes and check your spikes after every round. Replace them when they get worn down. It's an easy job that takes no more than five minutes. Spikes and spike wrenches are sold inexpensively at all golf shops.

Golf Balls

As an example of the number of golf balls on the market, the two golf ball plants at Titleist operate seven days a week to ship roughly 350,000 balls a day. With so many choices available, it's not surprising that many players just grab any sleeve off the shelf, assuming they are all alike. But there are nearly as many differences in ball construction as in manufacturers.

No matter which brand you select, they all have some common characteristics. A golf ball must not weigh more than 1.620 ounces, nor be smaller than 1.680 inches in diameter. Some larger balls, like the Spalding Magna, are manufactured with the goal of making good contact easier.

The beginning golfer would do well to buy the two-piece "distance balls." Constructed with a hard inner core and a durable Surlyn outer shell, they will stand up to being topped, rolled over cart paths, knocked into trees, and whatever other forms of abuse we can and will impose on them. This type of ball will be a bit more forgiving if you do not always hit it well, and also gives a bit more distance—something every player desires.

The *balata,* or three-piece ball, is quite a bit more expensive. Its center is liquid under wound thread and the "balata" skin (a kind of rubber) exterior is softer; offering more "feel" for the better players who can place spin on a ball. They also damage more easily.

Great care is taken throughout the entire golf ball manufacturing process, which is done in large part through robotics. X-ray technology is employed to ensure that the core of the ball has not been affected by any part of the manufacturing process. Defective balls are recycled in the early stages, but defects found in the later stages of production are destroyed.

Once the balls have come off the production line and are painted and stamped, they are sorted for compression, which determines the degree of hardness. Compression corresponds with the clubhead speed a player generates at impact. The lower handicap players most likely play with balls stamped with 100, which means that the clubhead is travelling at about 100 miles per hour when it hits the ball. Most pros play with 100-compression balls, while others prefer 90-compression. Eighty-compression, not available in balata, is popular with many novices, but may seem sluggish to the more advanced player.

Dressing for Success

You may add this to the verity of death and taxes: every golf course or club has a dress code. Be sure you dress like someone getting ready to play golf, and not like someone about to work in the yard. Shirts with collars (jewel necklines are now also considered acceptable for women if they coordinate with shorts or trousers), Bermuda length shorts (short shorts are a no-no) and tailored trousers are all you need to wear to gain immediate respect and recognition as a golfer. I can think of nothing more embarrassing than showing up at a private club as an invited guest of the company president and being turned away because of a failure to meet the dress code.

Over the years, I have found that 100% cotton tops work best in the summer heat and humidity because cotton is a natural fiber and breathes. Cotton wicks perspiration more readily than a

Getting Started

cotton/poly blend, even though the blends wrinkle less. For cooler weather, the blends are fine. Look for shorts and pants with an elastic inset in the waist band. The elastic allows for easier bending to tee up and to pick up balls and ball markers. Make sure shorts and trousers have deep front pockets so you can carry balls, tees, a ball mark repair tool and a ball marker. Shorts with shallow pockets will let your golf balls fall out when you are riding in the cart.

Invest in a good rain suit ($150-400), especially if you are planning to play in charity outings, since most don't cancel in the event of rain unless lightning is involved. A waterproof hat is a good idea, too. Keep these items stored in your bag, especially if you live in an area of the country where weather is unpredictable and changes are sudden. Rain suits make excellent windbreakers on cool, breezy days, as well. Be sure your suit and hat are dry before you stow them away in your bag.

A wind shirt is one item every golfer should have in her bag. Though not entirely waterproof, you'll be glad you have one when the weather turns cool and breezy on what had promised to be a short-sleeve day.

Bob Hope once said he'd give up golf if he didn't have so many sweaters. It seems we golfers have a tendency to collect quite a few, but you will find a sweater an absolute necessity, particularly if you like to get an early morning start. Aside from looking smart, they keep your muscles warm, which may help to prevent an injury while swinging. Be sure you warm up by stretching—especially on cool days—to prevent muscle pulls. Many pros and fitness trainers recommend stretching after you play, too (see Chapter 9).

Hats, visors, and sunglasses are a matter of personal preference: some people can't play with them; others can't play without them. I am of the latter conviction. I will only comment that while visors are stylish and provide shade for your eyes, hats protect your hair from sun and wind damage in addition to providing a bit more protection from the sun for your eyes and skin. Tucking up long hair under a hat will also keep it from blowing in your face and distracting you. Today's open-weave straw hats are fitted with a shade

29

screen just under the brim to protect your face and have a comfortable elasticized band to keep the hat securely on your head on windy days. Sunglasses protect your eyes from the sun's damaging UV rays and the wind, and will prevent dust irritation if you are riding in a golf cart without a windshield—especially if you are following another cart along a dusty path.

It's a good idea to buy a couple of gloves, one for regular play and one to keep in your bag as a backup. A dry glove for the back nine on a drizzly or blistering hot day will be most appreciated. If you are the fastidious type, use a plastic glove shaper to keep your glove fitting properly. If you are a bit more casual, just drop a ball into your glove to help keep its shape. If you live in the cooler climates where late fall and early spring golf means temperatures in the low fifties, a pair of winter golf gloves is a joy. Ask your pro shop. Be sure to replace worn or soiled golf gloves. Your golf glove can tell your pro quite a bit about your grip, too. If your glove is wearing out on the pad of your hand, instead of along your "lifeline," your grip may be incorrect.

Top this all off with a high-level sun screen, some lip balm, and you're ready to hit the links!

What's in Your Bag?
Being prepared isn't just for Boy Scouts

Do you have the following items in your bag or locker?

personalized balls	hand warmers	rain suit
feminine care products	winter golf gloves	aspirin
extra glove(s)	insect repellent	sunglasses
contact lens solution	snacks	extra socks
tees	bee sting salve	visor
ball markers	water bottle	tissues
pencils	band aids	rain hat
cash/coins	business cards	wind shirt
sunscreen	extra cleats	
USGA Rules Book	zippered jewelry pouch	
lip balm	cleat wrench	

2

Like every game, golf has its own set of rules. I must admit that reading the *USGA Official Rules Book*, which is updated every four years, can be a daunting experience. It's hard to imagine that in 1744, the first organized golf society in Scotland followed just thirteen rules. These rules endured for another decade, when they were adopted by the Royal and Ancient Golf Club of St. Andrews in Scotland in 1754.

Today, there are nearly three times as many rules, written in a way that is sometimes difficult to understand for even the most seasoned players, let alone the novice. This chapter will present the key rules so that you can learn them easily. Knowing the rules will enhance your enjoyment of the game, whether you are playing in leagues, amateur tournaments, or just with friends and colleagues. Keep in mind that golf, while lots of fun, is first and foremost a game of honor, and playing and winning by the rules will increase your enjoyment of the game, just as an acquaintance with the etiquette will increase your confidence.

The reason for learning the rules is not to transform you into a nitpicking, rules-reciting curmudgeon, but rather to give you a way to get the most enjoyment out of the game. You probably won't invoke every rule on every outing. I suspect you would not have many golfing companions if you did. Sometimes you will agree to play by different prearranged rules like winter rules, allowing mulligans, gimme putts, and perhaps even forgo stroke and distance to speed play.

For example, suppose a player can't find her ball where she thought it would be or the ball has rolled out of bounds and there is a foursome pushing you from behind on a crowded course. You could bend the rules and allow her to hit another ball from where it was lost rather than make her go back to the original spot. She would still have to add a one-stroke penalty. The rules were bent to speed play.

Although this chapter does not address every detail associated with the rules, it will provide you with enough information to let you decide how best to handle different situations that will inevitably arise as you make your way around the course. Because the rules and etiquette of golf are so closely intertwined, you'll find tips on how to conduct yourself in this section as well.

"I learned the game of golf playing in a league with men who delighted in teaching me the rules, one by one, after I broke them, one by one," said Bonnie Rafuse, who carries a 16-handicap and is president of Quality Journeys, a Massachusetts-based management consulting firm.

"Their delight came from adding the appropriate one or two stroke penalty to my score card. Sometimes I had fun, sometimes I got angry. But I got better and I learned the rules because I wanted to compete!"

While the rules of golf may seem complex and sometimes confusing at first glance, every player has the responsibility to learn them. Only when you have a thorough understanding of the rules and etiquette will you be alert to the many incidents that can occur during the round which, if not properly addressed, may spoil the round for your fellow players and brand you as an inconsiderate golfer.

So let's begin, as they say, at the beginning—on the first tee—and walk through the key rules all the way to the green. Among avid golfers, it is generally accepted that a player will be invited back even if she is not particularly skilled at the game if she knows the rules, practices the etiquette, and moves along. As my golf instructor, Susan Bond, always says, "If you are a polite and considerate person off the golf course, then you will be a polite and considerate person on the course."

Number of Clubs

The first rule to be addressed is the number of clubs you may legally carry in your bag. A player is allowed to carry fourteen clubs. You

Rules and Etiquette

may opt to carry fewer, but you may never carry more. If you are planning to play in any serious outings or tournaments, make sure you do not exceed this number—to do so risks disqualification.

On the Tee

The tee is an area which has been closely mown and leveled. It has colored balls or markers, placed several yards apart. They are usually painted gold, blue, white, red, and sometimes yellow. Traditionally, the gold markers are for championship play among men. The blue and white markers are also for men, with the exception of professional women golfers like my friend Susan Bond and top-ranked amateurs, who play from the white tees. The red or forward tees are largely used by women like you and me, and sometimes by junior golfers. The yellow markers, usually found in a private club or resort setting and located in front of the red tees, are ideal for novices because they cut a long course down to a more manageable size. You still have to deal with the hazards, but at least you won't be dragged around for five or six thousand yards.

While you are waiting for your nod from the starter to come to the first tee with your group, there are some "housekeeping" details that need to be worked out. Make sure introductions are made and decide what format you're playing, such as stroke or match play and decide what, if any, little side bets or "games within the game" you want to include (see Chapter 4). This is also a good time to stroke the score cards (see Chapter 3).

First honor (who will hit first) can be determined by tossing a tee in the air, with the players standing in a circle. The person to whom the tip of the tee points upon landing on the ground hits first. Toss the tee two more times to finish the order. Or you can go off according to handicap, with the highest or lowest handicap hitting first. Whatever the format, get it done before you are "on deck" to tee off and agree to play "ready golf" to keep the pace of play moving smoothly. The player who requires the fewest number of strokes to hole out will have "the honor" of going first on the second hole, and so on throughout your round. If the previous hole has been tied or halved (in match play), the person with the honor on the last hole would still retain the honor on the next hole. Once off the tee, the person who is furthest from the flagstick is the first to hit.

Make sure you carry two golf balls in your pocket. I like to carry tees and balls in my right pocket and my ball marker and repair tool in my left pocket. That way, I never have to fumble around looking for what I need. There are few things that announce your status as a novice more pointedly than fumbling with tissues, lipstick, tees, and whatnot, as you struggle to find a ball marker while the members in your foursome wait to putt.

Another suggestion with regard to golf balls is to use the same brand throughout the round (with one exception, which I will address in a moment). For example, using Pinnacle 3s will leave you one less thing to remember during your round. People who use a hodgepodge of balls forget what they have hit from one tee shot to the next, making it more difficult to identify their ball.

You should be playing from the forward or red tees and you may tee up your ball anywhere between the markers, up to two clublengths behind them, but never in front of them. You may take your stance outside the box, but your ball must be inside the box. You will incur a two stroke penalty in stroke play if you tee up anywhere outside of the box. In match play, you will be asked to re-tee the ball or replay the shot without penalty.

(Helpful hint: I have seen quite a few novices try to put the tee into the ground first and then put the ball on top. Try nesting the ball in your hand, with the cup of the tee under the ball and the shaft of the tee nested between your index and middle finger. Use the ball as a "tool" to insert the tee into the ground.)

Announce the brand of the ball you're playing (Titleist 4, Top Flite Magna 2, etc.) and any special mark you have placed on your ball with a felt tip pen. It could be your initials, a circle, a triangle—anything to distinguish your ball from others on the course. You'll see why as you read further.

I'd like to clear up a common misconception about knocking the ball off the wooden tee while you are standing in the tee box. It does not incur a penalty. The ball is considered in play only when you have taken your stance, grounded your club, and taken a stroke with the intention of hitting the ball.

You may also stop your swing at any point before hitting the ball, step back, collect your thoughts, and start over without penalty. However, if you intended to hit the ball, but swung and missed it (called a whiff), that is indeed a stroke and you must count it. In fact, whiffs occurring anywhere on the course—from tee to green—must be counted.

Just about every golfer has a set-up routine, i.e., an action or a series of actions performed each time before teeing off or hitting from anywhere on the course. Some players stand behind the ball and look down the fairway to select a point midway between where they stand and the target to assist with correct alignment. At address, taking one practice swing is most acceptable, taking three or four is frowned upon, and taking a divot on a practice swing is really in poor taste. Whatever set-up routine you decide on, please do not develop the habit of standing over your ball too long. Golf is not brain surgery—you cannot put off the shot forever!

Divots

If you take a divot during your actual swing, it's OK. In fact, it's quite normal, especially with an iron. Taking a divot means you are getting under the ball. Just be sure to replace the divot if possible. Take a scoop of ground repair material, usually a mixture of grass seed, fertilizer, and dirt located in a bucket with a cover in the tee box area, and spread it over the damaged area. Be sure to replace the cover to keep the mixture dry. Your motorized cart should have a plastic container filled with a seed mixture so you can fill fairway divots. If you are playing in Southern climates, replacing a divot means nothing, because the grass will not reseed itself. In this case, just spread some of the seed mixture provided in your cart.

People who play regularly take this routine seriously because it helps to keep a course in top condition. Further, once your ball has landed in an unrepaired divot, you'll appreciate how important this routine task is when you hear your fairway wood scrape over the concave canyon your ball is stuck in. If your ball rolls into a divot during a round, you cannot take relief. You must play the ball where it lies. This is also called "playing it down," or summer rules. Pros play this way.

Playing Your First Shot

If your tee shot clearly goes "out-of-bounds" (commonly called "OB" and defined by a white line, stakes, or other out-of-bounds markers like fences or a stone wall), the penalty you will incur is called "stroke and distance." Announce that you will play a second ball, step out of the tee box and let the other players tee off. After your fellow players have hit, return to the tee box for your second shot. Be sure to announce the brand of ball you are now playing.

What should you do if you think your first ball might be playable, but you can't see it to be certain? In this case, you will hit what is called a "provisional ball." This is a good time to use a different brand, or at least a different number within the brand, so that if it also slices to the right, you will be able to distinguish it from your first ball. Why? Suppose that when you arrive at the location, you find one ball playable and the other one OB. How will you be able to tell which is your first ball if you have used the same brand and number for both shots?

If your first shot is in fact OB and your second shot is playable, meaning it is in-bounds either on the fairway or in the rough, you will be lying three: one stroke for the first swing, a penalty stroke for going out-of-bounds, and the third stroke that put you back into play. "Stroke and distance" is not, as commonly thought, a two stroke penalty. Don't forget to pick up your "OB" ball (if you can find it quickly) and put it in your pocket. The official rules say you have five minutes to search, but everyone really wishes you would only take two minutes and then move on.

Let's further discuss the term "out-of-bounds" for a moment. To be considered out-of-bounds, your ball has to be completely on the other side of the painted white line or the imaginary line created by the white stakes. A ball that rests with any part of it on the line is considered in-bounds and playable. You may take your stance outside the line in order to hit your ball if it is lying on the line without penalty.

Once you have reached the area you believe your first ball to be in (remember you have no more than five minutes to search for your ball) and you find it "playable," you may pick up your second "provisional" ball—without penalty. However, if you find the first ball and it is out-of-bounds, or you can't find it at all, return to your second ball, where you will lie three, having taken the stroke and distance penalty.

Now you see why it's a good idea to carry an extra ball in your pocket in the event your drive goes out-of-bounds. It lets you get right back into play without having to walk back to your bag, thus saving time. Carrying a second ball also comes in handy on the fairway if you get into trouble with water hazards. The only time you should take a moment to get a different ball is when you are hitting a provisional ball.

Some other things to remember for good tee box etiquette:
1) Don't stand directly behind or forward of someone teeing off. In fact, stay completely out of the player's peripheral vision—preferably so that his or her back is to you.
2) Don't talk, whisper, or move around while someone is setting up to tee off. If you are standing still, be sure not to jiggle the tees in your pocket, a habit very common to male golfers. It is very distracting. Golfers are good sports, by and large, but can be unforgiving when they feel someone has interfered with a shot, particularly if it costs them a stroke or results in a poor hit.
3) Keep an eye on the shots of the people in your foursome. If it looks like it's going in the rough or out-of-bounds, find a tree, bush, rock—whatever—to visually mark the spot where the ball landed. It will help the player find it faster and keep the pace of play moving smoothly. If it looks like it will land too close to players in another fairway or on the next tee, don't hesitate to yell "Fore!"

4) Resist the urge to congratulate someone on a good shot until the ball hits the ground. I've seen hundreds of shots that looked great off the tee, only to be taken by the wind and land short of the target or fade in mid-flight and disappear into the woods.

5) If some of the players in your group are using the white or blue tees, and you are using the red tees, it is a good policy to go to the back tees first. You should never be in front of someone hitting, plus you can help to track the tee shots. Only after they have hit should you go to your tee box. As courteous golfers, they will wait quietly while you set up and should help you to track your drive.

6) Quite often, you may have to wait for the group ahead to move out of your range before you can hit. During this time, many players like to take practice swings. If you are one who enjoys this, please make sure you do so away from the people in your group.

During a charity outing last summer, I played with a woman who stood in front of us to take a practice swing. I explained to her that it was very easy to contact a stone or a clump of dirt and fling it into the faces of innocent bystanders. I have also seen clubheads come off for no apparent reason and go flying into the distance. I am sure she didn't realize how uncomfortable we felt and how dangerous her actions actually were.

Water Hazards

You're on the tee and there is a pond in front of you about 50 yards away. Funny thing about bodies of water—they can act like magnets, pulling our golf balls into their murky depths for no apparent reason! Sure enough, your tee shot lands in the middle of the pond and suffers a soggy death. You cannot hit a provisional ball, because your ball is not out-of-bounds. It is, instead, in a water hazard. Water hazards are defined by the USGA as "any sea, lake, pond, river, ditch, surface drainage ditch or other open water." While they may not always contain water, water hazards are always defined by yellow stakes or a yellow line painted around them. They can be located anywhere from just off the tee

Rules and Etiquette

to right in front of the green. To get your ball back into play, you have three choices:
1) You may play the ball where it lies in the hazard (if it is playable) without penalty. You may not, however, ground your club. To do so will earn you a two stroke penalty.
2) If your ball is unplayable off the tee, proceed to the designated drop area and hit (do not tee up) from there. If your ball goes into the water along the fairway, picture an imaginary line running from the hole to the point where the ball last crossed the margin of the hazard. Drop a ball on the extension of that line, adding a one stroke penalty, and go back as far as necessary to take relief.
3) The third, and least desirable, option is stroke and distance with a one stroke penalty. It is least desirable because you always want to be moving forward.

Dropping a Ball

You've now read the term "drop a ball" several times. Here's how to do it properly: stand straight, face the flagstick, hold your arm out at shoulder height, and drop the ball. If your dropped ball rolls closer to the hole or rolls back into the area from which you seek relief, you must drop it again. If it happens a third time, you may place the ball where it hit the ground before it rolled forward.

More Water Hazard Advice

If your ball went into the grassy or muddy area of the water hazard (defined by yellow stakes or a painted yellow line), and you feel it is playable, you may not ground your club or remove loose impediments made by nature. Doing so will incur a two stroke penalty. You may not pat the grass down behind the ball to clear a path for your swing. You may not declare your ball unplayable in a water hazard. Like everything in golf, there are set guidelines to help you with each situation that arises. Unlike the white "out-of-bounds" markers, where your ball can be on the line and still playable, the rule with regard to both yellow and red hazards is "if it's on the line, it's in the hazard."

41

Lateral Water Hazards

Defined by red stakes or lines, lateral water hazards run along the fairway on either side. The rules governing how you get out of lateral water hazards are the same as for water hazards (yellow stakes or lines), plus two more options. Again, taking a one stroke penalty:
1) You may drop your ball within two club lengths of the point where your ball went in, no closer to the hole.
2) You may drop your ball within two club lengths on the opposite side of the hazard from where your ball went in, no closer to the hole if you feel you can gain a better lie or have an unobstructed shot.

The penalty for not selecting and following one of the five options explained in this chapter is two strokes in stroke play or loss of the hole in match play, so be sure to commit these options to memory.

Bunkers

There is one more hazard we need to cover as we make our way down the fairway, and that's the "bunker," also referred to as a "trap" or "sand trap." In the bunker, you may remove paper, bottle caps, cigarette butts, and similar manmade objects, but you may not remove leaves, rocks, twigs, or other things made by nature. To do so incurs a two stroke penalty. You may not ground your club before you hit the ball in a bunker. If you do, add two strokes to your score. The grass that borders the bunker is not considered part of the hazard, and therefore a club may be grounded in the grass, but never in the bunker. A player may take a practice swing outside of the bunker.

Your ball might be plugged at the top of the high side of a bunker. Unlike being in a water hazard, you may declare your ball "unplayable." In this case, you have two options to get back into play with a penalty stroke:
1) Drop the ball two club lengths, no closer to the hole, but still in the bunker.
2) Return to the spot where you hit the last shot (even if it's the tee) and use the stroke and distance penalty.

Your ball may come to rest in casual water in a sand trap which entitles you to penalty-free relief no closer to the hole, but remaining in the bunker. Relief means you must drop the ball, not place it.

Some other things you'll want to know about being in a bunker have to do with the rake. First, the rake is a movable obstruction. If your ball moves while you're moving the rake, you can replace your ball without penalty. Should your ball come to rest on the rake, you may pick up your ball, move the rake, then drop your ball as close to its original position as possible, without penalty. When entering the bunker, always enter from the low side (it's easier than trying to slide down a deep, sandy slope) and take the rake with you. Do not drag it through the sand or rake any part of the bunker before you hit your shot as it could be construed as checking the density of the sand and will cost you two strokes in stroke play and loss of hole in match. Once you have hit your shot (remember, you can take a practice swing outside of the bunker), rake the sand smooth and replace the rake in the bunker with the teeth down.

Unplayable Lie

Suppose a shot on your way from the tee to the green causes your ball to roll under a bush, fall between large rocks, or come to rest against a tree or fence presenting you with a situation in which you cannot take a swing at the ball. You have an unplayable lie. Taking a one stroke penalty, you have three choices to get back into play:
1) Drop your ball within two club lengths, no closer to the hole, which will usually solve the problem.
2) Return to the spot you originally hit from, taking stroke and distance.
3) Drop your ball as far back as you like from the point it currently lies, keeping that point between you and the hole.

Whichever solution you select, remember to count the stroke that got you there, add the penalty stroke, and then count the stroke that gets you back into play from your new location. The penalty for not following one of the three options is loss of hole in match play or a two stroke penalty in stroke play.

Penalty-free Relief

Assuming you are feeling a bit tired of reading about penalties, this is a good time to tell you about penalty-free relief.

If your ball comes to rest in casual water, which is defined as any water that is not on the course 365 days a year (for example: a recent heavy rain has left a big puddle in the fairway or the bunker and your ball has rolled into it), you are entitled to penalty-free relief. That means you may select the closest point of relief, (the spot where you can comfortably stand to address the ball) plus one club length, no nearer the hole. If you are taking relief from casual water in a bunker, your ball must stay in the bunker. Once you've found the first dry spot behind the puddle where you can stand comfortably in the address position, insert a tee where your ball would be hit at address.

Lay your longest club—which is your driver—on the ground with one end touching the tee you just inserted into the ground, then put another tee at the end of the driver and pick up your club. The space between the two tees is the "area of relief." Stand straight, face the flagstick, hold your arm out at shoulder height, and drop the ball between the tees. When you are playing a casual round, it's acceptable to eyeball the area, but when you are in a serious tournament, you should know how to do this. The same procedure holds true for "ground under repair." The grounds crew will paint a white circle around the spot or have a "ground under repair" sign nearby. If it isn't marked, you must play the ball where it lies, no matter how badly the ground is damaged.

You also get penalty-free relief if your ball comes to rest in a hole made by burrowing animals or the greenskeeper, or if it comes to rest on the cart path or service road. You get relief if your ball comes to rest on a pile of grass or other debris intended for removal by the grounds crew too.

If you have to stand on the cart path or service road in order to hit the ball, you have the option to take relief in this case as well. If you like the lie of your ball, simply proceed to hit. Keep in mind that when you take relief, it must be full relief. For example, if you have a good lie after taking relief, but you still have to stand on the cart path to hit, that is not full relief. You must drop the ball again. Be sure to always take relief properly.

Finally, you get relief (one club length, no closer to the hole) when your ball lands on a green other than the green of the hole you are playing. Remove your ball from the green and drop it no closer to the hole, going as far back on the line as necessary.

In summary, relief without a penalty is one club length no closer to the hole. Relief with a penalty is two club lengths no closer to the hole.

Continuing Down the Fairway

We have already covered the toughest rules, applying to events that begin on the tee and take you along the fairway, into hazards, or the rough. Now it's time to discuss some other things that are going on as you continue to make your way to the green.

One thing that slows play is not tracking your shots and the shots of others. As a result, time is wasted looking for balls, which keeps you and other players waiting. To keep play moving, especially when you are riding, think about your next shot before you get to your ball. Find a distance marker en route and have an idea of which club you will be using.

Some courses have numbered yardage markers embedded along the fairway, others use color-coded stakes along the rough to tell you when you are 200, 150, and 100 yards away from the center of the green. Many courses use distinctive bushes at the 150-yard point. As you move along the fairway, take a moment to consider the markers in terms of which person in your foursome might find the distance relevant to her shot.

If your cart partner has hit her shot and is on the other side of the fairway and closer to the hole, drive to your ball, take out the clubs you'll be needing for the next two shots, and let her take the cart to her ball. Play "ready golf" whenever possible, which simply means whoever is ready to hit, providing it is safe to do so, should proceed.

If your shot has landed in the opposite fairway, and the foursome on that fairway is making its way to where your ball landed, it is a good idea to identify your ball and then retreat to the side until they have passed. Often players on other fairways will yield because they are waiting to make their next shots.

Unless the course states that you may play "winter rules," which means you may take a preferred lie (pertaining to balls in your fairway only), you must "play the ball down," which means you must hit it where it lies. If a player improves her lie or touches her ball before reaching the green when winter rules are not in effect, it is a two stroke penalty. When winter rules are in effect, you may mark your ball, pick it up, clean it, and place it (do not drop it) within one club length, no closer to the hole. This action is commonly referred to as "lift, clean, and place."

Although the *USGA Official Rules Book* does not recognize winter rules or preferred lies under any circumstances, some courses allow it to protect the course, especially if there is new grass or recent weather conditions involving heavy rain.

Damaged Ball

If your ball becomes damaged during the course of a hole either by hitting a rock, tree, or cart path, you may replace it without penalty because it is unfit for play. The time to do this is during the hole in which it becomes unfit or between holes. You may not put a different ball down if you are worried, for example, that your next shot won't clear the water. Keep in mind that you must 1) announce in advance to your opponent or fellow competitor that you intend to lift your ball to examine it and 2) mark the position of the ball before it is lifted. Failure to do either is a one stroke penalty.

Other Faux Pas and Penalties

It's always a good policy to identify your ball before you hit. That's why having your own symbol drawn on your balls is such a good idea. Sometimes we can become distracted or forget where our ball is (especially if we've been helping another player to look for a lost ball) and hit someone else's by mistake.

In match play, you will lose the hole; in stroke play, it's a two stroke penalty. If you do not rectify your mistake before teeing off on the next hole, or if you leave the green on the final hole without rectifying the error, you are subject to disqualification in stroke play. The only penalty-free exception to this rule is if you play another person's ball in a hazard. Just return the player's ball to the hazard, find your ball, and play accordingly. If someone hits your ball, which was not in a hazard, notify that person of the two stroke penalty to be applied to her score, and place your ball as close as possible to its original spot.

The importance of applying a special symbol to your ball comes into play again if, for example, you and another player are playing on parallel fairways and you both hit in the rough while playing the same brand of ball. If neither of you can positively identify your ball, then both balls would be considered lost for lack of identification. This is a very frustrating way to have unwanted strokes added to your score card.

It's never a good idea to ask someone what club she used on a shot, especially if she's your opponent. That question earns you a two stroke penalty in stroke play and loss of the hole in match play. In fact, since everyone hits the ball differently with varying strength levels, the club one player selects for a 130-yard shot may not be the right club for another player. Furthermore, the club you need from 130 yards in the fairway may not be the club you'll need from 130 yards in the rough. Best advice: find out at the driving range what you get for distance from each club and keep your own counsel. There are exceptions to this suggestion, especially when you are playing in a scramble. It may be helpful to your teammates to know which club you used on a given shot so they can better gauge what might work for them.

Loose Impediments and Obstructions

Sometimes a leaf, twig, or fallen branch will interfere with your ability to address the ball. You may move the "impediments" as long as you do not cause the ball to move. If you cause the ball to move, it is a one stroke penalty. You must replace your ball as close as possible to the spot from which it was moved. If your ball is in the rough in tall grass, you may not pat down the grass behind the ball to improve the swing path. You may not break branches from trees to improve your swing path.

If your ball comes to rest near the red or yellow stakes defining hazard areas, a cart sign, or the stakes that hold a length of chain or rope near the green to deter powered carts from going too close to the green, you may move these objects, take your shot, and then replace them.

However, if your ball comes to rest against a white out-of-bounds stake or the fence or stone wall that defines out-of-bounds, you may not move the stakes. You do not get relief because out-of-bounds markers are considered an integral part of the course. What you have then is an unplayable lie. Taking a one stroke penalty, you may drop the ball two club lengths, no closer to the hole, or take one of the two other unplayable lie options discussed earlier.

To reiterate, an obstruction is any man-made/artificial object on the course including buildings, roads, ball washers, benches, fences, signs, and stakes that do not indicate out-of-bounds. The objective of the free drop is to improve your stance and allow you to swing freely. If the obstruction is still in your line to the green, you must accept your fate and chip laterally to get back into play.

Don't Hesitate to Pick Up

If you are having the hole from hell and are at double par halfway down the fairway, pick up the ball. By picking up, you are doing yourself a favor by taking a little time to cool down. You can try again at the next hole. You are also doing the people in your foursome a favor by letting them move along, not to mention the foursome behind you, who will be singing your praises as a courteous player.

The Equitable Stroke Control lets you save some face, assuming you are not in a medal play tournament. Don't moan and groan about it. Just do it and be done with it. I have a much higher opinion of someone who has her ball in her pocket, having given the hole her best shot, than the duffer who stubbornly insists on just one more shot while we all have to stand aside for the next worm burner.

Driving the Golf Cart

Good manners as a cart driver are just as important as good manners as a golfer. Observe the rules for use of carts at the course you are playing. If the course wants you to keep the cart on the path at all times, please do so. To speed play, develop the habit of taking extra clubs from your bag when you head for your ball. Using a cart does not mean you have to ride to every shot—especially as you approach the green. In fact, searching for a lost ball on foot can be more efficient than riding through the woods in the cart.

Be mindful of where you park your cart when preparing to hit. Because the cart is considered to be part of your equipment, you will earn a two stroke penalty in stroke play and lose the hole in match play if either you or your partner hit it.

Make sure your cart partner is completely seated before you drive off to the next hole. Also make sure the clubs your cart partner is selecting are completely out of the bag before you drive away. If you're being bounced around by an inconsiderate cart driver, don't hesitate to speak up. If it's upsetting you, then it's affecting your game.

When a course asks you to "observe the 90 degree rule" they are telling you it is permissible to take the carts on the fairway, but they want you to drive in the rough as much as possible. When you do have to take the cart onto the fairway, turn onto the fairway at a 90 degree angle.

Always put the parking brake on, especially if you are playing a hilly course, and turn the wheels such that should the brake inadvertently release, the cart will roll to a safe place and not into people. If a parked cart does take off, do not chase it! It is only equipment. Make sure no one is in its path and let it come to rest on its own.

Be aware of where other players are on the course as you motor by in your cart. Don't drive up to the next tee if the foursome on it is preparing to tee off. Be mindful of putting the cart into reverse if people are putting or teeing off nearby. The beeping warning sound that some carts are equipped with could disturb someone's concentration.

It's good cart management to park the cart next to the side of the green which will lead you to the next tee when you hole out. Generally, it's best to take your sand wedge and putter with you and walk a few yards back to your ball after you park greenside, rather than ride to every single shot.

Finally, drive the cart as you would an automobile. By that I mean don't operate the cart from the passenger side. You'd be surprised how easily a golf cart can get away from you, resulting in accidents that cause serious injury to the driver, other players, or expensive damage to the cart—which in turn causes injury to the driver's wallet.

On the Green

The green is hallowed ground. More effort goes into building a green and more money goes into maintaining it than any other part of the course. This is also the place where players probably get into the most trouble in terms of etiquette and rules, so let's review everything you need to know, beginning with the etiquette.

Assuming you are driving the cart, observe the course rules about how close a cart can come to the greens. Usually, a course will paint a white line on the grass telling you that you may not cross that line with your motorized cart. If the course has not marked it off, a good rule of thumb is to stay at least 30 yards away. You may cross the line with your pull cart or when carrying your bag, but never take these items onto the green.

Park your cart close to the next tee and be sure to leave enough room for another cart or a course maintenance vehicle to get by, if necessary. If you are using a pull cart, leave it as close as possible to the next tee. The goal here is to get you to walk off the green just as soon as you have holed out and proceed to the next tee without delay. Having to walk back to a cart that was carelessly parked in front of a large green slows play for the foursome behind you and is just plain inconsiderate.

Mark your score cards only when you are off the green and heading to the next tee. I am hard pressed to think of anything more annoying than the player in my foursome who stands on the green,

Rules and Etiquette

faces the hole we've just completed, and begins to add up her score for the hole. Learn to count your strokes as you hit.

Marking Your Ball

Once your ball is on the green, mark it no matter where it lies. This gives you an opportunity to pick your ball up and wipe off any dirt or bits of grass. To properly mark your ball, place your marker behind the ball, without touching or moving it. Once the marker is in place, pick up your ball. To return your ball to play, place the ball in front of the marker and pick up the marker without moving the ball.

If your ball marker is in someone's line of putt, she may ask you to move your marker to the right or left. Here's how to do it properly: Keeping one end of the head of your putter on the marker, find an object on the course like a bush or a tree and line up with that object. Remove your marker from its current position at one end of the putter head and place it at the opposite end of the clubhead. When it's time to put your ball back into play, don't forget to move your marker back to its original position before putting the ball down.

Repairing a Ball Mark

Assuming you made an indentation on the green when your ball dropped down from that beautifully lofted wedge shot, now is the time to repair it. To do so properly, take your ball mark repair tool from your pocket and insert it at one end of the indentation, then push up from beneath the indentation to create a small mound. Do this all around the indentation, then gently tap the mound down with the bottom of your putter head so that it is level with the green.

Repairing ball marks keeps the greens smooth and in good condition. An unrepaired indentation dries out, causing the grass to die and leaving players a sandy, bumpy surface.

The six most important things to remember in the "good manners" department when you are on the green are:
1) Do not walk in someone's "putt line."
2) Pick up your feet so you do not scuff the green. (That's why so many courses are opting to adopt a "spikeless" shoes policy.)

3) Be careful not to damage the lip of the cup when replacing the flagstick.
4) Repair your ball mark (if you made one) and any others you see. This doesn't mean you should spend ten minutes repairing ball marks. A good rule of thumb: Fix yours and one other.
5) If someone has been kind enough to mark your ball for you, be sure to return the ball marker when you hole out.
6) Do not stand behind the hole or behind the player who is putting.

The Putt Line

What is the "putt line?" It's an imaginary line which runs from the location of a player's ball to the cup, taking into account the "break," or roll of the green. It is rarely a straight line, so step carefully. If you cannot see the other three markers, don't hesitate to ask, "Where are you marked?," to avoid stepping on someone's line. Some players don't mind if you step on their putt line, and will tell you not to worry about it. Others will hold you responsible if they miss a putt because you stepped on their putt line and will let you know in no uncertain terms. It is always better to be overly cautious and considerate on this particular point, especially if you're playing with people you do not know well.

You should pick up your feet on the green because a player may not repair scuff or cleat marks in her putt line before she putts. To do so results in a two stroke penalty on her score. In fact, you shouldn't repair scuff or cleat marks until after everyone has holed out. You may, however, repair ball marks in your putt line before you putt without penalty.

Holing Out

It's common courtesy for the first person to hole out (sink the putt) to replace the flagstick after everyone has holed out. Be careful not to damage the area around the hole when replacing the flagstick. The lip of the cup, like everything on the green, is very carefully maintained by the grounds crew. No one wants to putt into a damaged cup. An uneven rim could ruin a good putt.

Rules and Etiquette

Just as you would on the tee, do not stand too close to or in the peripheral vision of someone who's putting; be still and do not talk. If a player's ball comes to rest just a few inches from the cup, and you're playing a casual round, you can tell her "it's good" and let her pick it up, unless, of course, you are playing in a tournament. Then everyone must hole out. In casual play, when someone tells you "it's good," pick up your ball. It is considered rude to putt out if someone has given that putt to you. Be sure to add the stroke for the putt that was given to your score.

Tending the Flagstick

A player can have the flagstick tended from any point during a hole and also has the option of having it removed at any point during the hole. If you have been asked to "tend the flagstick" when someone is putting, keep the following in mind:

1) Don't stand on anyone's putt line.
2) Don't cast a shadow over the hole or the putt line. Everyone on the green should make sure she isn't casting a shadow on a player's line of putt or over the hole.
3) Stand to the side of the hole, never behind it.
4) Keep the flag from flapping if it's a windy day. Do not bend the flagstick as it can be visually distracting to the player putting.
5) Make sure to pull the flagstick out as the player's ball approaches. If a player's ball hits a flagstick, attended or not, while putting on the green, that player incurs a two stroke penalty. (There is no penalty if the ball strikes the flagstick if the player was hitting the ball from off the green and the flagstick was unattended.)

Now that you know how to "tend the flagstick," here are some tips to keep in mind when it's your turn to putt:

1) Remember that you may not repair scuff marks in your line of putt. It's a two stroke penalty if you do.
2) You may remove loose impediments in your line of putt, even if you are off the green. Loose impediments are sand, stones, leaves, insects, etc. You may pick them up or brush them away with your hand or clubhead. Do not use your glove (if you have

53

taken it off) or a towel. If you do, it's a two stroke penalty. If your ball is moved as a result of clearing loose impediments, just replace it without penalty.

3) If your ball comes to rest at the edge of the cup, it has ten seconds to go into the cup to be considered fair. You may not do anything to force it in. If it does not go in, or goes in after ten seconds have passed (a train rumbles by causing the ball to drop in), it is a penalty stroke, otherwise interpreted as the same score you would record if you had tapped the ball in. The same rule applies in match play.

4) If your ball hits another ball while you are putting in match play, there is no penalty. Just replace the ball you hit where it was, and play yours where it lies. However, in stroke play, it's a two stroke penalty. Return the ball you hit to its original position, and play yours where it lies.

5) If you hit an object while putting (for example, someone's club is lying on the green), or a person (specifically, your opponent or the caddie) in match play, just play your ball as it lies, penalty-free. Or you may elect to replay the stroke as long as no other players have taken a stroke. In stroke play, there is no penalty, but you must count the stroke and play your ball where it lies.

When everyone has holed out, take a quick look around the green to check if anyone has left a club behind. Having done that, it is time to head to the next tee. Remember to mark your score cards on your way to the next tee, not on the green.

Lightning: What to Do in an Electrical Storm

Imagine a sultry summer day, a little overcast, and humid. You've paid big bucks for your favorite Pro-Am and you have reached the 13th hole, way out there on the course, far from the clubhouse. Suddenly, you hear thunder in the distance and turn to see some very dark and ominous clouds over your shoulder. Rest assured that the pro shop has been monitoring the weather very closely, but before they decide to sound the horn to call all players into the clubhouse, a bolt of lightning rips from the sky. Obviously you want to get off the course immediately, and 99% of the time the horn would have sounded well before this point in the story.

But the storm hits too quickly and you're stuck out on the course with no shelter. Here's what you need to do:

1) Go into a dense, wooded area. Avoid isolated trees.
2) If you are caught in the open, take off your spiked shoes, and get on your knees in a tucked position.
3) Avoid the putting green. It is an open area.
4) Do not use your umbrella.
5) Stay away from your golf clubs; do not hold one.
6) Get away from the water.
7) Do not seek refuge in the cart; it is not safe.

Golf clubs take electrical storms very seriously and always act quickly to call players in when lightning threatens. It is vitally important to stop playing and head for the clubhouse the moment you hear the horn.

Committing the Rules to Memory

It may take a few readings before this chapter makes sense, especially if you are just starting to play. There is an old saying about how people learn that reads, "I hear and I forget, I see and I remember, I do and I understand." If you are told about a certain rule, you will probably soon forget it. If you take the time to read about it, you'll remember it, and when you are able to apply it accurately while playing, then you will understand it.

The best way to learn the rules, however, is to play with people who know them, follow them, and are willing to talk to you about them either during the course of a round or after. If you intend to be taken seriously, you must know the rules. Having a command of this critical part of the game will quickly earn you the admiration and respect of your golfing peers.

If you want to learn more about the rules, order a copy of *Decisions on the Rules of Golf* and the USGA *Official Rules Book* through Triumph Books at (800) 335-5323.

3

As mentioned in Chapter 2, the USGA Handicap System allows for a level playing field among all players. It is a nationally recognized and consistently practiced system that rates the difficulty of a golf course by assigning each course a "rating" and a "slope."

The course rating is based on the score a scratch golfer (zero handicap) would shoot on that particular course. It is based primarily on yardage and tells us how many strokes that expert player would require to complete a round.

The slope tells us how the course compares in its degree of difficulty, from the average player to the expert. A slope rating of 113 represents a low degree of difficulty. Higher ratings, like 128 for example, mean tougher courses that probably have a large number of bunkers and hazards.

The Handicap Index can range from zero (for the "scratch" golfer), up to a maximum of 40.4 for women and 36.4 for men. "Scratch" means an individual shoots par (usually 72) for 18 holes.

How Do You Get a Handicap?

Tell your pro shop you want to get a handicap. There is a modest annual fee (around $25.00) to join the USGA Handicap System. After you have submitted cards from about twenty rounds from your home course (it could be as few as five rounds at some clubs), your average score will be calculated according to the system created by the USGA. That number—taking into account the slope, course rating, and tees you play from—will give you your Handicap Index.

You will then be assigned a membership number in the USGA Handicap System and your handicap will be updated on a regular basis, usually every two weeks, with the results sent to your pro shop. You'll get a credit card-sized plastic card onto which you will affix your updated Handicap Index sticker. Carry it with you at all times or keep it in your golf bag.

```
Name  BOND LADD SUSAN    835   GHIN®
Golf Handicap and Information Network®
Club  WELLESLEY COUNTRY CLUB
Club # 08-109-3      GHIN #  2482-890
Effective Date  10/06/95         USGA
Scores Posted     2           HCP INDEX    HOME
       1-900-288-4446        0.8        1
       SCORE HISTORY — MOST RECENT FIRST *IF USED
  1  75*    80     79     73*    74*
  6  80     79     80     80     83
 11  74*    72*    75*    73*    74*
 16  72*    75*    80     81     79
```

A player can get a 9-hole or an 18-hole handicap or both. Nine hole handicaps are good if you plan to play in a twilight league. Turn in all your scores, including the good, the bad, and the ugly, because it's the only way to measure your true handicap. The handicap is calculated using your most recent lowest scores, so if you're usually playing in the mid-90s and a score of 105 gets put in, it will be thrown out assuming you go back to playing in the mid-90s. In some cases, players must present their Handicap Index Card to give evidence of playing ability before being allowed to play in particular tournaments or on certain courses.

Equitable Stroke Control

If you're like me, every now and then, you fall apart on a hole. Your ball has gone OB off the tee and then into the water once or twice, and the possibility of holing out before the sun sets in the West seems remote. The USGA designed the Equitable Stroke Control for those occasions so that the "hole from hell" will not artificially elevate your handicap. The Equitable Stroke Control sets the maximum number a player can post on any hole depending on the player's course handicap. There isn't a limit on the number of holes you can adjust.

Equitable Stroke Control Table

18 Hole Course Handicap	Maximum Number Posted on Any Hole		
	Par 3	Par 4	Par 5
9 or less (2 over)	5	6	7
10 through 19 (3 over)	6	7	8
20 through 29 (4 over)	7	8	9
30 through 39 (5 over, except Par 5, 4 over)	8	9	9
40 and above (6 over, except Par 5, 5 over)	9	10	10

However, if you are playing in a medal play tournament, you may not pick up. You must record every stroke. Then, at the *end* of the round, you may adjust your score for handicap purposes.

Visiting Other Courses

When you play other courses, you will want to check the Course Handicap Table, which should be posted in the locker room or pro shop. It will help you to adjust your handicap for the round you are about to play. There are separate tables for men and women as well as for the different tees at the course, so be careful when you are making your conversion. Let's say you have a 22.4 Handicap Index at your home course, which has a slope of 118. The course you are visiting today has a slope of 124. According to the Course Handicap Table, you will play the course with a 25 handicap. At the end of the round, you can enter your score right into the computer at the course you are visiting, or return the signed and attested score card to your home club within a reasonable period of time.

Stroking a Score Card

Stroking a score card is easy. Let's say you're playing with three friends and you all share the same home course. Imagine that your handicap is 22 and your friends have 13, 18, and 28, respectively.

BREAKING THE GRASS CEILING

The player with the 13 will play at scratch, because she has the lowest handicap. She will give five strokes to the woman with the 18-handicap, 9 strokes to you, and 15 strokes to the woman with the 28-handicap.

BLUE	WHITE	PAR	HDCP	Cheryl 18	Susan 13	HOLE	Lisa 22	Kim 28	HDCP	PAR	RED
348	318	4	13			1			11	4	290
442	417	4	1			2		✓	9	5	417
156	135	3	17			3			15	3	124
454	430	4	3	✓		4	✓	✓	1	5	410
436	422	4	5		✓	5		✓	5	4	276
181	163	3	15			6			17	3	136
409	363	4	11			7		✓	13	4	338
546	533	5	9			8	✓	✓	7	5	408
528	495	5	7	✓		9	✓	✓	3	5	406
3500	3276	36				OUT			38		2805
		INITIALS							INITIALS		
412	358	4	8			10	✓	✓	6	4	338
197	191	3	16			11		✓	12	3	150
397	373	4	6			12	✓		8	4	363
367	317	4	14			13			16	4	291
369	354	4	10			14		✓	14	4	300
450	438	4	2	✓		15	✓	✓	2	5	438
218	203	3	18			16			18	3	162
416	391	4	4			17		✓	10	4	315
458	448	5	12	✓		18	✓	✓	4	5	402
3284	3073	35				IN			36		2759
6784	6344	71				Tot			74		5564
73.3	71.3	RATING				HANDICAP			RATING	72.7	
133	130	SLOPE				NET SCORE			SLOPE	132	
						POSTING SCORE				1993	

Date: 4-Ball
Wellesley Country Club
Proper Golf Etiquette Is Your Responsibility

(Notice the rating and slope, in the lower right corner, for the course mentioned at the beginning of this chapter.)

Looking at the score card, you'll see that each hole is assigned a handicap number from 1 to 18. The #1 handicapped hole is the hardest hole on the course, while the #18 handicapped hole will be the easiest hole on the course. Place a check mark or a dot on the hole where the three players will "stroke" against the lowest handicap player. Therefore, the player with the 18-handicap will get strokes on handicap holes 1 through 5, the 22-handicap player will get strokes on handicap holes 1 through 9, and the player with the 28-handicap will get strokes on holes 1 through 15. At the end of the round, you will add up both gross and net scores. Net is the score minus the strokes.

If you are playing with golfers who are hitting from different tees, you may give or get strokes for that, too. The player hitting from the tees with the higher course rating gets more strokes. To calculate just how many strokes you get, subtract the difference between the course ratings. Let's say there is a 73.5 rating from the white tees and a 70.9 rating from the forward tees. Subtract 70.9 from 73.5 and round up to the nearest decimal from .5. Therefore, the player hitting from the whites would get three extra strokes (74 minus 71).

In some formats, you will "play against the field," which means you will stroke your card from zero. In other words, if you have a 22-handicap, you will get one stroke on each of the 18 holes, and two strokes on handicap holes 1 through 4.

I know this all sounds a bit confusing at first glance, but it will seem very routine once you've done it a few times.

Other Rules

When you play in certain outing formats, adjustments are made to keep play equitable, especially when there are significant differences in handicaps among team members. Generally, the Tournament Committee or the pro shop staff of the hosting club will work out all the details beforehand, and have the stroked cards ready for each team.

If you want complete background on how it's done, contact the USGA Order Department, P.O. Box 708, Far Hills, NJ 07931, and ask them for the *USGA Handicap System Manual*.

4

It is not uncommon at the beginning of a casual round of golf for someone to suggest a friendly wager. Everybody enjoys a little competition, even just a $2.00 bet. Many golfers claim that a small wager keeps them focused and challenged. The bottom line here is that if you want to play golf with your colleagues, prospects, and clients, you need to know some of the games that can keep a round interesting.

Match vs. Stroke Play

There are basically two forms of competition in golf. One is match play, the other is stroke play. Stroke play is sometimes also called medal play.

In match play, you are playing on a hole-by-hole basis. The team or individual winning the most holes during the round wins. In match play, the score doesn't determine victory, just the number of holes won.

Match play is a great format in which to compete because you are never out of the hole until the hole is over. For example, let's say you are playing match play against another individual:

You both tee off; her drive goes right down the middle, but your drive drifts to the right and goes into the woods, but not out of bounds.

Upon arriving at your ball, you are delighted to see that you have a clear shot. You hit and your ball lands just in front of the green.

Your opponent then proceeds to skull her second shot so that it only advances a few yards. Her third shot, however, lands on the green, but not close to the pin.

You then proceed to dump your third shot into the bunker. However, a splendid bunker shot places you about three feet from the cup.

Your opponent sends her fourth shot, which is a putt, way past the cup ending up on the fringe.

Her fifth shot, a chip, drifts by the hole and now she is about fifteen feet from the cup.

Lying four, you sink your putt, taking the hole with five.

Even though your opponent had a good drive and yours went into the woods, even though she was on the green in three while you were in the bunker in three, you still won the hole.

Add to this scenario the advantage of getting strokes (assuming your handicap is higher than your opponent's) and you might have won that hole 5, net 4.

The beauty of match play is that you can recover from a bad shot or a couple of bad shots and stay mentally focused because you never know what's going to happen to your opponent. It is easier to win a round "hole by hole" in match play than to win a round vying for the lowest score in stroke play.

In stroke play, the lowest score at the end of the round (counting every stroke) determines the victor. In professional and amateur competition, a tournament can take three or four rounds—or more—to determine the winner. In stroke play, there is a gross score (a score unadjusted by handicap) and a net score, which is simply gross minus handicap.

Nassau

The most common bet is called a Nassau. You and your fellow players will agree on how much to bet, but the standard is $2.00. You are betting $2.00 for the most holes won on the front nine, $2.00 for the most holes won on the back nine, and $2.00 for the most holes won overall. You may play as individuals or as two-person teams. The bet is settled at the end of the round, usually at the nineteenth hole.

The Press

No, it's not the *New York Times*. A "press" is just a new bet, most commonly used in a Nassau, that a team can introduce whenever they are two holes down. The original bet stays intact; the press is a side bet. It's a great strategy, because if you win the next hole, then you are just one hole down on the original bet, and one up on the new bet. It could throw your opponent off-balance, especially if you go on to win the second hole, going even on the original bet, and moving to two up on the press. At that point, your opponents may ask to press because they are now two holes down. You should accept the wager if you want to be a good sport. At the end of nine, you had better add up where you are because, if a team loses the front nine, they can press the back nine, making it a $6 bet. If it starts looking like they could lose the overall eighteen, they may press the eighteenth hole. Do your bookkeeping faithfully whether you are the collector or the debtor, but don't hold up the foursome behind you!

Better Ball

Sometimes called four-ball, better ball is a match-play format in which two players compete against two other players. The better score of the two-person team is recorded for each hole. For example, if you and your partner each score a four on a par 3, and the other players had a five and a two respectively, the two wins the hole for the opposing team. Be sure to stroke your cards to reflect individual handicaps in this game to make it fair.

Six Six Six

By switching partners after every six holes, Six Six Six is just a variation of better ball that allows players to play three different formats during one round. For the first six holes, team members alternate shots, for six holes they play their own ball, and for the final six they play a scramble.

Bingo Bango Bungo

Also referred to as bingle bangle bungle. Points are awarded for first on the green, closest to the hole, and the first to hole out.

Garbage

Hey, I didn't make up these names. Garbage, sometimes called "Trash," (honest!) are side bets. Here are some of the bets you may hear about. They generally range from $.25 to $1.00:

Gross birdies (as opposed to net birdies)
The score you got without using a stroke from your handicap.

Greenies
Whoever gets closest to the hole in regulation on par 3s and 5s.

Sandies
Making par out of the sand.

Barkies
Hitting a tree but still making par.

Hogans
Hitting the fairway, hitting the green, and making par or better.

Arnies
Missing the fairway, missing the green, and still making par or better.

Gurglies
Hitting the ball into the water but still making par.

Offie
A ball holed from off the green.

No doubt you can come up with your own side bets that compare with these in style and creativity.

Skins

Skins is probably the most popular game for three players, although it can be played with four players as well. The annually televised PGA Skins Games, for example, has a large and enthusiastic following.

In a skins game (sometimes referred to as scats or syndicates), the players agree to an amount for each "skin" or hole. Once again, this is match play for the number of holes won. If two players tie on a hole the skin is carried over, so the money can add up rather quickly. Sometimes when a hole is tied, the term "no blood" or it's a "push" may be used, because you are pushing the bet to the next hole.

Hawk, Pig, or Wolf

In this low-ball game, players toss a tee to determine the order of play for the first three holes. This order is kept for the entire round. So player #1 will tee off first on the first hole, player #2 will tee off first on the second hole, and player #3 will tee off first on the third hole. Player #1 will tee off first on the fourth hole, and so on.

The person teeing off is referred to as the hawk, pig, or wolf. She will look over the other players' drives and has the option of choosing a partner for the hole—perhaps a player who strokes on the hole or one who is in the best position—or she may elect to play the hole alone for all the points, in which case the bets are doubled.

Winning a hole gets you two points. Losing a hole costs you a point for each competitor. Add up your total points at the end of the round. Hawk, pig, or wolf can also be played with four players if you like.

Scramble

The scramble has become the format of choice for many charity outings because it speeds play for a large field (usually 144 players) and lets less accomplished players participate without undue pressure.

In a scramble, all the players drive off the tee, then the best drive is selected and all players hit their second shot from that spot, and so on into the hole. With the mulligans that are often sold, a team can potentially come in well under par. The scramble format may also be played at match, but the most familiar format is stroke.

Chapman

This is a great format when you have a couples event. In this format there are teams of two, usually a man and a woman. Both players drive and then each hits the other's ball for the second shot. (In other words, the men hit the women's drives and the women hit the men's drives.) Select the best of the two second shots, then play into the hole, alternating shots. Used by hundreds of golf clubs around the country, you may sometimes hear Chapman tournaments referred to as the "Divorce Open," particularly if one partner tends to hit long but not straight, and the other tends to whiff occasionally!

Stableford

Another interesting tournament format is Stableford, whereby point values are attached to scores. For example, a bogey gets one point, par is two points, birdie is three points, and an eagle is awarded four points. The player with the most points at the end of the round wins.

Regardless of what games you are playing, when you make your "bookkeeping entries" on your score card to keep track of all bets out, be sure you are not delaying play for the folks behind you. One last thing, be sure to pay off your debt immediately after the round.

If you would like some additional reading on this part of golf, look for the books *Golf Games: The Side Games We Play and Wager* by R. M. Ussak and *Golf Games Within the Game* by Linda Valentine and Margie Hubbard. Or you can call the National Golf Foundation at (800) 733-6006.

5

Think Golf

When making your initial call to a prospective client's office, you will want to be looking for signs of a golfer. Short of seeing a picture of Arnold Palmer or Nancy Lopez hanging on the wall, look for items that tell you your customer is a golfer.

Is there a brass golf ball paper weight on the desk, or a few pictures on the credenza with members of a foursome taken at a charity golf event? Maybe you'll see a few antique clubs displayed, or a putter and some balls in the corner. Somewhere, readily visible, there will be an artifact or two that will tell you this person plays golf.

Since we all know from Sales 101 that people like to talk about themselves, you might say something like, "Oh, I see you're a golfer. Where do you like to play?" You will soon find out that he or she is 1) a new golfer, taking lessons and perhaps playing at the local par-3 nine hole courses; 2) an intermediate or advanced player, playing and practicing as much as possible and therefore becoming a great prospect for accepting your outing invitation; or 3) a member of a private club and not only likely to accept your invitation to play in an upcoming charity outing (especially if it is at a terrific course), but a good contact if you want to meet more golfing executives. Further, if the relationship grows over time, this person might be willing to sponsor an outing at his or her club for your mutually favorite charity or trade association.

Leslie McQuillan, a sales representative with Charles River Lithographers in Rockland, Massachusetts, has been using golf for business for several years now.

"Since I took up golf seriously a few years ago, I found out that customers I've had for years play golf. We've gone out for a round and it has greatly enhanced the business relationship," she said. "In fact, one of my largest customers, ComputerWorld in Framingham, Massachusetts, holds an annual tournament and I have been invited to play in it for several years now. It's a great way to keep in touch with my customers."

Many company executives now take high level prospective hires out for a round of golf so they can observe how these people conduct themselves during the round. Golf reveals quite a bit about people in terms of personality traits. When I play golf with others, I observe their ability to make decisions, their willingness to take risks, whether they are able to laugh at mistakes, how quick they are to anger, and much more.

You can meet people at conventions, in airplanes, through associations, and dozens of other traditional business situations—and can forget people just as easily. But I will always remember someone with whom I have played golf. There is no doubt in my mind that we share a unique bond.

Get Involved in Your Community

Now that you are using golf as a business tool, you may begin to look at your current customers as potential golf partners instead of just customers. There are other ways you can expand your client base through golf as well. One way to meet successful and influential people who play golf is to become involved in community activities: museums, opera, symphony, ballet, and other performing arts and cultural events, athletic events, benefit dinners, political campaigns, etc., are all excellent vehicles for making new contacts. Becoming involved in activities beyond the scope of what your company does is an effective way to become known to the larger business community. You will be able to demonstrate your outstanding sales, marketing, planning, or research skills to leaders in other industries, which may have a positive impact on your future success.

It's not surprising that the group of business people who shape the political, cultural, and economic direction of a community have avid golfers among their ranks. They support political candidates, underwrite art exhibitions, attract conventions and expositions to their cities, recruit investors to build and expand local businesses; in short, they keep a pulse on the overall political, economic, and cultural well-being of their community.

If you took a poll of how many members of this elite business group are also members of golf or country clubs, you would find that the majority of these business leaders are somehow tied to golf. When you walk into the office of someone who plays golf, you are tapping into a very large network indeed. The old adage, "It's not what you know, it's who you know" rings true for the smart female executive who can use golf as a business tool. It is very easy to invite someone with whom you have worked on a special event out for a round of golf once the event is over and declared a success. It's one of the fastest ways to broaden your contacts and gain access to the power base in your community.

When Are You Ready to Invite a Business Associate to Play?

You're ready to host a round of golf with accomplished players once you begin to average around 115 to 125 for 18 holes, can play your round in four hours or less under normal conditions, and have familiarized yourself with the rules and etiquette of the game. There is universal agreement that a knowledge of the rules and etiquette is the most important thing to have mastered. It is now time to invite someone to play as your guest at a charity event, or at the course where you play regularly. As a beginner, you can still invite clients and colleagues to play if you know they are beginners as well. Just make sure you agree on an easy par-3 nine hole course. It can be great fun! Outings with a scramble format are another fun way to host guests.

I was looking for a fourth person to fill out my foursome at a charity outing to benefit a battered women's shelter during the summer of 1995. I called Christine Cahill, then a vice president for Small

Business Banking at the BankBoston branch in Wellesley, Massachusetts, to see if she'd like to round out the foursome. The branch of the bank she worked in was part of the community served by the shelter, and I thought it would give her office good exposure.

At first, she declined, saying she didn't think she was a good enough player to join us. "Nonsense," I told her. "You're playing in a league, I know you've just finished a clinic with Susan Bond, it's a scramble format, and it's for a great cause."

"You're right," she replied. "I really want to do this," and accepted the invitation. Needless to say, we had a great day and Christine sank some unbelievably long putts for our team. She also made several promising business contacts at the reception that followed. I might add that her self-confidence as a golfer went up a few notches, too.

Extending the Invitation and Organizing the Day

Give your clients a call a couple of weeks in advance so they can plan accordingly. Ask them if they have time for 18 holes, or if 9 would be better. Most people will opt for 18. Find out if they prefer to walk or ride and what their handicaps are so you can select an appropriate course. Give them the name and telephone number of the course and fax them clear directions if they don't know where it is. Be sure to include the names, titles, companies, and handicaps of the other players in your group so your guests will have a chance to familiarize themselves with the names of the other players and what their companies do. Tell them if the course has showers, lockers, what the rule is on spikes, and any special dress code rules. Determine if everyone can stay on for lunch or dinner after the round, as well.

Once you have reserved your tee time, call the members of your group, reconfirm the tee time and suggest that you meet in the pro shop at least forty-five minutes before you are scheduled to tee off. That gives everyone time to get there, stop at the bag drop, and change in the locker room if they are coming directly from the office. It's a good idea to call the course the day before you play to reconfirm your tee time directly with them.

Be sure you have a good supply of singles, fives, and tens to tip the various staff members who will help you with your day. Bag handlers, locker room attendants, and shoe shine staff get $3.00 to $5.00. If you take a caddie, plan on tipping a minimum of $7.00 per bag if you have a very young caddie, and up to $25.00 or more per bag on top of the caddie fee if your caddie was seasoned and outstanding.

In the Northeast and on the West Coast, caddie fees run around $15.00 to $20.00 per bag, plus a $10.00 to $15.00 tip. In the Southern region, expect rates to be a bit higher. The Midwest/Chicago area might well require $75.00 to $80.00 for a double (a caddie who carries two bags) plus tip.

If you want to walk and take a caddie, the best thing to do is to call the pro shop, find out what the fees and tipping practices are, and reserve a caddie or two, depending on the number of players in your group.

Some Thoughts about Playing with Caddies

There are those who could not even dream of a round without a caddie, while others are inveterate cart riders. Playing with an experienced caddie can be an uplifting experience—much entertaining fiction (and some hilarious true accounts) has been written about their role in golf's history. I am not referring to some of the youngsters who make us feel we should be carrying our own bags by the twelfth hole, but rather the men who have refined their skills and take great pride not only in their work, but in how well you play under their guidance.

To ensure a good experience when you opt to walk, follow these guidelines:

1) Get the fee structure before you head out. You are paying for someone to help track your shots, rake bunkers, clean clubs, tend the pin, replace divots, and offer strategic advice based on his knowledge of the course and the greens.

2) You do not always have to take the advice of your caddie, especially if you like to read your own greens.

3) Let your caddie put the golf bag down before you go rummaging around for a club. Better yet, just ask him to hand you the club you want. Don't feel badly about handing him your club when you are finished with your shot, or asking for one from him. That is his job and he takes pride in it, so don't coddle him.

4) It is your responsibility to buy him a snack or beverage at the turn. On a hot day, he needs just as much water as you do, maybe even more.

5) At the end of the round, he should clean your clubs, account for all of them (you'd best double check because I've pulled my clubs out of another bag being carried by the caddie more than once), and have them returned to club storage, or at the bag drop for you to put in your car.

Personal Belongings

Take care of your valuables. When you arrive at the course, you should have a system to keep your valuables, especially your jewelry, safe. A small pouch, with a zipper, will take care of your rings while you play. Rings can be uncomfortable under your golf glove, especially if you have large stones with high settings. Do not take them off and drop them in your pocket. I have seen too many women come in from a round and not be able to find their wedding and engagement rings, or other sentimental keepsakes because they dropped them in the pocket of their shorts. Imagine how many times you will bend down, go over bumps or look for a tee in those pockets over the next four hours. No wonder valuables are lost during the round.

You should either lock your handbag in the trunk of your car and put your car keys in your golf bag, particularly if you're walking, or take your handbag with you and store it in the basket on the motorized cart. Do not leave valuables in the locker room unless you can lock the locker. Also, be mindful of leaving your golf cart unattended if your handbag and other valuables are in it.

Meeting Your Guests

Once you meet your group in the pro shop and the proper introductions have been made, check in with the starter to tell him your group is present. Sometimes, the pro shop will do this for you, but never assume. Make sure your guests have pencils, score cards, and water. Arrange for shag bags or small buckets of balls for everyone as well. Many courses keep the balls at the driving range so you don't have to carry them with you from the pro shop. Escort your group to the driving range so you can all warm up—twenty to thirty minutes should do nicely. You should also offer your guests a chance to putt a few balls on the practice green. This will help them get a feel for the speed of the greens on the course.

Head back to the starter about ten minutes before your assigned tee time to wait for your nod to go to the first tee. Never go to the first tee without checking in with the starter. While you're waiting, use this time to stroke cards, agree on the format for the round, announce the ball you'll be playing, and determine the order of play.

At the first hole and at the beginning of each remaining hole, tell the other players a little about the hole if they have not played the course before. For example, "This is a sharp dogleg right, with two large bunkers on the front of the green. There's water on the right, so you'll want to stay left down the fairway." Tell them where the yardage markers are and brief them on any "local" rules and cart restrictions, as well.

Should You Discuss Business?

If your guest asks you a specific question about your product or service, then of course you should answer the question. But your time on the golf course is primarily to get to know people, for them to get to know you, and to have fun. If you can give a succinct answer, and promise to go into more detail after the round, it will allow everyone to concentrate on the game. The worst thing you can do is take the initiative and launch into an unsolicited pitch about how great your company is and what you can do for someone. Remember, these people have agreed to spend four or five hours of their time with you. Don't hold them hostage. Leave your cell phone and beeper in the car; they are the newest form of bad manners in golf.

Letting Others Play Through

If you are enjoying a leisurely but steady pace with your foursome, and a twosome is pushing you from behind, let them play through. If you are walking with your guests and there's a foursome in motorized carts pushing behind you, let them through, assuming you are not waiting for a group ahead of you. If you have to let more than one group through, you are playing too slowly and you should pick up the pace. A good way to measure your pace of play is to reach the turn in two hours. I like the sign that is posted at one of Boston's tonier clubs. It reads, "It is the duty of every golfer to be just behind the group ahead, not directly ahead of the group behind."

At the Turn

"The turn" is the expression used when golfers have finished the ninth hole, or front 9, and are moving onto the tenth hole to begin the back 9. At the majority of 18-hole courses worth their salt, a snack shack, with restrooms, will be located between the ninth and tenth holes. Most golfers take a short break after 9 holes to get something to eat (a healthy snack to take with you on the cart), make a quick visit to the restroom, and move on with as much speed as possible. In other words, the turn is not the place for a sit-down luncheon. It shouldn't take more than five to ten minutes.

If you are the first to hole out on the ninth hole, you may excuse yourself by announcing that in order to save time, you are going to go on ahead to the shack. The second person to hole out can do this to speed play as well. On this occasion, the last person to hole out will replace the flag (rather than the first) and join members of her foursome at the shack. You are the host at the turn, which means you should offer to pay for everyone's refreshments.

For most women, a trip to the ladies room after 9 holes is a necessity. The truly female friendly courses have additional comfort stations between the first and ninth holes and the tenth and eighteenth holes. As any pregnant woman (or a fellow with a prostate problem) will tell you, that's the kind of service that's worth repeat business and word-of-mouth recommendations. If not, vote with your feet and don't patronize those courses that can't (or won't) appreciate the needs of female golfers. Let them know in writing, too.

Nutrition and Hydration Impacts Your Game

During the round, it's important to keep your body hydrated. Drinking plenty of water during a round on a hot summer day, even if you don't feel thirsty, will keep you mentally sharp and your muscles happy and relaxed. Snacks such as bananas, apples, grapes, and dried fruit add the sugar you need for quick energy, but won't drag you down like candy, which gives a quick sugar high but then a sharp energy drop.

Dealing with Cheaters and Tempers

When someone is cheating, you can only point out the rule that covers the particular situation. If the person disagrees, take out your copy of this book or the *USGA Official Rules Book* (which you always carry in your bag) and explain the rule. Generally, if someone sees you know the rules, fair play will prevail.

While it is the rare person who will completely lose his or her self-control on the course, if it happens I strongly suggest you ignore it and go about your business. Unless clubs are being thrown directly at you (to exaggerate the point), just hope it will pass and that the player will calm down and apologize to everyone. After all, we can forgive bad shots and bad golf days, but it's harder to forgive bad manners. While it is most unlikely that you'll be faced with a real monster on the course, it could happen. Try to tell yourself it's just for half a day and then cross that person's name off your golf list. Life is just too short and golf is just too much fun to tolerate such childish behavior. If you have to talk to someone about unsportsmanlike conduct, do it after the round, in private, but never during the round.

If someone is complaining or making excuses after every poor shot, chances are that person is not a very good golfer to begin with, which is not the end of the world. But if a player analyzes every shot with "I should have done this or I meant to do that," and asks you if you can see what she is doing wrong, don't be tempted to give a lesson on the course. It takes up too much time, and if your advice doesn't work immediately, then you have made yourself responsible for tinkering with that person's game and are therefore responsible for all ensuing poor shots—at least in her mind.

All athletes must learn not only physical discipline, but mental discipline as well. If nothing else, golf demands self-control. While many people think golf builds character, I am of the opinion that golf reveals character. Being able to remain positive and unruffled when your game seems to be falling to pieces is very important if you intend to get refocused and concentrate on making your next shot a great one.

The Amateur Who Thinks He's a Pro

It's happened to all of us. You're playing in a group and there is a fellow who thinks he's going to teach you how to play golf. "You should turn this way," or "You should come down on the ball harder." I've heard enough for a lifetime, and the best way to stop it immediately is to politely say you are working with a pro. Or what of the man who picks up your 5-foot putt, telling you it's good, because there's a foursome behind you, and then proceeds to stand over his 2-footer as though $50,000 depended on it . . . and misses?

The late Mike Royko, the syndicated columnist, had me in fits of laughter with an article he wrote for the *Boston Herald* on July 4, 1995. He wrote about a woman who told her husband she wanted to take golf lessons. "What for?" he asked. "I can teach you anything you want to know."

"I already know how to hit a ball into the water," she retorted.

Should I Let my Boss or Guests Win?

Absolutely not! As Susan Bond says, "Never back down. I've played with men all my life and have had two 'playing interviews' on the course, which prompted me to play some of my best golf ever."

The thing to remember here is to play your best every time you play. The longer you play golf, the more you will realize that we all have bad days on the course. People who love and respect this great game know that an occasional bad day is as much a part of the game as the grass you stand on. But it is simply not right to throw your game because your fellow player is having a bad day, or because he has a higher rank than you do in the corporate pecking order. Be admired because you are a good player, not because you are willing to capitulate. It is a small-minded boss who would expect such an unreasonable sacrifice from an employee.

The Nineteenth Hole: Making the Most of Post-Round Time

At the end of the round, be sure to thank everyone and shake hands. It's time to post your scores and head for the nineteenth hole. Make sure you clean the bottom of your golf shoes before you go inside; there are special brushes set up outside the door of the pro shop or locker rooms for that purpose. Some clubs do not allow spikes in the clubhouse or bar, so check before proceeding. You may want to head to your car or the locker room to change into street shoes.

Although your guests may insist on buying a round of refreshments, you are still the host at the nineteenth hole. While a cold beer can be quite refreshing after a round, don't get carried away. Remember, especially if you did not drink plenty of water during the round, your body has lost a good deal of fluid through perspiration and exertion during the last several hours. Any alcohol entering your system at the nineteenth hole will be soaked up into your blood stream like a dry sponge absorbing water.

Begin with some water, juice, or a soft drink to rehydrate. Then if you want the ubiquitous cold beer or a gin and tonic, just have one and switch back to something soft. Carbonated mineral water with a wedge of lime looks like a cocktail, but doesn't give the kick. The bottom line here is that this post-round time is for making the final good impression. If you've played well out on the course and have gained the respect and admiration of your boss or prospective client(s), but end up face down in your soup because you blew it at the bar, you've lost the game of business golf, even though you may have had a good score.

Use this time to see if your guests who are prospective clients have any questions about your product or service if it came up during the round. If it didn't, do not initiate a business discussion. Wait a few days and then call to schedule a meeting. You already know you'll get the appointment. If your guests are current clients, use the time at the nineteenth hole to tell them how much you appreciate their business. Don't stretch post-round time out until the wee hours of the morning. You are a busy person with a demanding schedule. Be sure to compliment everyone on a good game and say good night.

Send a note the next day telling them it was a pleasure and that you'll do it again—if you say you will, make sure you do.

6

Just as any smart executive is going to join several membership organizations and trade associations to get her name and face into the public eye, the female executive who is willing to take her business acumen onto the golf course—to use golf as a business tool—is going to start by following announcements of charity golf outings in the local newspapers and association newsletters. Dozens of businesses, nonprofit organizations, health care providers, manufacturers, and retailers lend their names to golf outings every year. The cost to register can be as little as $100 per person and as much as $1,000 per person, but the average seems to be around $150 to $300. You may want to have golf outings as an annual budget item, perhaps allowing for one or two per month (if not more), depending on your sales goals and the degree to which your company has a golf culture.

Promoting Your Company

Successful charity golf outings are the result of months of hard work by a planning committee. If you want to put yourself and your company in the spotlight, there are several options. Should your schedule permit, and if you have a strong feeling toward the charity, volunteer to serve on the planning committee. Basically, you will be discussing the outing format, the budget, and fund-raising goals. You will also work on identifying corporate sponsors to support the event, either with monetary donations to help offset the operating expenses associated with the outing, or by soliciting product donations for the welcome bag, raffle, or auction. If you raise your hand, make sure your company gets behind you and the event.

Implied in being a member of this planning committee is the notion that you will put a few foursomes together, buy some advertising in the program book, and solicit some prizes. You must be prepared not only to make a commitment with your time, but to spend some money as well.

Or, for a few thousand dollars, your company could underwrite the luncheon or be the cart sponsor in exchange for recognition in all of the promotional materials. Alternatively, you might consider sponsoring a hole, which gets your name and logo on a sign that is displayed on one of the holes for a few hundred dollars. Still too expensive? Donate a prize for the raffle or auction, which in turn gets your name in the printed program. Many companies have tees, visors, or golf towels made up with the company's name to donate to the event, where they are included in the welcome bags handed out at the registration table.

In other words, there are dozens of opportunities to promote yourself and your company at charity outings. Decide which level of participation suits your goals and budget, then proceed with vigor. A well-run outing leaves a great impression, but keep in mind they demand good planning, superb management, and plenty of volunteers.

Many companies today create their own corporate outings and invite customers and prospects out to a great local course for an afternoon of golf, followed by dinner. Again, there are dozens of details that, if not properly executed, will do your company's image more harm than good. Get your special events people involved, talk to professional golf outing management companies, and establish a view of what you want to accomplish with this event.

If you want your company to get into the big league of golf sponsorship by being the title sponsor of a sanctioned PGA or LPGA tournament, you will have dozens of options to consider. There are several layers of sponsorship levels available, hospitality tents to promote, tickets to sell or give away, advertising to consider, security issues, television coverage, etc. The best way to survive is to engage a professional golf outing management company to handle the planning and marketing. They will be there for you from the first planning session, during the hectic days just before the event, and on the day of the event to make sure that everything you discussed over the previous months is executed without a hitch.

What to Expect on the Day of the Event

Whether you are playing alone or with a foursome, much of what we covered in terms of warming up in Chapter 5 will apply. However, since most charity outings involve two meals, usually lunch and dinner, you should arrive at least ninety minutes before the starting time. Stop at the bag drop first, unload your clubs, and tip the attendant a few dollars. Park your car, find the locker room, and get changed. Be sure to bring ample cash, because you are going to be asked to buy raffle tickets, mulligans, and who knows what else. Be sure to carry money with you through the day, because some donations will take place right on the course.

This time, instead of going to the pro shop, you will check in at the registration table, which is staffed by volunteers for that particular outing. It is usually set up outside the pro shop. Look for a banner or sign with the name of the charity. They will give you your welcome bag (filled with goodies like a sleeve of balls, a bag of tees, a shirt, visor or hat, some snacks, and maybe some samples of products donated by sponsors), tell you about the format for the day, give you your cart number, and supply any other pertinent information about special rules for the outing. By now the golf course staff member who took your bag at the bag drop has loaded it onto your assigned golf cart.

All the golf carts should be lined up nearby in starting hole numerical order. Look for your starting hole where the score card is kept on the steering wheel. There will probably be special instructions for the day, as well, like what holes have been selected for closest to the pin, longest drive, and any local rules.

Once you have registered, found your cart, and visited the pro shop for any last-minute purchases, it's a good idea to get something to eat before heading for the driving range and practice putting green. Return to your cart about fifteen minutes before the start time so you can meet other players in the groups around you. (Remember, you are there to network.) At some point in this time frame, a member of the staff at the club will address all the players and review the format and any special rules for the day.

Then you will head out to the hole you have been assigned to start on. Let's say the number on your cart reads "11 A." That means you will drive your cart to the eleventh hole and tee off first. You'll notice another foursome joining you. They will be "11 B," and they will tee off after you and your partners are out of range. There should be a map of the course on your score card so you can find your assigned hole quickly, or perhaps volunteers to guide the players to their respective starting holes. Once you have arrived at your assigned hole, listen for a few moments, and you will hear the starter's gun signaling to the field that it's time to tee off.

After the Round

Many people like to take a shower and change into clean clothes after the round and before cocktails and dinner. Don't be in the locker room all night. You want to rinse the dust of the day off, freshen your makeup and hair, and change into something casual.

Meet your guests at the bar, and remember what was mentioned in Chapter 5 about too much alcohol. If you have not had the opportunity to talk a little business out on the course (having done so only if your guests brought it up), use this time to answer their questions, or draw them out a bit more about their interest in your product or service. If you know other people at the club you are visiting, be sure to introduce your guests. If you are the guest and see someone you know, be sure to say hello and introduce your playing partners. Quite often people will know each other from college, church, previous business dealings, etc.

Pro-Am outings have a much higher registration fee than usual, but you can always expect a superb day from start to finish. You may also be expected to buy more raffle tickets or take an active role in the auction. Don't be shocked or intimidated. If you have the money, go after what you want. If not, let the high rollers do what they do best. Remember, it can be good theater and the money goes to charity.

Don't be the last to leave! Remember, this was a business round of golf, so be businesslike.

Be sure your notes of appreciation go out promptly, and follow up with new contacts to set up appointments as soon as possible.

7

In the two-and-a-half decades that I have been involved in the business world, I have had the good fortune of meeting some wonderful, successful people who took an interest in my career. If a mentor did not exist where I worked, I joined and actively participated in a number of membership associations that were either directly tied to the business I was in, or which brought me into contact with people I wanted to meet to further my own sales goals and career ambitions.

In the process, I have met dozens of men and women who were willing to share their knowledge and expertise, or who were able to introduce me to the people with whom I wanted to do business. The fastest way to achieve your goals is to have a mentor who is willing to help you to avoid the mistakes they themselves may have made or have seen others make.

Across the country, I am seeing more business associations, such as Chambers of Commerce, develop "Women's Business Networks" that foster networking and mentoring among the female members. On the whole, they are successful because they give younger women an opportunity to have access to seasoned, successful female executives and community leaders. Yet, I have heard some women sniff at the prospect of joining women-only business groups. They argue that they have worked very hard to attain their own senior positions, and that these single-sex associations are too narrow in focus. They claim they do not want to be singled out as "women executives," they just want to be known as executives. Period.

While I understand the difficulties associated with acquiring and maintaining senior level positions, I wonder if we sometimes either unconsciously close the door behind us once we reach the executive suite, or is it closed for us as a result of the corporate culture of our companies? The more "senior" we become, the more our calls are screened and most of our incoming mail is scrutinized by trusted assistants whose task is to help us economize our time. The net result is that we become insulated, and something that is insulated cannot, by definition, be a conduit. The more we stay behind the big glass doors, the more we miss connecting with interesting people with good ideas.

For women who have attained senior levels, either within a corporate environment or by owning their own companies, I would urge them to take an interest in women who are starting to "climb the ladder" by being a mentor. To my way of thinking, that means getting those women involved in golf, if they are amenable. As an established executive who plays golf, anything you can do to help other women accelerate their learning process and to prepare them to host their own round is as important as giving them the benefit of your experience as they set goals for their corporate careers. Introducing our female business associates to other women who play helps them plug right into the "old girl's network."

In fact, if you are of the mind that more women in your company should play golf, but they are unsure of how to get started, perhaps you might consider encouraging your company to underwrite a day-long clinic and include some female clients. I know of several companies and financial institutions who have done just that with great success.

I was watching CNBC in September of 1995 and there was a segment on how a nationally-known financial services company was paying for one of its female executives to take golf lessons. A huge company with thousands of capable women on the payroll was paying the way (and paving the way) for just one woman. At least it's a start. (Do you think she's under any pressure to improve quickly?)

If you are in the driver's seat in your company and you want to do something to boost morale among your golfing women executives, why not arrange for them to have a private lesson with a pro, send them to golf camp, or sponsor a female foursome in a charity outing. Your short term investment will reap huge dividends, and your company's reputation among your clients will be sterling indeed. If you really want to establish yourself as a golf mentor who cares, invite new golfers out occasionally for 9 holes at an easy course. While you cannot give lessons on the mechanics of the game, you can certainly show the ropes to newcomers by helping them to survive their first outing and perhaps coach them on the rules and etiquette.

I did just that for one of my friends. Susan Michaels, an insurance executive and friend for over sixteen years, decided she wanted to take up golf. She was a founding member of my golf association in 1993, but had yet to pick up a club. In the spring of 1995, however, Susan's husband, Stephen, became a golf member at the club where my husband, Larry, and I are members. Susan knew if she wanted to participate in the club golf events, accompany her husband to the many legal and insurance industry golf outings he was active in, and play in one of the BPWGA leagues, she would have to get started. She enrolled in the Novice Clinic that Susan Bond ran for BPWGA members at Wellesley Country Club.

"I loved it!," she said over the phone the morning after her first lesson.

I know that every time we try something new we are pushing ourselves out of our comfort zone. I think it takes some significant intestinal fortitude for a successful, poised woman to head for the driving range, grab a golf club, tee up a ball, and take a healthy, full swing at it with onlookers on all sides. But swing Susan did . . . all summer long. Every day, she would either swing in front of a mirror at home, or she would head for the driving range just a short distance from her office. She also told me she kept a club near her desk at work and would practice gripping the club over and over until it started to feel right.

She decided that the baseball grip felt better than the interlocking Vardon grip, and since she is quite petite and has small hands, the baseball grip may well give her better control. (A right-handed player who opts for the Vardon grip, named after Henry Vardon, will insert the pinkie finger of the right hand between the index and middle finger of the left hand. It is arguably the most universal method. The baseball grip simply means no fingers are interlocked and the leather on the club is held just as one would hold a baseball bat; all the fingers are in a row.)

In late September, I received one of the sweetest, most satisfying phone calls a golf lover could get from a friend who is learning to play:

"Hi, Cheryl, it's Susan. Do you have time for 9 holes?"

"Yes, I do, and I know just the place. Can you be here at ten tomorrow morning?"

We headed for Stony Brook, a 9 hole, par 3 "Mom and Pop" course just down the road in Southboro, Massachusetts. For a new golfer, it's heaven: no water hazards, no bunkers, no hole longer than 163 yards, and no wait to tee off. I did not bother to pick up a score card. Our mission was to have fun.

Ninety minutes later, Susan finished the ninth hole with these statistics (which I silently kept and only now reveal): She did not miss one short putt, her alignment on the tee was flawless, all of her tee shots stayed in bounds, she whiffed but once. Do you remember your first time on a course as an adult beginner? I remember mine, and I can tell you it wasn't half as good as Susan's. Jubilant, we proceeded to lunch with the promise that I would introduce her to some other women who are beginning their love affair with the great game.

Let's extend mentoring to our daughters and nieces, as well. If your daughter has an interest in golf, then try to help her get started by finding a good pro for regular lessons, enroll her in golf camps, and make time to play as a family. It can be a great way to watch your kids grow up and something that you will always be able to share together. If your daughter is a gifted junior golfer, I would urge you to look into the golf scholarships that are available from so many noteworthy colleges and universities. Oftentimes, those scholarship dollars go unused because parents were not aware of their availability. The most important idea here is that if your daughter chooses to follow a professional path, whether it's business, law, or the sciences, golf will open doors for her just as it has for me.

8

Research, Research, Research

Selecting a golf or country club is a serious undertaking. You have some homework to do before you write the first check. Being a member of a club is like joining a small community, so you need to know as much as possible about this "community"—its philosophy, values, and limitations, before you commit your money and time to join. Just as you researched the town or city you live in to learn about all of its benefits and possible detractions, you must find out what makes a golf club tick.

On the other hand, great progress has been made by a number of public courses which are run by people who have a pulse on America's ever-growing love for golf. They have skillfully targeted and developed a loyal cadre of women golfers by providing a well-maintained course, offering professional instruction, organizing leagues, and having a good place to congregate for post-round drinks, lunch, or dinner. No longer is a "good track" the exclusive domain of the private club set. While much has changed for the better in the public golf domain, even more has changed in the private golf world. In response to the demand for a good place to play on a regular basis without going broke, many clubs are being developed that are a bit more affordable.

Generally, you will be introduced to clubs through friends, relatives, or business associates. Sometimes you'll have the good fortune to be invited to a meeting, a social function, or a charity golf outing which will give you a chance to view the interior of the club house, including the locker room, lounge, and dining facilities. By the end of the day, you'll have a good idea as to the level of service and how well the club is managed. Also, the kind of service you receive will give you a feeling for the club's disposition toward women.

Learning how to play golf will seem easy compared to finding out about the inner workings of a private club before becoming a member. The word "private" refers as much to the attitude of the club's leaders and how their club is run as it does to the fact that the course itself is not available to the public.

The first thing you need to do, even before you recruit a sponsor, is find out as much as you can about how the club treats its female members. The first question you want to ask, particularly if you are going to be the primary member, is if a woman can have a full golf membership.

Full Membership Defined

With a full golf membership, you will be entitled to all the rights and privileges the club has to offer. Specifically, you will have an equity interest in the club (which means you'll own "a piece of the rock"), access to weekend morning tee times, a vote to cast on club issues, and the opportunity to run for office. If you are a single golfer or the only golfer in your family, work long hours during the week, or prefer to play on the weekends—preferably in the morning—then the full membership is the way to go. Finding a club that offers this may be a challenge. Some clubs simply do not offer full memberships to women, although the courts are seeing that this form of discrimination is coming to an end. You should also find out if they have women on the board of directors.

If the answer is no, be advised that this club is male-dominated, and you have some decisions to make. You may look for another club to join, or join and then try to change it from within. If you decide to stay the course and pursue a membership, you're going to need a little history of golf clubs in America, some of which follows.

Still in the Fifties

Historically, country clubs have been for the well-to-do: doctors, lawyers, senior executives, and successful entrepreneurs. But golf

Presenting Yourself for Membership in a Private Club

has become more attractive to many Americans these days, particularly two-income professional couples (many with children), and clubs have seen an increase in membership, particularly in younger people from a variety of professions.

For decades, clubs existed in a "Father Knows Best" mode. The men worked during the week and played golf on the weekend. The wives were homemakers and if they were taking care of young children, they often did not have time to play golf. If they had time, their use of the golf course was severely limited to one morning and one afternoon a week. They might have managed to serve on the entertainment or decorating committee (certainly not on the board of directors) or played bridge and tennis. Many waited to play golf until the children were older. If they did play golf, they were often relegated to Sunday afternoon and their accomplishments on the course weren't taken too seriously.

Title VII of the Civil Rights Act of 1964 started the ball rolling for women, so to speak, by barring sex discrimination in the workplace. Then in 1972, Title IX of the Education Amendments put our institutions of higher learning on notice that the federal funds they received for athletic programs must be used equally between men's and women's programs. Combined with the entrance of women into formerly "men only" schools, these events helped set the stage for a rekindling of the feminist movement, which had been smoldering since the suffragists rocked the nation in the infancy of this century. (You will note that it took until 1920 for the 19th Amendment to the Constitution to be ratified, which gave women the right to vote—so rights for women have historically moved slowly.)

In this new movement, women's voices were even more militant in their demand for equality. The struggle took place in the workplace and carried over to the homefront, right into the bedroom when necessary. Women, now armed with MBAs, law degrees, medical degrees, powerful pens, and united voices, were chipping away at the male-dominated status quo. Their voices were unwavering, their positions were unshakable, and their demands were for full equality

It has taken over twenty years for their hard work to produce the gains we enjoy today in the business and professional worlds. But many country clubs are still culturally in the fifties. When our high courts considered the value of equality, they also considered the rights of privacy and freedom of association, ruling that private clubs were exempt from the Civil Rights Act of 1964. So it is often the men who have the preferred weekend morning tee times while the ladies have weekend afternoons. It is the men who hold office; it is the ladies who decorate the club house for parties. It is the men who decide where the forward tees shall be placed; it is the ladies who must hit from them.

It's Not Like This Everywhere

Having read to this point, if you are now of the opinion that all clubs are male-dominated bastions, take heart. It's not like this everywhere. Stephanie Freeman, a resident of Weston, Connecticut, with a background in market research, has happily and successfully served not only on the board of her club, Redding Country Club in Redding, Connecticut, she also became its president.

Stephanie was the second woman on the board and she worked in various capacities therein for seven years before becoming president in 1993. She told me when we spoke that she is considering running again.

"Ours is a family-oriented club," she told me during our interview. "It's not stuffy and it is very female-friendly."

Redding had the "weekend morning tee time for working women" issue, just as hundreds of clubs do today.

"One club in the area decided to handle this issue by stating that one person in a family can play before noon on Saturday and Sunday. Then it is up to the couple to decide how to use that time," Stephanie said. "When the same issue came before the board at Redding, unlimited tee times were voted in, albeit by a narrow margin. We also have a 'one family, one vote' rule, so that both the husband and the wife have a say in how the club is operated and how expenditures are to be made," she continued.

Presenting Yourself for Membership in a Private Club

When I asked Stephanie if it made sense for female members to sue their clubs for parity, she allowed that it should be a last resort, but believes it will help women to gain equal status in their clubs in the long run. She maintains that the way her club handled the issues defused any problems before they got out of control.

When the Situation Gets "Out of Control"

Sadly, not all clubs have been able to settle these burning issues so easily and amicably. The year was 1988 and the place was Cedar Brook Golf and Tennis Club in Old Brookville, Long Island, New York. The story is taken from Marcia Chambers' extraordinary book, *The Unplayable Lie: The Untold Story of Women and Discrimination in American Golf.*

> After pressing club officials for weeks, Lee Lowell had finally received permission from the Club's management to tee off early one weekend morning. She would be the first woman at the club to do so. She wondered how hard that could be for the men, who were so used to their special weekend tee times. But that system couldn't last forever. This was America. It was 1988. It would be okay. She was a good golfer.
>
> She and her husband had joined Cedar Brook a few months before. She played there mainly in the summer and autumn months; the remainder of the year the couple lived in Florida and were members of a club that had no restrictions on tee times. She hated the tee-time restrictions at Cedar Brook and had vowed to change them when she joined. One could see why. On weekends the pecking order put women last. First men members teed off. Then men members with male guests. Then honeymooners, of all things. And finally, "Lady members with or without guests." Lady members were spouses.
>
> This day, Mrs. Lowell, a former art teacher, faced a special obstacle. She would be playing in a shotgun. A shotgun means golfers begin play simultaneously from all eighteen holes in order to get play moving quickly and to end the round together, usually at a gathering. Had it not rained the previous day, and had she gone out with men she knew, events might have turned out differently. As it was, a shotgun meant she would be playing with strangers.
>
> She arrived at the seventeenth tee. "The two gentlemen I was supposed to play with told me they wouldn't play with me." She was bewildered, stunned; she didn't know what to do or say. Being a golfer, she played the hole alone. She then jumped into her cart and went on to the eighteenth tee.

It was there that she met up with Ronald Forman, the chairman of the men's golf committee. He and a couple of other men were standing in the middle of the fairway, obviously unaware that she had been given permission to play. From where she stood it seemed they were trying to stop play. Mrs. Lowell couldn't understand what was going on. Suddenly, Mr. Forman erupted like Mt. Vesuvius. He began yelling obscenities at her and was joined by others. "They kept screaming I could not play," Mrs. Lowell said. Rather than keep to the order of the game and go to the first tee as required, Lee Lowell headed for what she thought was safer ground, the sixteenth tee. It was empty.

Forman and his men revved up their golf carts and went after her. They gunned their carts. That meant that when they floored it, they were trotting along at a solid ten miles an hour. They cursed at Lowell from 150 yards away. Undaunted, she teed off, her drive narrowly missing Forman. As she drove her cart to her ball, Forman walked up to it, picked it up, and put it in his pocket. He continued to curse at her. She fled again, now to the second tee. As she teed it up, a posse of golfers appeared on the horizon, racing toward her in their golf carts. It looked like a group of eight to ten men, including Forman. They stopped and got out in front of her. One of them unzipped his fly and peed in front of her. She coolly observed his penis. "If that's all you've got to show, it really wasn't worth taking it out, was it?," she inquired. Then Forman, who would have needed the Green Berets to stop him now, waved the ball he had picked up on the sixteenth hole and threw it at her. "He shook his finger in my face and told me, 'you will never hit another golf ball again.'" Still screaming at her, he kicked her ball off the tee.

Now she was really terrified. She tried not to show it, saying to herself, "Okay, I'll just leave." She took off in her golf cart. But this was not to be. As if in Dodge City, the golf posse, led by the fearless Forman, pursued her up and down the fairways in a frenzied golf-cart chase. You could see their brightly colored trouser legs hanging out the sides of their carts as they careened around turns.

Finally, they encircled her. The course appeared to fall silent. "I was alone. But I was determined not to let them run me off," she said. "Yet I was scared. I felt like a child who was afraid of being maimed or hurt. I felt the rage in these men. And Forman reduced me to a child. That's what angers me. I've raised my children, I got myself educated, yet that man diminished me. And where was I? I was in a wealthy country on the fairways of a private country club."

She said she felt as if she were being held prisoner. And for a few minutes she was. She glared at the scowling faces. The men were deep into analyzing their next move. How should they resolve what the judge would later describe as Lowell's gender invasion?

While the men were busy discussing it, she maneuvered her cart away and took off, playing the empty tees, moving quickly from seven to eight to nine and then onto one and five. Afterward, she went to the ladies' room and cried. "I love golf and that's what broke my heart," she said.

A few hours later, the club manager telephoned her at home. She learned that, without ever hearing her side, the golf committee, some of whom had chased her in their carts, had now suspended her for two weeks. The Lowells' life at the club would never be the same. They stayed on, but it wasn't pleasant. Her friends ignored her. "I can't in my heart look at weak women anymore," she now says.

She tried to stay active in the club. She signed up—not surprisingly—for the grievance committee. Learning that, the club's officials disbanded the grievance committee. Her scientist husband was denigrated, too. He would be summoned from lunch to the locker room to find no one there. Both received threatening telephone calls at home. "You better not play or your life is at stake," said one caller.

Not until after a long court battle and several hearings covering some seven years did Mrs. Lowell find peace. They eventually joined another New York club that had no restrictions on women. As a result of the incident, Cedar Brook has made some dramatic reformations, including the establishment of a mixed grill and allowing equal access on weekend mornings.

How sad that events had to take such a shameful turn to get a club to examine its conscience by forcing it to reevaluate its unfair practices. It is even sadder when one considers that so often members of private clubs are the political and business leaders of a community. If their actions reflect their true feelings about women, what real chance do we have as we look for career opportunities in the companies that they run?

Different Levels of Membership, Different Costs

As you continue to gather information on the club you are interested in joining, you will want to find out what exactly your investment will be: What is the initiation fee? What are the annual dues? Is there a bond you must buy? How much is it and can you spread the investment out over a period of time? What are the club's bylaws with regard to divorce? Can you stay if you and your husband split up? Can you assume a full membership in the event of his death?

If you join as a single, full member, will that status be transferred to your spouse should you marry? Will you be relegated to a "B" member in the event of marriage? What are the monthly food minimums? Are the pool and tennis courts extra? Is the driving range extra? Are they planning to remodel the clubhouse or the course in the near future? All of these financial questions are essential in determining if this is the place for you. Also, in the event of a serious injury, onset of a health problem, or if you are moving or being transferred and you are no longer able to maintain your membership, you will want to know what portion of your investment, if any, will be returned to you. Remember, every club is different because the rules and regulations are established by the members. Be sure to get all the facts up front.

How Long is the Waiting List?

Once you have determined that this is the place for you, it will be helpful to get an idea of how long it will take before you get your golf membership. Some newer clubs may have a waiting list just a few months long; other more established clubs have a five-, ten-, even twenty-year waiting list. Some clubs publish the order of the names on the waiting list; others keep that information confidential. If a club publishes the list, you can be assured you will indeed be the next in line. On the other hand, if the club plays its cards close to the vest, you may be bumped if a local celebrity wants to join.

The Probation Period

Many clubs have a "probation period" for all new members, just to make sure it's a good fit all the way around. If a new member turns out to be a quarrelsome, difficult, and downright unpleasant character, the club has a chance to terminate the membership, usually within ninety days. By the same token, if the member is disappointed with the environment, she may depart gracefully. Since most clubs require you to have, at a minimum, one sponsor who is a member of the club, the chances of such unfortunate occurrences are drastically reduced, but sometimes the chemistry just isn't right and both parties agree to go their separate ways.

After the probation period (it sounds more intimidating than it really is), you may become a "social member" with limited access to the golf course. A long waiting list for full golfing privileges often makes this necessary. Perhaps you will be able to play once or twice a month, with or without a member. Maybe you can play on weekend afternoons after 3 PM, or in some of the Scotches that are so popular. Just make sure you know what you can and cannot do before you join and follow the rules.

Nothing will get you into hot water faster than breaking the rules of the club. Golf and country clubs are, by and large, homogeneous societies and the nail that sticks out will be hammered down.

Are You Getting What You Paid For?

Here, perhaps, is a good place to discuss under what circumstances women might consider legal action. If you have joined a club as a full member, which means you have paid the initiation fee, bought the bond, paid your dues, etc. with the understanding that you would be a full golf member, including having a vote and access to weekend morning tee times, but are getting neither, you have a legitimate complaint.

On the other hand, if you have joined a club as a "spouse," and your husband has the full or "A" membership, at let's say $9,000 a year in dues (remember, this is after the one-time initiation fees are paid, which can run from $10,000 to $50,000 and up), and you pay a mere $1,000 in dues as a "spouse" member, then it is purely a matter of economics and you must abide by the "spouse" member or "B" member rules, unless you want to pay for an "A" membership for yourself.

If you are a member of a club and have a legitimate complaint, try to work it out within the confines of the head of the women's golf association or the club's board of directors first. It may take a few overtures to get them to see your side of the situation. Be patient and be reasonable. No one wants to have the club's "laundry" aired in public—especially by the news media. Remember, clubs are owned by the members. They are not public entities. Clubs are places people pay handsomely to join in order to enjoy the amenities and the privacy. They have little tolerance for people who would heap a large legal expense on the operating budget. However, if you are blatantly being discriminated against, and you are willing to endure the icy stares and harsh comments of some disgruntled fellow members, then take legal action to right the wrong. Do so, however, with the knowledge that you will lose some friends. Perhaps you will make others—people who were afraid to do what you did.

Taking a Stand

What can corporate America do to end discrimination against women and other minorities? Again, drawing from Marcia Chambers' book, I will present the story of two top corporate leaders and the steps they took to end discrimination at clubs in their areas.

> When Paul H. O'Neill became chairman of the Aluminum Company of America in 1987, he learned that one of the perks of running Alcoa was membership at Laurel Valley Golf Club in Ligonier, Pennsylvania. According to the *Washington Post,* when he inquired if the club admitted women and blacks as members, and was told, "No," he refused to join. But he didn't stop there. The company adopted a policy that it would not pay dues for any of its executives to organizations that discriminated, or reimburse expenses incurred at such clubs.

Another example reads . . .

> In 1994, John F. Smith, Jr., president and chief executive officer of General Motors, resigned from Bloomfield Hills Country Club in Michigan, long an exclusive bastion of the auto industry's top executives, because Roy S. Roberts, a black vice president, was rejected for membership. This was not racism, the club's president said. But he offered no other reason for the action.

After Mr. Smith resigned from Bloomfield Hills, his story could be found in the major newspapers and TV shows.

Are We Seeing a Trend?

With the popularity of golf enjoying a steady rise, more people will be looking into membership in private clubs as tee times at upscale public courses become more and more difficult to book. Clubs are wonderful retreats for leisure time activities, provide a splendid backdrop for entertaining friends and clients—despite the current tax laws—and may well lead you to new business opportunities as you come to know the members. For busy two-income couples, meeting for dinner at your club after a hectic day can be a great way to unwind. If you are looking for a place where you can get a tee time with little or no difficulty, especially on the weekends, where the condition of the course and clubhouse will always be top notch, and where you can host friends, family, and business associates, joining a private club could be a very satisfying investment.

The amendments of individual states' civil rights laws to end discrimination against women and minorities in private clubs is gaining momentum, buoyed by responsible corporate and political leaders. In addition, the IRS and state tax departments have considerable clout to impact the nonprofit tax exemption enjoyed by so many "private" clubs if the clubs discriminate "against any person on the basis of race, color, religion or gender," while the state can easily pull the liquor license of a club that discriminates. Further, how private can a club be if it is serving meals to non-members, allows non-members to buy goods at the pro shop, gives lessons to non-members, permits business and trade to be conducted within the club between members and non-members, receives payments or fees for use of the space or facilities from non-members, and acknowledges corporate tax deductions for memberships as business expenses?

And what of the fathers who would let their daughters be shoved aside by the club at which they spent their childhood, when they grow up and take on their own responsibilities as business leaders and professionals? How can these men say they want women to help them to lead their companies, and then retreat behind archaic, discriminatory practices at the golf club?

My own experience at our club has been a positive one, with many changes and improvements occurring every year. Women at my club can have a full membership with a full vote and weekend morning tee times. Our grill room is coed and is often quite fun and boisterous. We have plenty of 9- and 18-hole Scotches to play in, member/member tournaments, guest days, and intraclub matches at some of the area's finest clubs. We also have a terrific junior golf program. The men and women at our club respect what all golfers respect: those who have worked on their games to develop their skills, know the rules and etiquette, don't hold up play, show up on time, and pay their bets off at the end of the round. It's really pretty simple; I expect to live happily there for many years to come.

9

At one of the meetings I arranged for the members of the Business and Professional Women's Golf Association back in November of 1994, a personal fitness trainer came to talk to us about exercises we could do over the winter months to stay fit for golf. She also gave us some insight into the minds of the Olympic athletes she has helped train over the years.

The speaker, Cathy Von Klemperer, whom I mentioned in the introduction, shared this with us: "Positive thinking is a key to self-confidence. Unlike physical skills, it is a mental skill that can be observed only by you. You must be aware of what you think and say to yourself when you practice and play. Ask yourself if you are thinking about your skills or if you are doubting yourself. Remember: Winners think about what they want to happen; losers think about what they fear might happen. You must use your thoughts to direct your attention and behavior."

Cathy invited one of her clients to come and speak with us. A young mother of three, who had just finished another road race that day, had this to say, "I never was an athlete. I thought having asthma meant I couldn't run. That was three months ago. Since then, I run three miles four times a week and have entered many two mile races. I feel more confident, adventurous and proactive in all areas."

Making My Own Commitment

It took me six months of thinking about all the things Cathy and her client had said to us that day before I finally picked up the phone and asked for an appointment.

"I want to be a better golfer," I told her over the phone. "I'm taking lessons, I'm practicing, but I'm not building strength and I'm not training my mind to think about being a better golfer."

Cathy suggested a time. In fact, she suggested six times—once a week for six weeks. I was going to boot camp!

The first visit was spent talking about my business, my schedule, what other sports I enjoyed (tennis, skiing, biking, and walking), the power of meditation, the benefits of daily stretching, and some athletic goals we could set for a six-week period, to be followed by goals for a six-month period. She gave me some reading to do, some stretches to incorporate into my day, and suggested I come the following week in workout clothes. She also gave me a daily log to fill out each time I completed an activity: stretch, meditate, walk, golf, bike, etc.

Each time I meditated (really another name for deep breathing exercises), I told myself I had a smooth golf swing, along with my other positive affirmation for the week. Each time I rode my bike 5 miles, I could feel my legs getting stronger. In a very short period of time, I had totaled 100 miles. Then I tried 10 miles in one ride. It was exhilarating. Me, forty-something, pedaling along with the wind, over hills, on back roads—feeling very empowered.

When I went to play golf, I did the stretches included in this chapter and before I got on the first tee, I would do a deep breathing exercise and tell myself, "I am a good golfer. I have a smooth swing." Then, I would picture my friend Susan Bond's elegant swing in my mind's eye. Let me tell you, it worked. Not every time, but often enough to make me believe you can think your way to achievement in sports and in business.

Is There a Correlation between Mind and Muscles?

Research is currently underway at the Institute of Neurology in London, as well as here in the United States, on the impact of mentally rehearsing a technique or movement and how it translates into enhanced physical ability. It seems that swinging a club in mental practice turns on most of the brain circuits used when a person swings for real at the golf course.

That's why a practice swing can be so helpful during your round. You're giving your body a signal that you will be requiring it to perform a task in a few moments, and you are giving your mind a chance to envision the shot you are about to make. While nothing can replace the benefit of practice to build muscle memory, thinking about performing a task well does help.

Golf Exercises

When most people think about golf, they do not necessarily think about fitness, especially when we see players riding about in motorized carts. While golf is more of a skill sport than an endurance sport (like swimming, tennis, or running), it still requires muscles to be in good shape for optimum performance.

Since most of the power in a golf swing comes from the lower half of the body, exercises that build strength in the legs are the place to start. Walking, cycling, and weight training are all great ways to tone muscles and build strength. Tennis, swimming, and rowing will build additional upper body strength and expand aerobic capacity.

In the following photos, Susan Bond is demonstrating some stretches you can do before you play to loosen your golfing muscles. As with any stretching exercise, do not force the stretch—turn gently to avoid injury. Be sure to bend your knees as you take the club down to the ground.

With the club behind her back, Susan transfers her weight, coiling power around her right side with her weight on the right leg, and releasing with a smooth follow-through as the weight shifts to her left side.

You can practice these stretches every day in the comfort of your home or office.

With the club over her head, Susan gently moves from side to side to loosen muscles in her torso and arms. Do ten repetitions.

Keeping her knees bent, Susan loosens her lower back muscles and hamstrings. Do ten repetitions.

Exercises for Your Body and Stretches for Your Mind

With this exercise, Susan is working on her turn. Notice how her weight is loaded onto the right side in the first pose, then shifts to the left, simulating her follow-through. Do ten repetitions.

Here Susan is coming through and shifting weight onto the left side. Notice how she finishes with her right knee facing the target and her right foot up. Do ten repetitions.

Mind Stretches: Think your way to better golf

Course management is as much a part of your mental training as putting practice is to developing a smooth stroke on the green.

Suppose you have a shot off the tee that slices to the right and comes to rest on another fairway. The ball lands at the beginning of a stand of pine trees that divides the fairways and is about 100 yards in length. You can see your ball and, according to the local rules, it is not OB. Upon reaching your ball, here is how the situation looks. Ahead of you, there's a narrow opening in the trees that a perfect 4-iron shot could get through. Maybe you could lob the ball over the trees with a perfect 9-iron shot, and advance the ball that way. But would you consider another option like laterally "punching" the ball out with a hooded 4- or 5-iron to get it back into play in your fairway?

Let's play out a possible scenario for each option. I've used the word "perfect" in the first two cases for a reason. As amateur golfers, we occasionally hit a perfect shot. The pros, on the other hand, occasionally hit a bad shot. Suppose your 4-iron shot hits a tree and bounces right back at you. In fact, it flies past you by about 10 yards. You've lost yardage and added at least another stroke to get back into play. Suppose your 9-iron lob over the trees is hit fat, and now you're in the trees. Add another stroke to get out from under the trees and back onto your fairway.

Now, let's look at what good course management would dictate. Punch your shot out with a low iron and the ball will roll into the middle of your fairway. You'll be able to see the green and you could be on in three. Being in the middle of your fairway and seeing the target will give you the confidence to execute a good third shot.

Keeping our minds focused and under control is one of the most important parts of our golf game. The sooner we can teach ourselves to think about the next shot, and only the next shot, the stronger we will be as players. It's easy, after three or four bad holes in a row, to start saying, "I'm a lousy player. I can't do this."

In fact, this is the time to reach down inside yourself and say something like, "I am going to pull myself together, slow that backswing down and follow through." You have to tell yourself that you can do it. It may take a few more shots for the thought process to kick in, but it will kick in!

Never give up, never give in. Once we begin to train ourselves to stay focused, to "treat our thoughts and images as though they are subject to our control," as Cathy Von Klemperer says, "we will begin to feel the power of mind over body."

If someone told you that you were not qualified to run a company, drive a car, or run for office, wouldn't you take the challenge to demonstrate to your detractors that you most certainly can attain the goals that you set for yourself? Well, in golf, we have to keep telling ourselves we can. We have to keep showing ourselves, through mental discipline, that good shots will follow a series of poor shots if we only stay focused and think about performing better.

Anger Is Your Worst Enemy

There are few emotions that will take your game apart quicker than a flared temper. The best golfers I know keep their emotions in check. A bad shot is not automatically followed by a string of expletives. Accept what has happened, and then visualize the success of your upcoming shot. Anger disrupts our ability to think clearly. What is called for is logic, self-control, and the ability to make the next shot. Poor sports throw clubs and carry on. Winners (regardless of score) are those who maintain their dignity and are mindful that they are with friends or colleagues who should not have to endure a childish outburst.

"Play Within Yourself"

The legendary Patty Berg gave me the best advice when I participated in the Pat Bradley Thyroid Foundation Pro-Am a few summers ago. Addressing a gallery of anxious amateurs who were about to tee it up with LPGA players, Patty turned to us and said, "Play within yourself."

At that precise moment, golf took on a whole new meaning for me. I no longer had to try to hit the ball as far as the men I played with. I would never again feel embarrassed after hitting a bad shot. Everyone hits a bad shot now and then, even the pros. I no longer worried when someone used a pitching wedge as I stood near the same spot clutching my 9-iron. I had just received "the sermon on the Mount" and all was right in my universe.

As we made our way to the first tee that day, I watched as the men teed it up at the blues, then our LPGA pro, Carrie Wood, hit from the whites, and then I, Cheryl A. Leonhardt, all-American amateur, walked calmly to the red tees and launched the proverbial rocket. We used my drive on the first tee!

The moral of the story is this: be yourself on the course. Don't put undue pressure on yourself to perform the way other players perform. Think in terms of playing to the best of your ability. Your skills will come with time, practice, and patience.

Golf is supposed to be fun, first and foremost. The sooner we learn to not take ourselves too seriously on the course, the sooner we will relax and enjoy not only the game, but the fine company and the beautiful surroundings. Golf is not, as Mark Twain once said, "A good walk spoiled." No, to me, it is a wonderful way to enjoy a lovely summer day, to smell the fragrance of newly-opened flowers floating over a gentle spring breeze. I feel so alive when I am on the golf course. I love watching a red wing hawk float gracefully over the seventh hole and I readily admit to cooing over the new ducklings, all small and fuzzy, as they make their way to the water as a bossy, squawking mother duck leads the way. I love playing golf with my friends, with my husband, and with people I've just met, because they'll be strangers for only a hole or two. I know I'll find some silly, funny thing to say and everyone will laugh and with that burst of laughter we'll be on our way to becoming friends.

I really appreciate every game because I am looking down at the tee instead of looking up at it, if you know what I mean. So lighten up. Enjoy each time you get to go out. Goodness knows, we've all spent enough time at our desks on sunny days, and enough nights burning the midnight oil to finish a report or meet a deadline. Remember when you were stuck at the airport in a blizzard or sat trapped in a plane on the tarmac while the rain pounded down? Think for a moment about the last tacky hotel room you stayed in while preparing for the next day's crucial meetings.

We all work hard. We all sacrifice. We all worry about every last detail. So when it's time to go out and play some golf, stop feeling guilty, and try putting a little more emphasis on the word *play*! The golf part will come in good time.

Appendix I

This directory, which is organized alphabetically by the 31 most populated U.S. cities, was compiled with assistance from the presidents of several chapters of the Executive Women's Golf League. It lists more than one hundred "female friendly" courses around the country, and I hope you will find it helpful as you look for fun places to learn and play near your home or office.

The Executive Women's Golf Association is a national membership organization designed to help unite career-oriented women who want to learn and enjoy the game of golf in a positive, accepting environment. While activities vary from chapter to chapter, the focus is on league play, clinics, charity outings, and regional events. There are chapters in most major cities, which translates into thousands of EWG members who share your interest in golf. For more information, call EWG headquarters at (800) 407-1477, or find the nearest chapter in Appendix V.

When deciding on a course, be sure to use the rating and slope as a gauge, taking into consideration not only your own skill level, but that of your client or colleague. Also, keep in mind that the ratings here are from the red tees. If you need a refresher course on slope and rating definitions, you'll find it at the beginning of Chapter 3.

The following fees guide will help you determine which courses best fit your budget and outing purpose.

$	Under $25
$$	$25-40
$$$	$40-60
$$$$	$60-80
$$$$$	Over $80

Atlanta

The Champions Club $$$-$$$$
151135 Hopewell Road   **4,470 yards**
Alpharetta, GA 30201-3140   **65.2/108**
(770) 343-9700
http://www.championsclub.com
A hilly, heavily wooded 180-acre course in suburban Atlanta.

Fox Creek Golf Club $-$$
1501 Windy Hill Road   **3,055 yards**
Smyrna, GA 30080   **57.1/96**
(770) 435-1000
FAX: (770) 434-2350
An 18-hole executive course.

Olde Atlanta Golf Club $$$
5750 Olde Atlanta Parkway   **5,081 yards**
Suwanee, GA 30024   **69.3/119**
(770) 497-0097
http://www.oldeatlanta.com
Designed by Arthur Hills, offering tree-lined fairways and rolling, hilly terrain. Thirty minutes from downtown.

Baltimore

Bay Hills Golf Club $$
454 Bay Hills Drive   **5,057 yards**
Arnold, MD 21012   **69.2/121**
(410) 974-0669
An abundance of bunkers and water hazards places a premium on strategy and shot placement.

Bear Creek Golf Club $$
2158 Littlestown   **5,270 yards**
Westminster, MD 21158   **Not rated/123**
(410) 876-4653

Clifton Park Golf Course $
2701 Saint Lo Drive   **5,314 yards**
Baltimore, MD 21213   **Not rated/107**
(410) 243-3500

Appendix I: Recommended Courses

Geneva Farm Golf Club $-$$
217 Davis Road **5,427 yards**
Street, MD 21154 **71.4/116**
(410) 836-8816

This championship course is built on the site of an historic farm. A restored, century-old barn serves as the clubhouse.

Boston

Colonial $$$
427 Walnut Street **5,280 yards**
Lynnfield, MA 01940 **70.5/119**
(781) 245-0335

Juniper Hill Golf Club $$
202 Brigham Street **Lakeside: 4,707 yards; 65.3/102**
Northborough, MA 01532 **Riverside: 5,373 yards; 70.2/117**
(508) 393-2444

Juniper Hill offers two courses to choose from: Lakeside and Riverside.

Sandy Burr $$
103 Cochituate Road **4,561 yards**
Wayland, MA 01778 **66.2/110**
(508) 358-7211

Chicago

Marriott's Lincolnshire Golf Course $$$
10 Marriot Drive **4,900 yards**
Lincolnshire, IL 60069 **68.9/117**
(847) 634-0100

Pine Meadows $$$-$$$$
1 Pine Meadow Lane **5,203 yards**
Mundelein, IL 60060 **70.2/120**
(847) 566-4653

Steeple Chase $-$$
Mailing address: 100 North Seymour **4,831 yards**
Mundelein, IL 60060 **68.1/113**
Physical address: 200 North La Vista Drive
Mundelein, IL 60060
(847) 949-8900

Ranked in Chicagoland's top ten public courses for four years running.

Cincinnati

Crooked Tree $$
5171 Sentinel Oak Drive **5,295 yards**
Mason, OH 45040 **69.7/118**
(513) 398-3933

The Golf Center at King's Island $$$-$$$$
6042 Fairway Drive **North/South: 5,143 yards; 69.2/114**
Mason, OH 45040 **North/West: 5,176 yards; 69.4/117**
(513) 398-5200 **South/West: 5,139 yards; 69.2/116**

Designed by Jack Nicklaus and named the Grizzly Course, the Golf Center has 27 holes of championship golf. There is also a midlength course named the Bruin. Has hosted numerous LPGA events.

Sugar Ridge Golf Club $$$
21010 State Line Road **4,812 yards**
Lawrenceburg, IN 47025 **66.9/109**
(513) 333-0333

Cleveland

Astorhurst Country Club $
7000 Dunham Road **6,075 yards**
Walton Hills, OH 44146 **73.3/124**
(216) 439-3636

Mallard Creek Golf Club $$
34500 Royalton Road **36.6/118**
Columbia Station, OH 44028
(440) 236-8231

Three separate 9-hole courses: 2,887, 2,890, and 2,915 yards each.

Manakiki $
35501 Eddy Road **5,390 yards**
Willoughby Hills, OH 44094 **72.8/121**
(440) 942-2500

Columbus

Cooks Creek Golf Club $$$
16405 US HWY 23 South **Red tees: 4,995 yards; 68.2/120**
Ashville, OH 43103 **White tees: 5,972 yards; 71.5/127**
(614) 983-3636

Twenty minutes south of Columbus. Two women's tee placements. Global Positioning System.

Appendix I: Recommended Courses

Foxfire Golf Club **Foxfire course:**
10799 State Route 104 $-$$; 5,175 yards; 71.1/111
Lockbourne, OH 43237 **Players Club:**
(614) 224-3694 $$-$$$; 5,255 yards; 70.3/121

Boasts two 18-hole championship courses: the Foxfire course and the Players Club at Foxfire.

Raymond Memorial Golf Course $
3860 Trabue Road **5,113 yards**
Columbus, OH 43228 **66.9/113**
(614) 645-3276

A Robert Trent Jones design, with his trademark large elevated greens, bunkered on both sides. Built in the 1950s.

Shamrock $-$$
4436 Powell Road **5,520 yards**
Powell, OH 43065 **67.8/119**
(614) 792-6630

Dallas

Hyatt Bear Creek Golf and Racquet Club $$$$
3500 Bear Creek Court West course: **5,570 yards; 72.5/122**
DFW Airport, TX 75261 East course: **5,620 yards; 72.4/124**
(972) 615-6800

Two 18-hole championship courses, minutes from the Dallas-Ft.Worth Airport.

Pecan Hollow Golf Course $
4501 East 14th Street **5,300 yards**
Plano, TX 75074 **71.3/118**
(972) 423-5444

Ridgeview Ranch $$
2701 Ridgeview Drive **5,335 yards**
Plano, TX 75025 **70.4/117**
(972) 390-1039

Denver

Buffalo Run Golf Course $$
15700 East 112th Avenue **5,227 yards**
Commerce City, CO 80022 **68.1/119**
(303) 289-1500

Fox Hollow $$
13410 West Morrison Road **Canyon/Meadow: 5,203 yards; 69.9/121**
Lakewood, CO 80028 **Links/Meadow: 5,396 yards; 71.5/119**
(303) 986-7888 **Canyon/Links: 7,461 yards; 71.6/124**
Three separate 9-hole courses, just minutes from downtown Denver.

Lake Valley Golf Club $$
4400 Lake Valley Drive **5,713 yards**
Longmont, CO 80503 **71.7/126**
(303) 444-2114

Links-style course designed by Press Maxwell, situated in the naturally rolling terrain of the Rocky Mountain foothills.

Detroit

Copper Creek $
27925 Golf Pointe Boulevard **2,428 yards**
Farmington Hills, MI 48331 **33.9/118**
(248) 489-1777

Copper Creek has a 9-hole public course combined with an elegant restaurant.

Fox Hills Golf and Convention Center
8768 North Territorial Road **Golden Fox: $$$; 5,040 yards; 69.7/122**
Plymouth, MI 48170 **Hills/Woodlands: $-$$; 5,588 yards; 70/100.2**
(313) 453-7272 **Woodlands/Lakes: $-$$; 5,548 yards; 69.9/107.2**
 Lakes/Hills: $-$$; 6,028 yards; 72.6/108.1

With 27 holes of golf, including the Golden Fox, Fox Hills is a championship course with a Scottish flair, designed by Arthur Hills. Three 9-hole courses are available as well: the Lakes, Hills, and Woodlands.

Sycamore Hills $$$
4787 North Avenue **West/South: 5,122 yards; 68.5/120**
Macomb, MI 48042 **South/North: 4,934 yards; 67.2/121**
(810) 598-9500 **North/West: 5,070 yards; 68.3/119**

Three 9-hole courses: West, South, and North.

Fort Worth

Fossil Creek $$-$$$
3401 Clubgate Drive **5,066 yards**
Ft. Worth, TX 76137 **68.5/111**
(817) 847-1900

Appendix I: Recommended Courses

Riverchase Golf Club
700 Riverchase Drive
Coppell, TX 75019
(972) 462-8281
$$$
5,125 yards
70.5/119

Squaw Valley
HCR 51-45B
Glenrose, TX 76043
(254) 897-7956
$$
5,014 yards
70.0/117

Houston

Bear Creek
16001 Clay Road
Houston, TX 77084
(281) 855-4720
Masters: $$-$$$; 5,544 yards; 72/123
Presidents: $-$$; 5,728 yards; 71.2/112
Challenger: $-$$; 4,432 yards; 65.7/104

Three courses to choose from: Masters, Presidents, and Challenger.

Old Orchard Golf Club
13134 FM 1464
Richmond, TX 77469
(281) 277-3300
$$$
Range/Stables: 5,020 yards; 68.1/111
Stables/Barn: 5,035 yards; 69.0/113
Barn/Range: 5,167 yards; 69.4/114

Three 9-hole courses: The Range, Stables, and Barn.

Southwick
2907 Clubhouse Drive
Pearland, TX 77584
(713) 436-9999
$$$
5,145 yards
70.5/120

Kansas City

Bent Oak Golf Club
1300 Southeast 30th Street
Oak Grove, MO 64075
(816) 690-3028
$
5,500 yards
Not rated/119

Dub's Dread Golf Club
12601 Hollingsworth Road
Kansas City, KS 66109
(913) 721-1333
$
5,454 yards
Not rated/113

Windbrook Country Club
10306 Northwest 45 Highway
Parkville, MO 64152
(816) 741-9520
$
4,939 yards
Not rated/112

Los Angeles

Malibu Country Club $$$$
901 Encinal Canyon 5,523 yards
Malibu, CA 90265 71.4/119
(818) 889-6680
Nestled in a canyon in the middle of the Santa Monica mountains.

Rancho Park Golf Course $
10460 West Pico Boulevard 6,000 yards
Los Angeles, CA 90064 73/121
(310) 838-7373

Recreation Park Golf Course $
5001 Deukmejian Drive 5,793 yards
Long Beach, CA 90804 72.6/120
(562) 494-5000

Miami

Bayshore Golf Course $-$$$
2301 Alton Road 5,538 yards
Miami Beach, FL 71.6/120
(305) 532-3350
FAX: (305) 532-3840

Crandon Park Golf Course $$-$$$$
6700 Crandon Boulevard 5,662 yards
Key Biscayne, FL 33149 73.1/129
(305) 361-9129
FAX: (305) 361-1082

Miami National Golf Club $-$$$$
5401 Kendale Lakes Drive **Marlin (2,743) + Dolphin (2,579):**
Miami, FL 33183 5,322 yards; 69.6/119
(305) 382-3935 **Barracuda: 2,702 yards; 70.6/118**
FAX: (305) 382-3996
Three 9-hole courses: The Marlin, Dolphin, and Barracuda.

Appendix I: Recommended Courses

Milwaukee

Country Club of Wisconsin   **$$$**
2241 Highway W   **5,499 yards**
Grafton, WI 53024   **72.4/126**
(414) 375-2444
FAX: (414) 375-4187
Twenty minutes north of Milwaukee, nominated for Golf Digest's "Best New Public Course" in 1995.

Muskego Lakes Country Club   **$-$$**
S100 W14020 Highway 36   **5,493 yards**
Muskego, WI 53150   **71.7/123**
(414) 425-6500
FAX: (414) 425-7165
E-mail: mark/proaol.com

Western Lakes Country Club   **$$**
W287 N963 Oakton Road   **5,662 yards**
Pewaukee, WI 53072   **71.8/122**
(414) 691-0900
FAX: (414) 691-9893

Minneapolis/St. Paul

Baker National Golf Course   **$**
2935 Parkview Drive   **5,395 yards**
Medina, MN 55340   **Not rated/129**
(612) 473-0800

Bunker Hills Golf Course   **$$**
1313 Coon Rapids Boulevard   **5,863 yards**
Coon Rapids, MN 55433   **74.2/128**
(612) 755-4141
Thirty-five minutes northwest of Minneapolis.

Edinburgh USA   **$$**
8700 Edinbrook Crossing   **5,255 yards**
Brooklyn Park, MN 55443   **70.7/128**
(612) 424-7060
Pro shop: (612) 315-8550
This 18-hole championship course, designed by Robert Trent Jones, Jr., is fifteen minutes northwest of Minneapolis. Site of the Minnesota LPGA Tour Classic since 1990.

New York City

Brigantine Golf Links $$$
Roosevelt Boulevard & the Bay   **5,460 yards**
Brigantine, NJ 08203   **71.2/123**
(609) 266-1388
(800) 698-1388

This Scottish links-style course was named to Golf for Women's *Top FairWays list of the country's 175 most "women-friendly" courses in 1997.*

Latourette Park Golf Course $
1001 Richmond Hill Road   **5,493 yards**
Staten Island, NY   **70.9/115**
(718) 351-1889

Rancocas Golf Club $$$
Clubhouse Drive   **5,284 yards**
Willingboro, NJ 08046   **70.9/122**
(609) 877-5344

This Robert Trent Jones course is named after a former local Indian tribe.

Van Cortlandt Golf Course $-$$
Van Cortlandt Park South   **5,388 yards**
Bailey Avenue   **72.9/118**
Bronx, NY 10471
(718) 543-4595

Philadelphia

Ashbourne Country Club $$-$$$$
Oak Lane and Ashbourne Roads   **5,263 yards**
Cheltenham, PA 19019   **71.5/125**
(215) 635-3090

Eagle Lodge Country Club $$$$
Ridge Pike and Manor Road   **5,260 yards**
Lafayette Hill, PA 19444   **70.74/123**
(610) 940-4787

Wyncote Golf Club $$-$$$$
50 Wyncote Drive   **5,454 yards**
Oxford, PA 19363   **71.6/126**
(610) 932-8900

Appendix I: Recommended Courses

Phoenix

Camelback Golf Club $$$$$
7847 North Mockingbird   **The Padre: 5,586 yards; 72/124**
Scottsdale, AZ 85253   **Indian Bend: 5,917 yards; 72/118**
(602) 596-7050

Two courses laid out in the shadows of Scottsdale's Camelback Mountain. The Padre offers a "classic Arizona golf experience," with well-bunkered greens and tall stands of eucalyptus trees. Indian Bend is a links-style course, winding its way through water holes and the southwestern landscape.

The Pointe Golf Club on Lookout Mountain $$$$$
11151 North 7th Street   **4,557 yards**
Phoenix, AZ 85020   **65.3/113**
(602) 866-6356

This Bill Johnston-designed course is on the edge of the Phoenix Mountain Preserve, with views of both Lookout Mountain and Squaw Peak. Combines desert and traditional golf layouts. Part of the Pointe Hilton Resort at Tapatio Cliffs.

Red Mountain Ranch $$$
Lakes at Ahwatukee   **3,177 yards**
13431 South 44th Street   **56.4/86**
Phoenix, AZ 85044
(602) 893-3004

Pittsburgh

Black Hawk Golf Course $
644 Black Hawk Road   **First and Second Nines:**
Route 251   **5,365 yards; 70.9/112**
P.O. Box 1538   **Third and Fourth Nines:**
Beaver Falls, PA 15010   **5,552 yards; 71.4/112**
(412) 843-5512

Two sets of nine holes.

Deer Run Golf Club $$
4321 Monier Road   **5,238 yards**
Gibsonia, PA 15044   **70.9/127**
(412) 265-4800

Semi-private club. Tee times are difficult to get, but worth it.

Lindenwood Golf Course
260 Galley Road
McMurray, PA 15317
(412) 745-9889
Twenty-seven holes total.

$
5,199 yards
66.4/119

Portland

Eastmoreland
2425 Southeast Bybee Boulevard
Portland, OR 97202
(503) 775-2900

$
5,646 yards
71.3/117

Rated one of Golf Digest's *top 25 public courses*—a 36-hole championship course in downtown Portland, yet surrounded by lakes and woods.

Heron Lakes
3500 North Victory Boulevard
Portland, OR 97217
(503) 289-1818

Greenback:
$; **5,240 yards; 69.4/113**
Great Blue:
$$; **5,285 yards; 69.8/120**

One of Golf Digest's *top 75 public courses*. The two distinct courses, the Greenback and the Great Blue, are designed by renowned golf architect Robert Trent Jones, Jr.

Ghost Creek at Pumpkin Ridge
12930 Old Pumpkin Ridge Road
North Plains, OR 97113
(503) 647-9977
FAX: (503) 647-2002

$$$$-$$$$$
5,206 yards
70.4/117

This Bob Cupp-designed course hosted the 1997 U.S. Women's Open and was named Best New Public Course in 1992 by Golf Digest.

Sacramento

Ancil Hoffman Park Golf Course
6700 Tarshes Drive
Carmichael, CA 95608
(916) 482-5660

$
5,954 yards
72.8/128

Bing Maloney Golf Course
6801 Freeport Boulevard
Sacramento, CA 95822
(916) 428-9401

$
5,889 yards
68.5/106

Features full-length 9- and 18-hole executive course.

Appendix I: Recommended Courses

Del Webb's Sun City Roseville $$
7050 Del Webb Boulevard   **5,182 yards**
Roseville, CA 95747   **70.8/122**
(916) 774-3851

San Antonio

Cedar Creek $
8250 Vista Colina   **5,216 yards**
San Antonio, TX 78255   **67/122**
(210) 695-5050

Hill and dale terrain plus a great view from the clubhouse.

Tapatio Springs Resort $$$$
P.O. Box 550   **5,179 yards**
Boerne, TX 78006   **70.9/122**
(800) 999-3299

Situated in San Antonio's hill country, Tapatio Springs is recognized as one of the top ten golf resorts in Texas, with an 18-hole Billy Johnston-designed course plus an executive 9-hole.

Willow Springs $
202 Coliseum Road   **5,792 yards**
San Antonio, TX 78219   **73.7/115**
(210) 226-6721

Built in 1923, this course has hosted several Texas Open tournaments.

San Diego

Aviara $$$$$
7447 Batiquitos Drive   **5,007 yards**
Carlsbad, CA 92009   **69.1/119**
(760) 603-6900

Coronado Golf Course $$
2000 Visalia Row   **5,784 yards**
Coronado, CA 92118   **73.7/126**
(619) 435-3121

Steele Canyon Golf and Country Club $$$
3199 Stonefield Drive Canyon/Ranch: 5,657 yards; 72.9/131
Jamul, CA 91935 Ranch/Meadow: 5,600 yards; 72.8/131
(619) 441-6900 Meadow/Canyon: 5,291 yards; 70.5/124

Twenty-seven unique holes, each nine designed by Gary Player. Twenty minutes from downtown San Diego.

San Francisco

Half Moon Bay Golf Links $$$$$
2000 Fairway Drive Ocean Course: 5,109 yards; 70.7/115
Half Moon Bay, CA 94019 Links Course: 5,745 yards; 73.3/128
(650) 726-4438

Within an hour of downtown San Francisco, Half Moon Bay features two courses: the traditional Links and the newer, appropriately named Ocean, running along the water.

The Presidio Golf Course $$-$$$$
P.O. Box 29603 **5,785 yards**
San Francisco, CA 94129 **69.2/127**
(415) 561-4653

A Robert Johnstone design, built in 1914, the course occupies an often fog-shrouded corner of the nation's oldest military post. One of the three oldest courses in continuous operation west of the Mississippi.

San Juan Oaks Golf Club $$$-$$$$
P.O. Box 1060 **Red tees: 4,770 yards; 67.1/116**
San Juan Bautista, CA 95045 **Gold tees: 5,785 yards; 72.8/128**
(408) 636-6113

Five different tee placements, two for women.

Seattle

Jackson Park Golf Club $
1000 NE 135th Street **5,636 yards**
Seattle, WA 98125 **71.8/118**
(206) 363-4747
For tee times: (206) 301-0472
http://www.cybergolf.com/Jacksonpark/

An 18-hole championship course and a 9-hole executive course located just north of downtown in the Olympic Hills area.

Appendix I: Recommended Courses

Jefferson Park $
4101 Beacon Avenue S **5,490 yards**
Seattle, WA 98108 **70.2/116**
(206) 762-4513
For tee times: (206) 301-0472
http://www.cybergolf.com/Jefferson

An 18-hole championship course plus a 9-hole executive course offering views of downtown Seattle and Mt. Rainier.

Willows Run Golf Club $$-$$$
10442 Willows Road NE **5,571 yards**
Redmond, WA 98052 **Not rated**
(206) 883-1200 or (206) 869-7607
FAX: (206) 869-7607
http://www.willowsrun.com/
Links-style course.

St. Louis

Forest Park Golf Course $-$$
5591 Grand Drive **5,528 yards**
St.Louis, MO 63112 **71.5/117**
(314) 367-1337

Quail Creek Golf Club $$$*
6022 Wells Road **5,244 yards**
St. Louis, MO 63128 **69.2/109**
(314) 487-1988

*Designed by Hale Irwin. * Discount for soft spikes or tennis shoes.*

Spencer T. Olin Community Golf Course $$-$$$
4701 College Avenue **5,049 yards**
Alton, IL 62002 **65.6/110**
(314) 355-8128 or (618) 465-3111

Rated number one public golf facility in St. Louis. Designed and managed by Arnold Palmer. Global Positioning System used. Host of 1996 USGA Women's Amateur Pub Links Championship.

Tampa

The Eagles Golf Course $$-$$$
16101 Nine Eagles Road **Islands/Forests: 4,911 yards; 67.6/120**
Odessa, Tampa Bay, FL 33556 **Oaks/Lakes: 5,375 yards; 70/114**
(813) 920-6681

Two sets of 9-hole courses: Islands/Forest and Oaks/Lakes.

Saddlebrook Resort $$$$$
5700 Saddlebrook Way **Saddlebrook Course:**
Wesley Chapel, FL 33543-4499 **5,147 yards; 70.8/124**
(813) 973-1111 **Palmer Course:**
(800) 729-8383 **5,212 yards; 70.2/121**
FAX: (813) 973-4504
http://www.saddlebrookresort.com
Two championship courses, both designed by Arnold Palmer.

Westchase $$-$$$
10217 Radcliffe Drive **5,205 yards**
Tampa, FL 33626 **69.1/121**
(813) 854-2331

Virginia Beach/Norfolk/Newport News

Kiln Creek Golf and Country Club $$-$$$
1003 Brick Kiln Boulevard **5,316 yards**
Newport News, VA 23602 **69.5/119**
(757) 988-3220
Designed by Tom Clark; numerous lakes and sandtraps.

Ocean View Golf Course $
9610 Norfolk Avenue **5,470 yards**
Norfolk, VA 23503 **70.0/115**
(757) 480-2094
One of the oldest and most scenic courses in the region.

Red Wing Lake Golf Course $
1080 Prosperity Road **5,282 yards**
Virginia Beach, VA 23451 **68.1/102**
(757) 437-4845
A classic-style course designed by George Cobb.

Washington, DC

Goose Creek Golf Club $$-$$$
43001 Golf Club Drive **5,235 yards**
Leesburg, VA 22075 **71.3/120**
(703) 729-2500
FAX: (703) 729-9364

Appendix I: Recommended Courses

Little Bennett Golf Course   **$-$$**
25900 Prescott Road   **4,921 yards**
Clarksburg, MD 20871   **68.2/115**
(301) 253-1515
EWG host club.

Needwood   **$**
6724 Needwood Road   **5,112 yards**
Derwood, MD 20855   **69.2/105**
(301) 948-1075
Very commutable. Full-length course plus an executive 9-hole.

Appendix II

Do Your Homework

With more than 13,500 golf courses in the United States today (discounting some 5,500 private clubs), it would be beyond the scope of this book to attempt to list each and every one. One must also bear in mind that due to the growing popularity of the sport, the demand for more courses has resulted in the addition of about 300 new courses per year, with little abatement in sight. For brevity's sake, an average of two courses was selected from each state, except in the case of those states and vacation destinations known for great golfing spots. For other course recommendations refer to the several golf magazines that annually list the "100 best" and "best new" courses. The Internet is also a growing resource for golf courses, resorts, and events.

While there is clearly no shortage of courses and resorts to visit, you would be well-advised to do some research before making a reservation. Questions like price for the round, dress code, soft spikes or not, and cost for caddies are probably the most common issues to consider for a round locally. But what if you are thinking about a golf resort holiday in another part of the country . . . or the world?

Things to Consider

Do you want to stay at a golf resort and enjoy a golf package and the related pampering for a few days, or do you need to economize by staying at a hotel located near the resort? (If you don't check to see if the resort will book tee times for "non-resort guests" you may end up playing the less desirable nearby courses.)

If the former is your goal, start by calling the hotel and asking for information on their golf packages. They run from what many call a Platinum Package, which could include 36 holes a day for four days, driving range privileges, breakfast and dinner, a welcome gift (resort logo golf shirt, logo towel, logo sleeve of balls, logo ball mark repair tool, etc.) to a more scaled-down arrangement that still offers the amenities of the resort.

Although staying at a golf resort can be rather expensive, it is the best way to take a golf vacation. With outstanding courses, fine food, and a highly trained staff who all share the philosophy that this should be a memorable experience for guests, your money is seldom wasted.

Is this a family trip that includes toddlers or teenagers? Or is it a trip for adults? If it's a family vacation you're after, make sure the resort has babysitting services so you can enjoy one or two dinners alone. Many fine resorts also have supervised activities during the day for children so you can get in a couple of rounds without your youngsters in tow.

Are there other attractions nearby to fill up a rainy day? Assuming not everyone wants to or is physically able to play 36 holes of golf every day, or if your day of golf is threatened by foul weather, there should be other things to do or places to visit in the area you plan to stay. At courses in remote areas, you will be completely dependent on the resort for culture and entertainment. If you enjoy antiquing, shopping, museums, local theatre, etc., and feel that is an important part of a trip, make sure the area you intend to visit has the added cultural amenities you desire. Either the resort or the local chamber of commerce can provide you with brochures on nearby attractions.

Possible Restrictions to Keep in Mind

Restrictions vary among courses and resorts, and you will want to find out:

- If the course has restrictions on public play, or if tee times are readily available
- If the course is reserved for resort guests and guests from certain hotels

Appendix II: Golf Courses and Resorts

- If the course gives first priority to its hotel guests, which means non-hotel guests can play, but only at specified times (which are most likely the least desirable ones)
- If the course will assign a tee time to you once its members with reservation privileges have been assigned times (again, times available may not suit your holiday schedule)

The Cost of Play

Other things you will want to ask when thinking about new places to play:

- Do the fees vary depending on the season?
- Are the fees lower during the week?
- Is there a lower fee for a "twilight" round?

You should also always clarify whether the price includes a cart. If not, plan to add an extra $18 to $30. If it's a caddie you want, be sure to ask the rate and plan on a $10-15 dollar tip per person, assuming two golf bags are carried. Some areas of the country demand more money for caddies, so be sure to ask the pro shop what the standard practice is for the area you are visiting.

Prices for a round of golf run from a very reasonable amount to the kind of money you might not want to spend if you are not a somewhat accomplished player. The following outline will help you with your choices.

$	Under $25	Could be a good place to take the kids or a great place for a novice. If you get tired or the weather turns sour, you won't feel bad walking off.
$$	$25-40	A good value if the course is in decent shape.
$$$	$40-60	Hope you get some attentive service, good greens, and a nice snack at the turn.
$$$$	$60-80	You're in heaven. The club house is beautiful, the pro shop is packed with top-of-the-line equipment and fashionable golf clothing, the course is magnificent, the staff is well-trained and attentive, and you can't remember your last bad day at the office.
$$$$$	Over $80	All of the above multiplied by two! This should be an almost otherworldly experience. If you have not digested the concept of pace of play, cultivated the habit of replacing divots and repairing ball marks on the green, please don't even think about playing here.

BREAKING THE GRASS CEILING

(To make this directory easier to use, the continental United States has been divided into regions. The $ symbols refer to greens fees only. You should check with the hotel/resort about room rates.)

Rocky Mountain
Colorado
Idaho
Montana
Utah
Wyoming

Midwest
Illinois
Indiana
Iowa
Kansas
Michigan
Minnesota
Missouri
Nebraska
North Dakota
Ohio
South Dakota
Wisconsin

Northeast
Connecticut
Delaware
Maine
Massachusetts
New Hampshire
New Jersey
New York
Pennsylvania
Rhode Island
Vermont

Western
Alaska
California
Hawaii
Nevada
Oregon
Washington

Southwest
Arizona
New Mexico
Oklahoma
Texas

Southern
Alabama
Arkansas
Florida
Georgia
Kentucky
Louisiana
Mississippi
Tennessee

Mid-Atlantic
Maryland
North Carolina
South Carolina
Virginia
West Virginia

Appendix II: Golf Courses and Resorts

NORTHEAST REGION

Connecticut

Blackledge Country Club $$
180 West Street
Hebron, CT 06248
(203) 228-0250

A fairly easy track designed by Geoffrey Cornish. The fairways are wide and the greens are generous.

Delaware

Ron Jaworsky's Garrison's Lake Golf Club $
Route 13/101 Fairways Circle
Smyrna, DE 19977
(302) 653-9847

Built in the early 1960s on farmland, Garrison's Lake is just a short drive north of Dover. The topography is relatively flat, offering large greens with just a hint of undulation. There aren't many fairway bunkers or water hazards, but the greens are well protected by bunkers, and the narrow fairways and an abundance of trees make the course a challenge. Walkers are welcomed and there is a fully appointed clubhouse.

Maine

Samoset Resort Golf Club $$
200 Warrenton Street
Rockport, ME 04856
(207) 594-1431

More "Down Maine" than this is hard to find. This oceanside course designed by Robert Elder offers views of the rocky coast from nearly every hole. Located in a town accustomed to summer tourists for over a century.

Sugarloaf Golf Club $$
Route 27
Carrabassett Valley, ME 04947
(207) 237-2000

While the Samoset Club is oceanside, Sugarloaf offers a different perspective of the beauty of Maine. Situated deep in the woods, this Robert Trent Jones Jr. course offers striking views of the mountains of Maine. White birches, babbling brooks, and the Carrabasset River offer players a grand sense of nature. A year-round resort, there are lots of things to do and see postround.

Massachusetts

Crumpin-Fox Club $$
Parmenter Road
Bernardston, MA 01337
(413) 648-9101

Locals argue Crumpin-Fox is the best public course in the state and beyond. Offering the serenity of the Berkshires, with ample local attractions like Tanglewood, the summer home of the Boston Symphony Orchestra, and the Norman Rockwell Museum, there are also several unique spots for food and lodging.

Ocean Edge Resort $$
832 Villages Drive
Brewster, MA 02631
(508) 896-5911

No visit to Massachusetts is complete without a trip to Cape Cod. The Ocean Edge Resort offers fine golf and elegant accommodations, with lots to do and see nearby. The course has hosted the annual New England PGA Championship for several years running.

New Hampshire

Mt. Washington Resort Golf Club $
Bretton Woods, NH 03575
(603) 278-1000

Situated in the heart of the White Mountains, this Donald Ross course offers some of the most beautiful vistas in New England. The hotel is breathtaking and takes you back in time. (A bit of little-known history; it was the site where the papers were signed to establish the IMF, or International Monetary Fund, after World War II.)

Sky Meadow Country Club $$$
2 Sky Meadow Drive
Nashua, NH 03062
(603) 888-9000

A somewhat newer course (1989), Sky Meadow makes up in challenge for what it lacks in age. Carts and precision are prerequisites to negotiate the steep hills and water hazards.

Appendix II: Golf Courses and Resorts

New Jersey

Hominy Hill Golf Course $$
92 Mercer Road
Colts Neck, NJ 07722
(908) 462-9223

About a fifty-minute ride due south from Manhattan, Hominy Hill is situated in farm country and continues to earn accolades as one of the top public courses in the country.

Marriott's Seaview Resort $$$$
Route 9
Absecon, NJ 08201
(609) 652-1800

A short drive from Atlantic City, the Seaview Resort offers two 18-hole courses: Pines and Bay. The Pines, as indicated by its name, has tree-lined fairways, while the Bay is a links course. The latter is another work by Donald Ross, who is credited with designing dozens of the northeast region's finest courses.

New York

Leatherstocking Golf Course $$$
Nelson Avenue
Cooperstown, NY 13326
(607) 547-9853

This is a mountain goat course and while it might not be as wonderful as many others in New York, it is included because Cooperstown is a good family vacation destination. Home of the Baseball Hall of Fame, this charming, friendly town should be on every little baseball player's list of places to visit. The Otesaga Hotel is a vintage upstate New York resort-style hotel, complete with early and late dinner seatings, tennis, dancing, and good service. The large veranda, which is lined with comfy, wooden rockers, is perfect for enjoying a cocktail as the sun sets over pristine Lake Otsego.

The Sagamore Resort $$$$
Sagamore Road
Bolton Landing, NY 12814
(518) 644-9400

If you're a fan of Donald Ross courses, here is a course you will not soon forget—the first hole offers a panoramic view of Lake George. From there, your tour of the course is punctuated with mountainous terrain, undulating, slick greens, and no shortage of bunkers. Get your short game in top working condition! The resort is large, elegant, and offers something for everyone—including parasailing.

Pennsylvania

Tamiment Resort $$
Tamiment, PA 18371
(800) 233-8105

Whether you are planning a golfing honeymoon or just heading to the Poconos for some much needed R & R, a round at this Robert Trent Jones course will do you a world of good.

Toftrees Resort $$$
1 Country Club Lane
State College, PA 16803
(800) 458-3602

Located near the center of the state, Toftrees continues to earn top reviews from Golf Digest *as a fine golf destination. It requires some skill to play here; the course demands strategic thinking for shot placement and the greens are subtle and undulating.*

Rhode Island

Triggs Memorial Golf Course $
1533 Chalkstone Avenue
Providence, RI 02909
(401) 272-GOLF

The Ocean State has a gem of a course here, designed by Donald Ross, that hosts the annual Providence Open. Enjoy a view of downtown Providence while you play. Providence is a city for food lovers, boasting more than its share of trendy restaurants. Be sure to visit the Brown University Campus during your stay.

Vermont

Stratton Mountain Country Club $$$
Stratton Mountain Access Road
Stratton Mountain, VT 05155
(802) 297-1880

A terrific destination for all levels of golfers. This resort offers three 9-hole courses—the Mountain, the Lake, and the Forest. Stratton houses a fine golf school here and is also home to the annual LPGA Stratton Mountain Golf Classic.

Sugarbush Inn $$
P.O. Box 307
Warren, VT 05674
(802) 583-2722

Boasting spectacular views of the Green Mountains, this Robert Trent Jones layout has everything going for it including lush fairways, generous greens, and plenty of challenges. Particularly beautiful in autumn, when the trees are awash in red, yellow, and orange leaves.

MID-ATLANTIC REGION

Maryland

Swan Point $$
1 Swan Point Boulevard
Issue, MD 20645
(301) 259-2074

With tall pines and marshlands offering shelter to a variety of wildlife including deer and osprey, this course is situated along the Potomac River.

North Carolina

High Hampton Inn $$
Highway 107
Cashiers, NC 28717
(704) 743-2411

A gem of a course (no bunkers) set on a family estate high in the Blue Ridge Mountains. Each hole offers a breathtaking view, especially in the spring when the wildflowers are in bloom.

Pinehurst Resort and Country Club $$$
Carolina Vista
Pinehurst, NC 28374
(800) 634-9297

Like the pilgrims on their hadj to Mecca, we are drawn to Pinehurst to pay homage to some of the finest golf courses in the country. Whether you stay in the great white hotel or settle into one of the condos, start your day with a good breakfast and head out to one of Pinehurst's eight courses. The jewel in the crown has to be the No. 2 Donald Ross masterpiece, with the new No. 8 Centennial Course designed by Tom Fazio running a close second. The town offers lovely shops and charming little places for lunch.

While Pinehurst courses are for hotel guests only, there are twenty fine public courses in the area and several smaller resorts and clubs. Check with the Chamber of Commerce for more details.

The Pit Golf Links $$$
Highway 5
Aberdeen, NC 28315
(919) 944-1600

Heading south from Pinehurst, this public course has received high marks from the golf magazines who proclaim it as one of the top fifty public courses. Created on the site of an old sand-mining pit, it has abundant nooks and crannies as you descend "into the pit" along the front nine. By the turn, the topography changes to water country, as you work your way along a large lake.

Springdale Country Club $
Highway 276 South
Cruso, NC 28716
(704) 235-8451

This is a challenging track set on mountainous terrain with the Great Smoky Mountains looming in the background. Lots of tiny streams interrupt the fairways.

Myrtle Beach, NC and SC $-$$$$$

The number one destination for golfers from around the country, Myrtle Beach stretches some fifty miles, beginning at Ocean Isle Beach, North Carolina, and ending in Georgetown, South Carolina. Within the "Grand Strand," as many call the area, there are over 70 golf courses. Some of them are outstanding, others need a second look before putting your money down.

If you want some funny stories about Myrtle Beach, pick up a copy of David Owens's My Usual Game. *The tales of Owens and his buddies on a golf safari in "the man van" make for great 19th hole chatter.*

Since there is such variety in housing and course qualities, your best bet is to call Myrtle Beach Golf Holiday at (800) 845-4653. Keep in mind that there are dozens more courses and comfortable places to stay just a few miles beyond the Myrtle Beach empire, so be sure to do some additional research.

Oyster Bay Golf Links $$$
Highway 179
Sunset Beach, NC 28459
(800) 647-8372

Ranked by Golf Digest *as one of the top fifty public courses in America, this Dan Maples layout has water on fifteen holes. With those famous, tall Carolina pines waving in the breeze on one side, and marshlands beckoning an errant shot on the other, you'll have to stay focused on each shot for the entire round.*

Appendix II: Golf Courses and Resorts

South Carolina

Kiawah Island Inn and Villa $$$$$
1 Kiawah Island Drive
Kiawah Island, SC 29455
(803) 768-2121

If it's rest and relaxation you want, head for the magnificent beach at Kiawah. It stretches far in both directions and is a pleasure to walk at sunrise or sunset. If it's unparalleled golf you're after, Kiawah is the place. Let's begin with the Ocean Course, home of the 1991 Ryder Cup. Designed by the legendary Pete Dye, this true links-style course demands precision as you make your way along the Atlantic Ocean. Calculating what the sea breezes will do to your next shot is half the fun; the other challenge is negotiating the greens. Not inexpensive, but well worth the experience.

There are three other great courses at Kiawah: Marsh Point, Turtle Point, and Osprey Point. Each has its own personality. Marsh Point, which was designed by Gary Player, brings marshlands and trees into play-rewarding good shots and punishing poor ones. Turtle Point, a Jack Nicklaus track, plays along the ocean a bit more like the Ocean Course, but the fairways are narrower and the greens are smaller. Finally, Osprey Point was designed by Tom Fazio, and has a different personality altogether. Offering wide fairways and varying sized greens, his challenges come in the form of dunes and vast waste areas.

For fun things to do, Charleston is a short ride away and is a city proud of its heritage. The straw market is a good take on any afternoon and Rainbow Row is a must-see. Restaurants feature delicious local seafood and places of historic interest abound. There are other hotels and public courses in the area that are more reasonable, but for a luxury golf vacation, Kiawah ranks high on the list.

Tidewater Golf Club $$$$$
4901 Little River Neck Road
Myrtle Beach, SC 29582
(803) 249-3829

With five sets of tees to select from, this award-winning course continues to get high marks from the golf magazines as one of the top ten best. Lovingly created by Ken Tomlinson, who was careful to use the land as he found it, Tidewater is situated on a peninsula with half of its holes running along the Intracoastal Waterway and an inlet. The remainder of the course stretches through deep forest graced with several lakes.

Hilton Head Island, SC

As famous as Myrtle Beach, but much more compact (12 miles long and 5 miles wide), Hilton Head Island is separated from the mainland by the Intracoastal Waterway. A year-round resort by virtue of the Gulf Stream influence, boating, bicycling, fishing, and golf are just some of the local activities.

Port Royal Resort $$$$
Port Royal Plantation
Hilton Head Island, SC 29928
(803) 686-8801

Boasts three 18-hole courses surrounded by lagoons and magnolias with Civil War memorabilia at each tee.

Sea Pines Resort $$$$$
P.O. Box 7000
Hilton Head Island, SC 29938
(800) 752-7463

Perhaps the most famous destination on the island is the Harbour Town Golf Links course, a Pete Dye design which holds the distinction of being rated among the top thirty courses in the world. Two more courses grace this outstanding resort: Sea Marsh and Ocean Course, each a bit less expensive than Harbour Town but just as scenic. Put this destination on your "must visit at least once in a lifetime" list.

Shipyard Golf Club $$$$
Shipyard Plantation
Hilton Head Island, SC 29928
(803) 842-2400

Another lush course featuring the ubiquitous pines and wildflowers so long associated with Carolina golf. Accommodations are with the Marriott Hotel.

Virginia

The Homestead $$$$
Route 220
Hot Springs, VA 24445
(703) 839-5500

This magnificent resort, with its elegant, rambling hotel, has a long and venerable association with the game of golf. With three courses to test your skills, the toughest is the Cascades. The Lower Cascades and the Homestead round out the trio.

Appendix II: Golf Courses and Resorts

Kingsmill Resort $$$$$
1010 Kingsmill Road
Williamsburg, VA 23185
(804) 253-1703

Another superb resort with much to see and do in historic Williamsburg when your round is over. Kingsmill has two outstanding 18-hole championship courses: the River Course and the Plantation Course. The River Course, a Pete Dye design, plays along the James River and is host to the PGA Tour Anheuser-Busch Golf Classic. The Plantation Course, an Arnold Palmer design, works its way through deep woods with ample water hazards. There is also the Bray Links, a par 3 executive course which is perfect for the kids. Its longest hole measures 110 yards!

West Virginia

Canaan Valley Resort $$
Route 1
Davis, WV 26260
(304) 866-4121

Situated in the northeast corner of the state, Canaan Valley is a Geoffrey Cornish course. If you like the great outdoors, this course is part of a 6,000-acre state park.

The Greenbrier $$$
300 West Main Street
White Sulphur Springs, WV 24986
(800) 624-6070

A classic golf resort boasting three 18-hole courses: the Old White Course, the Greenbrier Course, and the Lakeside Course. Host to the 1979 Ryder Cup, the Old White Course—with its deep bunkers and sloped greens—is considered the most difficult of the three.

SOUTHERN REGION

Alabama

Alabama has something special when it comes to great golf: it is called the Robert Trent Jones Trail and encompasses just about the entire state. Seniors, juniors, and AAA members enjoy an extra discount. The state publishes a "Trail Guide" which lists addresses, phone numbers, maps, and detailed descriptions of each course. There are even operators to help you book tee times and answer questions. Call (800) 949-444 for complete details.

Marriott's Grand Hotel at Lakewood Golf Club $$$$
Scenic Highway 98
Point Clear, AL 36564
(334) 928-9201

With an island green to test even the best player's skills and fairways lined with moss-draped trees, this "for hotel guests only" resort is a fine golf destination. Choose from the Dogwood Course or the Azalea Course.

Arkansas

Cherokee Village South Golf Course $
P.O. Box 840
Cherokee Village, AR 72525
(501) 257-2555

There are two courses at Cherokee Village, but only one is open to the public. The South Course looks like it would play easily with open fairways and only two water holes, but the hilly terrain and length must be factored in.

Mountain Ranch Golf Course $$
P.O. Box 3008
Fairfield Bay, AR 72088
(501) 884-3333

Drive about ninety minutes from Little Rock and check into your condo or rental unit in the foothills of the Ozark Mountains. Then head out to the first hole for a round of golf that Golf Digest has ranked among the top five in the state.

Appendix II: Golf Courses and Resorts

Florida

With over 1,000 courses to choose from, Florida is without peer when it comes to planning a golf holiday. Home to scores of professional golfers who discovered the joys of the "Sunshine State," this vacation destination has something for every player, every budget.

At one time, the educated opinion of Florida golf was that the courses were flat and watery, but no longer is this the case. Golf course architects have designed contoured, challenging layouts which, in many instances, have resulted not only in exciting, beautiful tracks, but in new homes for various birds and fish. For more information on how to plan your Florida golf holiday, call the Florida Division of Tourism, Visitor Inquiry Section at (904) 487-1462. Be sure to specify which section of the state you are interested in.

Amelia Island Plantation $$$$$
Highway A1A South
Amelia Island, FL 32034
(800) 874-6878

Whether it's 9, 18, 27, or 36 holes you have planned to fill your day, this resort has it all. The Long Point Club Course is a Tom Fazio gem with beachside holes that, depending on the prevailing winds, may require a long or a short iron to reach the green.

The Oakmarsh, Oysterbay, and Oceanside courses, all from the mind of Pete Dye, make use of wetlands, marshy areas, and clusters of palmetto thickets.

Bardmoor North Golf Club $$$
7919 Bardmoor Boulevard
Largo, FL 34647
(813) 397-0483

Here is an outstanding public course, minutes from Tampa, which is the former host of the JCPenney Mixed Team Classic. Always in great condition, this course provides outstanding customer service.

Boca Raton Resort and Club $$$
501 East Camino Real
Boca Raton, FL 33431
(407) 395-3000

A true Florida paradise, this resort offers two courses for guests only: the Resort Course and the Country Club Course, which is considered the more difficult of the two.

Bonaventure Country Club $$$
200 Bonaventure Boulevard
Fort Lauderdale, FL 33326
(305) 389-3300

Open to the public, Bonaventure Country Club boasts two courses. The East Course is one of Florida's top ten courses. The much easier West Course is a good place for the newer golfer to enjoy a lush resort environment without the intimidation of a difficult course layout.

Doral Golf Resort and Spa $$$$$
4400 NW 87th Avenue
Miami, FL 33178
(305) 592-2000

Lush, luxurious, meticulous: these are the words to describe one of the finest resorts in the world today. Select from four 18-hole courses and a 9-hole course. Enjoy pampering by the resort staff, swim, shop, and save some energy for Miami night life. By the way, Doral has no restrictions, so the public is welcome—just bring your credit cards!

Eastwood Golf Course $$
4600 Bruce Herd Lane
Fort Myers, FL 33905
(941) 278-7264

A municipal course in a park-like setting featuring spectacular birds. Golf Digest continues to keep this challenging course in the top 50 public course rankings.

Golden Ocala Golf Course $$
7300 US Highway 27 Northwest
Ocala, FL 34482
(800) 251-7674

North of Orlando, and most unique in its offering, this course has replicated eight of the world's most famous golf holes, including the Road Hole at St. Andrews, the Postage Stamp at Royal Troon, two holes from Augusta National, and two that celebrate Muirfield and Baltusrol.

Grand Cypress Golf Club $$$$$
1 North Jacaranda
Orlando, FL 32836
(407) 239-4700

For resort guests only, 45 Nicklaus-designed holes await the golfer who wants a Scottish links-style experience. The first 27 holes are called the North, South, and East Courses. In 1988, the New Course opened, presenting players with 145 bunkers, with one in particular named "Hell." Grand Cypress has a superb golf academy which is considered to be one of the best in the United States today.

Appendix II: Golf Courses and Resorts

Innisbrook Hilton Resort $$$$$
P.O. Box 1088
Tarpon Springs, FL 34688
(800) 456-2000

If you've followed the JCPenney Mixed Team Classic for PGA and LPGA Tour Pros, then you've seen the Copperhead course's famous 14th hole—the tree-lined, double dogleg par 5, complete with not one but two water hazards, with the famous Innisbrook name proudly displayed on the large bunker that protects the green. There is also the 18-hole Island course, plus three nines at Sandpiper, so getting a round in here is never a problem.

The Links at Key Biscayne $$
6700 Crandon Boulevard
Key Biscayne, FL 33149
(305) 361-9129

Just a short ride from Miami, expect wonderful views of the Miami skyline and the Bay. Open to the public, you may ride or walk in the afternoon.

Palm Beach Polo and Country Club $$$$
13198 Forest Hill Boulevard
West Palm Beach, FL 33414
(407) 798-7020

Another resort for hotel guests only, the PBPCC offers two 18-hole courses and a 9-hole course. The Cypress Course and The Dunes Course are both challenging with the latter working around lakes and trees and the former being a links layout. The Olde Course is perfect if you need more time for shopping in those fabulous Palm Beach shops!

Pelican's Nest Golf Club $$$$
4450 Pelican's Nest Drive
Bonita Springs, FL 33923
(800) 952-6378

"The Nest" is located just a short ride from Fort Myers and is famous for its Tom Fazio-designed four 9-hole courses. The names sound like they play: The Gator, The Panther, The Hurricane, and The Seminole. Plan to stay at the nearby Ritz-Carlton in Naples.

PGA National Golf Club $$$$
1000 Avenue of the Champions
Palm Beach Gardens, FL 33418
(407) 627-2000

Moving now to the East coast, this resort, which is for hotel guests or members only, has five 18-hole courses to suit every ability level. The Champion Course was redesigned by Jack Nicklaus about eight years ago. It is the home of the PGA Seniors' Championship. The Haig Course, by Tom and George Fazio, is ideal for the high handicap golfer because it allows you to play around the fifteen water hazards rather than forcing shots over the water. The Squire, another track by the Fazio team, requires precise shot placement and sound course management skills, while the General Course, the work of Arnold Palmer, is more open and undulating. Finally, the Estate Course is the quintessential marriage of bunkers and water.

Ravines $$
2932 Ravines Road
Middleburg, FL 32068
(904) 282-1111

Moving east toward Jacksonville, the Ravines presents players with a hilly terrain with drops as much as 100 feet. The course is heavily wooded and serene.

The Resort at Long Boat Key Club $$$$$
301 Gulf of Mexico Drive
Longboat Key, FL 34228
(800) 237-8821

As laid-back as this part of Florida is, the Islandside Course will pump you up in no time. Water, water, water on every hole. The Harbourside Golf Course, with 27 holes, is also available. Nearby Sarasota offers lovely ambiance with fun shopping and good restaurants.

Saddlebrook Resort, Tampa $$$$$
5700 Saddlebrook Way
Welsey Chapel, FL 33543
(813) 973-1111

Only a short ride from the Tampa airport, this resort offers two courses to choose from, both by the hand of Arnold Palmer. The Saddlebrook Course and the Palmer Course offer hills and lakes, plenty of bunkers, and some lovely, tropical plantings. Nearby Tampa offers some sizzling night life.

Tiger Point Golf and Country Club $$
1255 Country Club Road
Gulf Breeze, FL 32561
(904) 932-1333

Just east of Pensacola, in the Florida Panhandle, Tiger Point offers two courses. The East Course combines links-style golf laced with pine trees and water. The West Course is a bit more traditional.

Appendix II: Golf Courses and Resorts

Tournament Players Club at Sawgrass $$$$$
110 TPC Boulevard
Pointe Vedra Beach, FL 32082
(904) 285-7777

Ranked by Golf Magazine *as one of the 100 greatest courses in the world, the Stadium course, a Pete Dye creation, has everything to test a golfer's skills. From difficult greens and lush fairways to very large waste bunkers, you'll need some great shots in your bag to get around this spectacular layout.*

The Valley course, also from the drawing board of Pete Dye, has water on every hole, but is a little less difficult.

There are two more courses available to guests of the Marriott at Sawgrass: Marsh Landing and Oak Bridge, both 18-hole courses.

Turnberry Isle Resort and Club $$$
19999 West Country Club Drive
Aventura, FL 33180
(305) 932-6200

Located just north of Miami, both courses at Turnberry Isle are the work of Robert Trent Jones. With trees, wind, water, and ample bunkers, they are a challenge for even the most skilled players.

Walt Disney World Resort $$$$
Lake Buena Vista, FL 32830
(407) W-DISNEY

Knowing Disney's reputation for ingenuity, quality, and service, rest assured that one of the five courses located here will tickle your fancy. In case you're thinking that Goofy or Donald Duck did the work, we are happy to report that three are the work of Joe Lee and the other two are by Tom Fazio and Pete Dye. Feel confident that if you're golf day is rained out, there are a few other things you can do to fill up the day!

Georgia

Chateau Elan Golf Club $$
6060 Golf Club Drive
Braselton, GA 30517
(404) 658-1868

If you're looking for something a little different from your southern hosts, you might consider this golf resort, which has a French chateau and a winery on site, for your next golf holiday. Chateau Elan has a fine reputation as a preferred Georgia course, with plans for two more courses under development.

Port Armor Club $$

1 Port Armor Parkway
Greensboro, GA
(404) 453-7366

About 85 miles inland from Atlanta, some reporters claim this track is close on the heels of Augusta National in popularity. The club is private, but guests of the Inn on the Green can get on. The course is laid out among rolling hills and glimmering lakes.

The Sea Island Golf Club $$$

100 Retreat Avenue
St. Simons Island, GA 30642
(912) 638-3611

Part of the luxurious Cloister hotel, which boasts a five-star, five-diamond rating, this is a golfer's paradise. Sea Island has four 9-hole courses, each with a unique personality. Choose from Seaside, Plantation, Retreat, and Marshside courses. Keep in mind that in March and April you must be a hotel guest in order to get a tee time.

Sheraton Savannah Resort and Country Club $$

612 Wilmington Island Road
Savannah, GA 31410
(800) 325-3535

A traditional Donald Ross course that hosts the Georgia State Open. You will need accuracy and control to avoid the 84 bunkers that await a poor shot.

Stouffer Renaissance PineIsle Resort $$$

9000 Holiday Road
Lake Lanier Island, GA 30518
(404) 945-8921

Georgia has a world-renowned reputation for welcoming golfers with an elegance and gentility almost forgotten in our day and age. PineIsle is often said to be one of Georgia's finest public courses and the hotel enjoys a Mobil 4-Star/AAA-4 Diamond Rating. The course is laid out next to Lake Lanier and the Gary Player/Ron Kirby design makes good use of the water, elevated tees, and challenging greens.

Kentucky

Kearney Hill Golf Links $
3403 Kearney Road
Lexington, KY 40511
(606) 253-1981

While reasonably priced, this is a highly regarded links-style course which is ranked among the top five in the state. Nestled in the heart of horse-farm country, Kearney Hill is one of the few courses in the region to offer bentgrass fairways and greens.

Marriott's Griffin Gate Resort $$$
1720 Newtown Pike
Lexington, KY 40511
(606) 231-5100

With a "top 75 resort courses in the country" rating from Golf Digest, *this Rees Jones layout has enough bunkers and water hazards to keep you on your toes throughout the round.*

Louisiana

Belle Terre Country Club $$$
111 Fairway Drive
La Place, LA 70068

Just about a thirty-minute drive from New Orleans, Belle Terre (French for "beautiful land") must be someone's idea of humor. Built around swamps, bayous, and ponds, "terra firma" at this Pete Dye course is at a premium.

The Bluffs on Thompson Creek $$$
P.O. Box 1220
St. Francisville, LA 70775

A truly historic area, rich with whitewashed plantations, fertile deltas, and Civil War artifacts, the Bluffs was designed by Arnold Palmer, Ed Seay, and Harrison Minchew. (Audubon painted dozens of his "Birds of America" series at the Bluffs.) The land has been kept as natural as possible, so look for mature trees, generous fairways, and very difficult greens. There is a lodge here with a proclivity for comfort and easy living.

Mississippi

Pine Island Golf Club $
P.O. Box 843
Ocean Springs, MS 39564
(601) 875-1674

This course, designed by Pete Dye, meanders over lakes and marshlands, while alligators sun themselves on nearby banks. If you have an uncontrollable slice or hook, you'd better try another course or bring a few dozen balls!

Timberton Golf Club $$
22 Clubhouse Drive
Hattiesburg, MS 39401
(601) 584-4653

A ninety-minute ride from the Jackson Airport. Landing areas are generous, but the greens demand accuracy. Thumbs up from Golf Digest *and* Golf Week.

Tennessee

Bent Creek Golf Resort $$
3919 East Parkway
Gatlinburg, TN 37738
(615) 436-2875

An unusual track where the front nine flows through a valley filled with mature trees and flowers while the back nine charts its way over mountainous terrain featuring vistas of the Great Smokies.

Stonehenge Golf Club at Fairfield Glade Resort $$$
Fairfield Boulevard
Fairfield Glade, TN 38558
(615) 484-3723

With a high slope and mountainous terrain, Stonehenge has played host to the Tennessee State Open for many years. Earning its stripes in 1985 with a Golf Digest *"best new resort course" award, this track is a challenge for more experienced players.*

MIDWEST REGION

Despite long, harsh winters and acre after acre of farm land, the Midwest has some remarkable golf courses.

Illinois

Cog Hill Golf and Country Club   **$$ Courses 1-3**
12294 Archer Avenue   **$$$$ Course 4**
Lemont, IL 60439
(708) 257-5872

With four excellent courses to choose from and an ample practice area, Cog Hill has more than earned its reputation as one of the most outstanding public courses in the country. Located just a short ride south of Chicago, the number 4 course, called Dubsdread, is by far the most difficult. Loaded with bunkers, it is a traditional layout requiring accuracy off the tee and a light touch on the greens.

Golf Club of Illinois   **$$**
1575 Edgewood Drive
Algonquin, IL 60102
(708) 658-4400

Drive about forty minutes northwest of Chicago and leave urbane Michigan Avenue behind for rolling, verdant farmland. The lay of the land and the constant windy conditions invoke a Scottish-links layout with target fairways and greens amid waving prairie grasses. Bring extra balls for this experience at a truly outstanding public course.

Indiana

Golf Club of Indiana   **$$**
6905 S 525 E
Lebanon, IN 460520
(317) 769-6388

If your travels take you to Indianapolis, this course is just about twenty minutes from the city. A perennial favorite with the golf magazines and open to the public, it is a pleasant way to conclude a day of business.

Iowa

Amana Colonies Golf Course $$
Route 1
Amana, IA 52203
(800) 383-3636

A superb public course which earned the honor of being in the top ten of new public courses by Golf Magazine *earlier this decade. Created from mature, lush acreage, it is blessed with wide fairways and rolling greens.*

Kansas

Terradyne Resort Hotel and Country Club $$
1400 Terradyne Drive
Andover, KS 67002
(316) 733-2562

Touted as one of the top five in the state, there is a Scottish-links feel to this layout which is open to the public and is about ten miles from Wichita.

Michigan

Garland $$$
Country Road
Lewiston, MI 49756
(800) 968-0042

Michigan is a fine destination for summer golf, with many excellent courses and resorts from which to choose. With 63 holes to play over some 3,500 acres, Garland, with its AAA and 4-diamond ratings, is perhaps the most well-known. Three 18-hole courses and a delightful 9-hole course were all designed by the owner. Open to the public, the only restriction is that you must ride.

Grand Traverse Resort $$$$$
100 Grand Traverse Village Boulevard
Acme, MI 49610
(800) 748-0303

Who else but Jack Nicklaus could have designed a course called The Bear? It is a tough test of your skills with tree-lined fairways and lots of wet stuff. There is also a second 18-hole, easier track here called Spruce Run designed by Bill Newcomb. Grand Traverse is open to the public, but you must use a cart.

Appendix II: Golf Courses and Resorts

Minnesota

Izatys Golf and Yacht Club $$
Mile Lacs Lake
Onamia, MN 56359
(800) 533-1728

Situated about 90 minutes from the St. Paul/Minneapolis area, this public course runs along the shores of Minnesota's second largest lake and offers magnificent scenery and a challenging Pete Dye layout.

Madden's on Gull Lake $$
8001 Pine Beach Peninsula
Brainerd, MN 56401
(800) 642-5363

Thoughtfulness and quality describe this spot. There are two 18-hole courses called Pine Beach East and Pine Beach West, plus a charming, aptly named 9-hole course called the Social Nine.

Missouri

Lodge of the Four Seasons $$$
State Road
Lake Ozark, MO 65049
(800) 843-5253

Imagine teeing off on a misty morning on one of the two Robert Trent Jones courses offered here in the Ozark area. The terrain is hilly, the fairways are narrow, and the scenery is beautiful. Try the 9-hole executive course.

Nebraska

Heritage Hills Golf Course $
6000 Clubhouse Drive
McCook, NE 69001
(308) 345-5032

Treeless yet challenging, this links-style course has earned Golf Digest's *top seventy-five public courses rating.*

Sand Hills Golf Club $$$
P.O. Box 8
Mullen, NE 69152
(308) 546-2237

Ben Crenshaw and Bill Coore designed this new links-style course, which is like Ballybunion in Ireland. Very little was done to change the topog-

raphy, leaving the wind, sand, and tall grasses to present you with a natural challenge. The greens are dramatically contoured and provide many opportunities for run-up shots. Although a private club, some limited play may be arranged with prior permission.

North Dakota

Edgewood Golf Course $
North Elm Street
Fargo, ND 58102
(701) 232-2824

Open to the public and featuring a lovingly maintained course, Edgewood welcomes both riders and walkers.

Ohio

Bent Tree Golf Club $$
350 Bent Tree Road
Sunbury, OH 43074
(614) 965-5140

Minutes from Columbus, this public course has slick greens and ample bunkers. The terrain rolls alongside ponds and looks more like a private club thanks to a dedicated maintenance crew.

South Dakota

Meadowbrook Golf Course $
3625 Jackson Boulevard
Rapid City, SD 57702
(605) 394-4191

If you're planning a visit to Mt. Rushmore, Meadowbrook is nearby and is ranked as one of the top fifty public courses in the United States.

Wisconsin

Sentry World Golf Course $$$
601 Michigan Avenue
Stevens Point, WI 54481
(715) 345-1600

The chairman of the Sentry Insurance Company thought this would be a good spot for a course, and he convinced Robert Trent Jones, Jr. as well. Open to the public and lush with flowers (one hole has 90,000 flowers arranged around the green), it earned high marks when it opened in 1983 and still is considered a local gem.

Appendix II: Golf Courses and Resorts

Blackwolf Run $$$
1111 West Riverside Drive
Kohler, WI 53044
(800) 344-2838

Two Pete Dye courses truly test a golfer's mettle here. Steep hills, water, and pot bunkers join dramatic changes in elevation to make the River Course and the Meadow Valley Course memorable. Several sets of tees are available, but accuracy is the key to success or disappointment. Blackwolf is open to the public and you may walk or ride.

SOUTHWEST REGION

Arizona

Arizona has over 200 golf courses and resorts with about two-thirds welcoming the public. For more details, contact the Arizona Department of Tourism at (800) 842-8257.

The Sedona Golf Resort $$$
7260 Highway 179
Sedona, AZ 86351
(602) 284-9355

Nestled in the heart of an area known for red rocks and talented artists, this is a fine public course that invites walkers to enjoy the scenery and the wildlife.

Tournament Players Club of Scottsdale $$$$
17020 North Hayden Road
Scottsdale, AZ 85255
(602) 585-4848

Staying at the elegant Scottsdale Princess is an experience you will not soon forget. The amenities are first class, truly in keeping with the venerable Princess reputation. The desert-links style TPC features the challenging Stadium Course, which was designed by Tom Weiskopf and Jay Morrish, and the easier Desert Course, also from their drawing boards. There are no restrictions to non-hotel guests. You may walk the Desert Course, but not the Stadium Course.

Troon North Golf Club $$$$$
10320 East Dynamite Boulevard
Scottsdale, AZ 85255
(602) 585-7700

Opening in 1990 to great reviews, this course is a prime example of what is called "desert links." Lacking the aid of the gentle heather of Scottish links, Arizona players must hit their shots over rocky terrain to very small fairways. Riding is required and preference is given to the nearby homeowners.

Ventana Canyon Golf and Racquet Club $$$$$
6200 North Clubhouse Lane
Tucson, AZ 85715
(800) 828-5701

A year-round resort, Ventana Canyon's two 18-hole desert courses were created by Tom Fazio. Guarded by the Catalina Mountains and canyons, both courses are considered outstanding resort courses by Golf Digest. Walking is not allowed and there are some restrictions on play for nonguests so be sure to get all the details if you aren't planning to stay on site.

New Mexico

Inn of the Mountain Gods $$
Route 4
Mescalero, NM 88340
(800) 545-9011

Owned by the Apache tribe of Mescalero and considered to be on ancient sacred grounds, this course is picturesque and challenging, as it makes its way over hills and through wooded areas nurtured by water.

University of New Mexico Golf Course $
3601 University Boulevard, SE
Albuquerque, NM 87131
(505) 277-4546

This course overlooks the city in one direction and the mountains in the opposite. Challenging but fair, it is a desert terrain and quite hilly. There is also a 9-hole course on site.

Oklahoma

Karsten Creek Golf Course $$$
Route 5/ P.O. Box 159
Stillwater, OK 74074
(405) 743-1658

Situated close to Oklahoma State University, this Tom Fazio-designed course gets high marks from Golf Digest for a number of outstanding features. This is a challenging course (140/75.3 from the red tees and 127/70.1 from the forward tees) that pits players against the wind so prevalent in this part of the country. The practice area, spread out over 40 acres, is a golfer's dream come true: a double-ended practice range with targets and a designated area for short game practice, featuring a Bermuda grass green and a bentgrass green.

Appendix II: Golf Courses and Resorts

Forest Ridge Golf Club $$$
7501 East Kenosha
Broken Arrow, OK 74014
(918) 357-2282

Minutes from Tulsa, this links-style course gets its challenge from the native grasses that border the Bermuda grass fairways and the unpredictable wind. The fairways are wide and friendly and the greens are large and slightly undulating. The clubhouse has all the amenities and there is a sizeable practice area. There are plenty of activities to fill non-golfing hours, with nearby amusement and water parks, art museums, the Tulsa Zoo, and seasonal festivals.

Texas

Four Seasons Resort and Club $$$$
Tournament Players Course
4150 North MacArthur Boulevard
Irving, TX 75038
(214) 717-2530

Located just north of Dallas, the TPC at the Four Seasons is for hotel guests only. Known for fast greens and a creek that crosses half of the holes, the course has a reputation for always being in top condition. Riding is required.

Horseshoe Bay Resort $$$$$
Horseshoe Bay Boulevard
Horseshoe Bay, TX 78654
(512) 598-2511

In grand Texas style, complete with luxurious accommodations, Horseshoe Bay presents its guests with three 18-hole courses all designed by Robert Trent Jones. Slickrock, Applerock, and Ramrock await your tee shots with waterfalls, woods, rocky passages, and rolling fairways. Only 45 minutes west of Austin.

Waterwood National Resort and Country Club $$
1 Waterwood Parkway
Hunstville, TX 77340
(409) 891-5211

Tucked in the middle of a national forest and adjacent to Lake Livingston, this is a very challenging course with little room for error. Open to the public, and welcoming those who like to walk, it is a good value for the quality of the course.

ROCKY MOUNTAIN REGION

Colorado

Arrowhead Golf Club $$$$
10850 West Sundown Terrace
Littleton, CO 80125
(303) 973-9614

This layout represents the perfect marriage between man and nature. Enormous sandstone monoliths abound along this Robert Trent Jones Jr. course, telling tales from the ice age, while mortals make their way over fairways that turn this way and that, trying to reach greens that are full of surprises.

Breckenridge Golf Club $$$
200 Clubhouse Drive
Breckenridge, CO 80424
(970) 453-9104

An amusing bit of golf trivia: Breckenridge is the only municipal golf course designed by Jack Nicklaus. It has open fairways and is surrounded by majestic mountains.

The Broadmoor $$$
1 Lake Avenue
Colorado Springs, CO 80906
(719) 634-7711

Probably one of the largest resorts in the area, The Broadmoor has three courses designed by three famous architects. The East Course is by Donald Ross, the West Course by Robert Trent Jones, and finally the South Course, which is the work of Arnold Palmer and Ed Seay. You must use a cart and play is for guests only.

Tamarron Resort at Durango $$$$
40292 US HWY 550 N
Durango, CO 81302
(970) 259-0955

Considered by Golf Digest *to be one of the top 75 resort courses in the country, Tamarron requires the right club selection (remember your shots will go about 20% further in this thin air) and rewards accuracy. With mountains in the background and thick pines everywhere, it is ideal for photography buffs.*

Idaho

Coeur d'Alene Resort $$$$
On the Lake
Coeur d'Alene, ID 83814
(208) 765-4000

This is something out of the ordinary. Built in the early 1990s by two local men, this resort, with a $60 million price tag, is both opulent and capacious. Conde Nast Traveler *has ranked it as the best mainland resort in America. The course, which takes advantage of a spectacular lake and lush forests, is challenging yet user-friendly, with several sets of tees. Beginners and weekend hackers can attend the Floating Green Golf School.*

Elkhorn Resort $$$
Elkhorn Road
P.O. Box 6005
Sun Valley, ID 83354
(208) 622-2309

Situated in Sun Valley, one of the nation's most popular winter destinations, this Robert Trent Jones gem is regarded as one of the best public courses in the U.S. by Golf Digest. *Hilly, well-bunkered, and sporting ample water holes, the 125 slope from the forward tees tells you that you're in for a challenge. With an elevation of six thousand feet, players can expect to hit some unusually long drives.*

Montana

Big Sky Golf Club $$
1 Lone Mountain Terrace
Big Sky, MT 59716
(406) 995-4211

With Yellowstone National Park just down the road, you might well imagine the scenery here—mountains, wildflowers, pristine meadows, and incredibly fresh air. This is the only Arnold Palmer course in the state and is fairly easy considering the skills and reputation of the designer. Big Sky is open to the public and invites walkers.

Utah

Jeremy Ranch Golf Club $$$
8770 North Jeremy Road
Park City, UT 84060
(801) 531-9000

With ample tees from which to play, Jeremy Ranch offers something different on each hole. But don't kick back and relax—there are 129 sand traps and plenty of water.

Park Meadows Golf Club $$$
2000 Meadows Drive
Park City, UT 84068
(801) 649-2460

Here is a links-style course from the mind of Jack Nicklaus, located some 7,000 feet above sea level. There is plenty of room to use your driver, as the fairways are wide, but the greens are staunchly protected by bunkers. Park Meadows is open to the public and walkers are welcome in the afternoon.

Wyoming

Jackson Hole Golf and Tennis Club $$
5800 Spring Gulch Road
Jackson, WY 83001
(307) 733-3111

It might be difficult to keep your mind on your game with the Grand Tetons looming in the background. The course, however, is flat, while the greens are somewhat more contoured. Everyone is welcome and walking is encouraged.

Teton Pines Resort and Country Club $$$$
3450 North Clubhouse Drive
Jackson, WY 83001
(800) 238-2223

As described above, the Grand Tetons are truly the focal point of this Arnold Palmer-Ed Seay course, but there is an equally natural wonder on the ground: 42 acres of streams and lakes that come into play on many of the holes.

WESTERN REGION

Alaska

Anchorage Golf Course $$
3651 O'Malley Road
Anchorage, AK 99516
(907) 522-3363

Do the Official Rules of Golf consider a wandering moose a moving obstacle? You might check that rule before you head north to Alaska and this beautiful course. As Mt. McKinley looms in the background, you will have to negotiate narrow fairways, undulating greens, and the usual array of water hazards. It's not a long course, so walk it if you can to drink in the unspoiled splendor of Alaska.

Appendix II: Golf Courses and Resorts

California

Bodega Harbour Golf Links $$$
21301 Heron Drive
Bodega Bay, CA 94923
(707) 875-3538

Seaside marshes, unpredictable winds, and breathtaking water views all characterize this lush course nestled in the heart of wine country. A true test for better golfers, Bodega Harbour has double doglegs, ample bunkers, and contoured, well-protected greens.

Chardonnay Club $$$
2555 Jameson Canyon Road
Napa, CA 94558
(707) 257-8950

Imagine playing a links-style course which meanders through the region's vineyards. The Chardonnay boasts two such courses that are etched over hilly, rocky terrain. There are some tee restrictions, so schedule ahead of time and plan to ride. Enjoy a glass of wine at the 19th hole.

The Golf Resort at Indian Wells $$$$$
44-500 Indian Wells Lane
Indian Wells, CA 92210
(619) 346-4653

An elegant, whitewashed hotel gives you lots of comfort after a day on the links. Indian Wells has two 18-hole courses nestled in the verdant, mountain-flanked Palm Springs Valley. Priority is given to hotel guests and riding is a must.

La Costa Resort and Spa $$$$
Costa Del Mar Road
Carlsbad, CA 92009
(619) 438-9111

Let yourself become rejuvenated at this internationally known spa. When the kinks are worked out, head for the two golf courses here—they just might put the kinks back in. Both challenging layouts, the North and the South Courses present the player with scores of bunkers and water hazards. Good shot-making and proper club selection are the keys to success here.

The Links at Spanish Bay $$$$$
Seventeen Mile Drive
Monterey, CA 93953
(408) 624-381
Pebble Beach Resorts (800) 654-9300

If there is heaven on earth, then it is Monterey. It is difficult to imagine that the Links at Spanish Bay was created by mere mortals. Every detail

181

has been considered for this layout, right down to the fescue grass to provide players with the old-world feeling. The only hint of the present is the surfers riding the waves off in the distance. Beware of the unpredictable wind, the pot bunkers, and the heavy grass. They will all have an impact on your shots. The experience of playing this course is well worth the potential for a high score.

Northstar-at-Tahoe $$$
Highway 267
Truckee, CA 96160
(800) 466-6784

Just forty miles from Reno, this tree-lined, majestic course is also about 6,000 feet above sea level, so you can expect your shots to travel about 20% further. Open to the public, the course is on what was once sheepherding land. Artifacts from a turn-of-the-century sheepherding area, on which the course has been built, still exist.

Pebble Beach Golf Links $$$$$
Seventeen Mile Drive
Monterey, CA 93953
(408) 624-3811
Pebble Beach Resorts
(800) 654-9300

If there is one course every dedicated golfer dreams of playing, it is Pebble Beach. Just the mention of the name, Pebble Beach, conjures up images of the finest players—Nicklaus, Watson, and Kite were all U.S. Open winners here. One of the top ten courses in the country for years, Pebble Beach is considered by many to be the best and the most beautiful of courses.

PGA West $$$$$
Stadium Course
56-150 PGA Boulevard
La Quinta, CA 92253
(619) 564-PGAW

Arguably the toughest course Pete Dye ever designed, it even unnerves some of the finest pros. The desert-links layout has water, water, and more water (thirty-five acres of it to be exact), deep bunkers, and table-top fast greens. The holes have intimidating names like Eternity, Amen, Double Trouble, Moat, and Alcatraz. Also located here is the PGA West Jack Nicklaus Resort Course. It, too, has a demanding design, but will play a little easier.

Appendix II: Golf Courses and Resorts

Sandpiper Golf Course $$$$
7925 Hollister Avenue
Goleta, CA 93117
(805) 968-1541

Close to Santa Barbara, this challenging oceanside course reserves its title as one of the country's favorite public courses. Some dare to compare it to Pebble Beach.

Torrey Pines Golf Courses $$$
11480 North Torrey Pines Road
La Jolla, CA 92037
(619) 453-4420

Torrey Pines is a user-friendly resort with two courses to enjoy. The first, the South Course, is the more difficult, but many say it is fair. The North Course, with a lower slope of 116, is a good spot for the newer golfer and offers wonderful ocean views. Open to the public and welcoming walkers, this is a terrific oasis from a day of meetings in the San Diego area.

Hawaii

Kaluakoi Golf Course $$
Kaluakoi Road
Molokai, HI 96770
(808) 552-2739

A delightful oceanside course that welcomes all visitors to the island. Anticipate ocean breezes to play with your shots and beware of the 88 sand traps along the course.

Kapalua Golf Club $$$$
300 Kapalua Drive
Maui, HI 96761
(800) 367-8000

An outstanding resort with three championship courses, Kapalua is Hawaiian golf at its best. The Bay Course, perhaps the most well-known, meanders through pineapple fields and thick vegetation, while granting players panoramic ocean views. The Village Course works its way uphill for the first six holes, and then it's a nine-hundred-foot stroll downhill to the finishing hole. The newer Plantation Course is hilly with ample fairways and inviting greens.

Ko Olina Golf Club $$$$$
92-1220 Alii-Nui Drive
Oahu, HI 96707
(808) 676-5300

Famous for hosting the LPGA Hawaiian Open and having the reputed toughest finishing hole on the LPGA Tour, Ko Olina is a superb layout featuring waterfalls, streams, and lakes.

183

Mauna Lani Resort $$$$$
Hawaii Kohala Coast, HI 96743
(808) 885-6655
Ritz Carlton Mauna Lani (808) 885-2000
Mauna Lani Bay Hotel (808) 885-6622

Located on the big island, Mauna Lani is known by many to be one of the most beautiful courses in the world. The North and the South Courses are there to challenge you with ocean breezes, lush foliage, black lava flows, and vistas that are impossible to forget.

Princeville Resort $$$$$
5-3900 Kuhio Highway
Kauai, HI 96722
(808) 826-9644

The Princeville Resort has a royal heritage; it is built on land once owned by a Hawaiian prince. There are two courses here, the Prince Course and the Makai. The Prince is considered to be the best course in Hawaii. There are five sets of tees, and only single digit handicappers are allowed to play from the back two. From the forward tees, the yardage is only 5,338, so the course can be played by just about anyone willing to take the challenge.

The Makai Course has twenty-seven holes and enjoys the reputation of being in the top 100 of great American golf courses by Golf Digest. No matter which layout you choose, you will have an unforgettable experience.

Volcano Golf and Country Club $$
Hawaii Volcano National Park, HI 96718
(808) 967-7331

Situated on the east coast of the big island near Hilo, this unusual location uses the volcanic mountain slopes and high elevation (4,000 feet) to offer players something a bit out of the ordinary.

Wailea Golf Club $$$$$
100 Wailea Golf Club Drive
Maui, HI 96718
(808) 879-2966

Just off the Main Island, Maui is home to several outstanding courses and the Wailea is no exception. Offering three courses, all with breathtaking views of the Pacific, the mountains, and the tropical vegetation, it is difficult to decide which one to play first.

Appendix II: Golf Courses and Resorts

Nevada

Desert Inn Golf Club $$$$$
3145 Las Vegas Boulevard South
Las Vegas, NV 89109
(702) 733-4290

Desert Inn is the course where the rich and famous play. It is also the host of many PGA and LPGA events. Located in the heart of the casino "Strip," you would never know it thanks to the abundance of trees. Priority is given to hotel guests, so when you get tired of "21," try 18.

Emerald River Resort and Country Club $$$$
1155 West Casino Drive
Laughlin, NV 89029
(702) 298-0061

About an hour from Las Vegas, along the banks of the Colorado River, Emerald River is a magnificent course which has combined traditional holes and links-style to create one of the toughest courses in the state. Yet, with four tee boxes, even a high handicapper can get around this track.

Incline Village Golf Resort $$$$$
955 Fairway Boulevard
Incline Village, NV 89450
(702) 832-1144

Moving northwest from Las Vegas to the Reno area, Incline Village is aptly named as it perches some 6,400 feet above sea level. With two fine courses, the Championship Course designed by Robert Trent Jones Sr. and the Executive Course by Robert Trent Jones Jr., you can decide how much challenge you want in a day. Both offer panoramic views of Lake Tahoe. The Championship has more difficult greens and numerous water hazards, while the Executive is only 3,002 yards from the reds with a slope of 94.

Oregon

Sunriver Lodge and Resort $$$
P.O. Box 3609
Sunriver, OR 97707
(503) 593-1221

Near Bend, Sunriver Lodge has two challenging courses which have earned it the reputation as an outstanding golf resort. With elevated greens built with different levels and ample doglegs to keep you thinking, both courses are a good test of any golfer's skills.

Tokatee Golf Club $$

54947 McKenzie Highway
Blue River, OR 97413
(800) 452-6376

Situated in the McKenzie River Valley, about fifty miles east of Eugene, Tokatee gets its name from a Chinook word which means "place of restful beauty." With a slope of 119, it is a relatively easy course with few bunkers, but the thousands of towering pines and mountain scenery make it a top-rated public course.

Washington

Indian Canyon Golf Course $

West 4304 West Drive
Spokane, WA 99204
(509) 747-5353

Bring your pull cart for this charming, short, but tricky course. It has a view of Spokane and a reputation as being one of the best twenty-five public courses around, according to Golf Digest.

Semiahmoo Golf and Country Club $$$

8720 Semiahmoo Parkway
Blaine, WA 98230
(800) 770-7992

Long considered Washington's finest resort and with a top twenty rating from Golf Digest, *this Arnold Palmer-Ed Seay course is as well designed as it is beautiful. (Nearby woods and lakes offer a natural habitat for bald eagles.)*

BERMUDA AND THE CARIBBEAN

The Bahamas

Atlantis, Paradise Island $$

Nassau, Bahamas
(809) 363-3000

Open to the public and welcoming walkers at times, the Atlantis is well named if the intention was to make one think of water. With lateral water hazards (13 holes to be exact) and the ocean as guardian of the green for two more, the challenge here is to not run out of golf balls before you finish the round. Despite the challenge, the beauty of this course lies in the fact that it was designed on a bird sanctuary and is graced with lush tropical foliage like hibiscus, oleanders, ficus trees, and bougainvillaea.

Cotton Bay Club $$
Rock Sound
Eleuthera, Bahamas
(809) 334-6101

Only resort guests can enjoy this Robert Trent Jones gem. Loaded with bunkers and Bermuda grass greens, this links-style course offers scenic ocean views. Yachts decorate the bay and the sound of the ocean will calm even the most frustrated golfer. A good course to walk.

Divi Bahamas Beach Resort and Country Club $$$
Nassau, New Providence, Bahamas
(800) 367-3484

A bit unusual for this part of the world, the Divi offers more rolling fairways and less water than its cousins and is considered to be the best course in the area. At 5,908 yards from the forward tees, you'll need some good drives to score well here. It is open to the public, but requires carts.

Bermuda

Belmont Hotel and Golf Club $$$
P.O. Box WK 251
Warwick, WK BX
(809) 236-1301

Just four miles from bustling Hamilton, the Belmont is famous for narrow fairways and small, elevated greens. The flora and fauna so famous in Bermuda offer a visual feast, as do the views of Hamilton Harbour and the Great Sound. You may walk or ride and priority is given to guests of the hotel. This is an ideal course for novices.

Castle Harbour Golf Club $$$$
Paytner Road
Tuckers Town
(809) 293-2040

Situated within the Marriott Castle Harbour Resort, this course begins from an elevated tee and takes you up and down the island terrain. The ocean views are abundant, as are the ocean breezes, which come into play on just about every hole. A steady short game will serve you well as greens are small and well-bunkered. Carts are required and priority is given to hotel guests.

Port Royal Golf Course $$$
P.O. Box 189
Southhampton, SN BX
(809) 234-0972

With a high slope and rating, this Robert Trent Jones course was commissioned by the Bermudian government. Like all the courses in Bermuda,

Port Royal offers panoramic ocean and harbor views. Its 16th hole is arguably one of the most photographed holes in the world. Ocean breezes will play tricks with your ball, so be prepared. There are no restrictions here; the public is welcome and walking is allowed at certain times.

Jamaica

Half Moon Golf Club $$$$$
P.O. Box 80
Montego Bay, Jamaica
(809) 953-2615

Another Robert Trent Jones course, situated among thousands of palm trees and awash with color from oleander and hibiscus. The ocean is only two hundred yards away and offers additional challenges with unpredictable breezes. Half Moon has hosted a number of international tournaments, including the Jamaica Open, yet welcomes the public.

Tryall Golf, Tennis and Beach Club $$$$$
Hanover, Jamaica
(809) 952-5110

Host of many tournaments, yet open to the public, Tryall has an extremely beautiful layout. The front nine runs along the ocean, providing you with plenty of sea breezes to play with your shots. The back nine is quite different in that it is located in the foothills of the island and has ample palm trees and bunkers to foil even the best shots.

Puerto Rico

Hyatt Dorado Beach $$$$
Dorado, PR 00646
(787) 796-1234 or (800) 233-1234

The East and West Courses here were designed by Robert Trent Jones and built back in the 1950s on the Rockefeller estate. Over the years, a number of renovations have taken place, but the lush, mature landscape is still intact.

The East is considered the more challenging with its hilly terrain and oceanside holes. The West Course plays a bit more inland and has lakes, lagoons, and lots of trees. As with the Cerromar courses, priority is given to hotel guests.

Hyatt Regency Cerromar Beach $$$
Dorado, PR 00646
(787) 796-1234 or (800) 233-1234

Golfers have two courses from which to choose, both designed by Robert Trent Jones. The North Course is oceanside and loaded with water and palm trees. *The South Course travels inland a bit and might well feel a bit more "open." It also has a tropical feeling to it, with ample palms and coconut groves to add to its charm. Priority is given to hotel guests for tee times, but all are welcome. Walking is not allowed.*

Palmas del Mar $$$$$
Bo. Candelero Abajo
Route 3, Road 906
KM 86.4
Humacao, PR 00791
(787) 852-6000

Just thirty miles from San Juan, this golfer's paradise was designed by Gary Player in 1974. The course rolls over hills and offers ocean views on some holes, but the challenge comes from narrow fairways and small greens. Priority is given to hotel guests and walking is not allowed.

St. Croix

Carambola Beach Resort and Golf Club $$$
Estate River
St. Croix, USVI 00851
(809) 778-3800

Lush, tropical, and meandering through a valley, Carambola has quite a few dogleg holes, especially on the front. On the back, you must carry across water on a couple of holes. Walking is not allowed and priority is given to hotel guests.

Mahogany Run Golf Course $$$
1 Mahogany Run Road
St. Thomas, USVI 00801
(809) 775-5000

You'll wish your golf cart had seat belts to play this mountain goat course. While the course is located primarily in the rain forest, it does come perilously close to the ocean on three holes, known as "Devil's Triangle." Although the course is not long, it makes up in beauty and difficulty for what it lacks in length.

CANADA

Alberta

Banff Springs $$$
Spray Avenue
Banff, Alberta T0L0C0
(800) 828-7447

Banff Springs offers three courses, the Rundle, Sulphur, and Tunnel Courses. It's a bit of a drive (one hour and forty-five minutes) from the closest airport, but don't think you'll be "roughing it." This is a luxurious hotel complete with boutiques and creature comforts like masseuses and hot tubs. Once you settle into your room, turn your attention to the mountains that adorn the golf courses. They are breathtaking in their majesty and relentless in the illusions they cast over the courses. Situated in a Canadian National Park, wildlife abounds here—including bison, elk, bear, moose, and sheep.

British Columbia

Royal Colwood Golf Club $$$
629 Golfstream Avenue
PO Box 7428 Depot D
Victoria, British Columbia V9B5B8
(604) 478-9591

With a 135 rating from the forward tees and stretching out some 5,912 yards, this semiprivate course is not for the novice. Although flat and easy to walk, it's filled with traps and strategically placed water. A favorite of British Royalty from years gone by, it is always in top condition despite the over 90,000 rounds of golf played here per year.

Whistler $$$$
Chateau Whistler Resort
Highway 99/Chateau Blvd
Box 100
Whistler Village, British Columbia V0N1B0
(800) 828-7447

Three courses named for three golf legends await you just two hours from Vancouver airport: Nicklaus North, Arnold Palmer Golf Course (The Whistler Golf Club), and the Robert Trent Jones Jr. at the Chateau Whistler Golf Club. Offering an array of activities après golf, such as horseback riding, hiking, boating, fishing, and shopping, there is good reason why Whistler has been viewed as one of North America's top ten resorts for many years.

If you would like more information on golf in British Columbia, contact the Ministry of Tourism in Victoria at (800) 663-6000.

Manitoba

Wasagaming Golf Course $
Riding Mountain National Park
Box 52
Wasagaming, Manitoba R0J280
(204) 848-7445

A public course that invites walkers, Wasagaming is a bit scaled back compared to some of the fancier courses around, but makes up for it by offering players some truly beautiful scenery. Some 175 miles northwest of Winnipeg, this course is peacefully situated in the 1,150-square mile Riding Mountain National Park. The layout is hilly, with plenty of blind shots leading to well-protected greens which are rather slick.

For more information on golf in this vast area of Canada, contact Tourism Winnipeg at (800) 665-0204.

New Brunswick

The Algonquin Resort $$
184 Adolphus Street
St. Andrews, New Brunswick E0G2X0
(800) 268-9411

Another fine bit of work by Donald Ross, the courses at the Algonquin are appropriately named Woodlands and Seaside. Seaside is a test for all levels of players, with the sea breeze and water coming into play on 13 holes. The Woodlands course is a bit more tranquil, offering golfers an opportunity to work on their short game. The resort is located about two hours by car from Bangor, Maine, or 90 minutes from the Saint John airport.

The New Brunswick Office of Tourism will be happy to provide you with more information on courses in this part of Canada. Call them at (800) 561-0123.

Newfoundland

St. Christopher's Resort $$
Twin Rivers Golf Course
Trans Canada Highway
Port Blanford, Newfoundland A0C2G0
(709) 543-2525

A one-hour ride from Gander International Airport, Twin Rivers is best described as rustic, as it meanders through thick forests, over rocks and rivers, and uses the vast Atlantic ocean as a backdrop. If you are a bird-

watcher, the bald eagle can be spotted in this territory, as well as some large four-legged critters like moose and bear. It is a challenging course that demands good course management skills and careful club selection to score well. The hotel consists of 90 luxury rooms offering numerous services and amenities.

For more information on golf in Newfoundland, contact the Department of Tourism and Culture at (800) 563-6353.

Nova Scotia

Keltic Lodge $$
Ingonish Beach
Cape Breton, Nova Scotia B0C1L0
(902) 285-2880

The Highland Links course at Keltic Lodge, a true Scottish-links style layout, is a walker's paradise set firmly on a peninsula between mountains and the ocean. You'll have a new appreciation for the term rough on this track—the greens are small, undulating, and protected by bunkers. Add to this the unpredictable sea breezes that at times pound the terrain, and you have all the ingredients for an unforgettable round. With fewer than 20,000 rounds played here each year, it is easy to understand why so many golf magazines rate this as one of the top courses in North America. The Keltic Lodge is well-appointed with 32 guest rooms.

The Sports and Recreation Commission will provide you with more golf locations in Nova Scotia by calling (902) 424-7512.

Ontario

Angus Glen Golf Club $$$
4495 Major Mackenzie E.
Markham, Ontario L6C1N9
(905) 887-5157

A relatively new public course, built in 1994, presents you with its number one handicap hole at the first tee. Built on a former cattle farm, hence the name "Angus," this track received "the best new public course" for Canada from Golf Digest *in 1995. Riding is mandatory and the course has everything a golfer wants: a driving range, bunker practice area, putting green, instruction area, well-stocked pro shop, and locker rooms with showers.*

About twenty-five miles north of Toronto, you could easily combine a great golf experience with the sites and attractions of downtown Toronto for a memorable Canadian vacation.

Glen Abbey Golf Club $$$$
1333 Dorval Drive
Oakville, Ontario L6J4Z3
(905) 844-1800

Built by Jack Nicklaus in 1976 and just about 20 miles west of Toronto, here is one more course to add to your Toronto holiday. A large course with open fairways and fast, undulating bentgrass greens, Glen Abbey is the home of the Royal Canadian Golf Association and hosts the annual Canadian Open. It is still fully accessible to the public. The club house is comfortable and well-appointed and a practice area is in place. The Royal Canadian Museum and Golf Hall of Fame are also on the property—add these to your list of places to visit.

There are dozens of superb golf courses in the Province of Ontario and the Ministry of Culture, Tourism and Recreation has information on all of them. Call them at (800) 668-2746.

Prince Edward Island

The Links at Crowbush Cove $$$
P.O. Box 204
Morell, Prince Edward Island C0A1S0
(902) 961-2800

Minutes from Charlottetown, this course was designed by Thomas McBroom in 1993 to great critical acclaim. Set along the shore with ocean views from every hole, the challenging layout will keep you more focused on your next shot than on the surrounding scenery. The greens are challenging, there are plenty of pot bunkers, and a mixture of wild and natural grasses present you with a links-style layout. If you are a birder, Crowbush is set in an Audubon conservation area so you're likely to view heron, wood ducks, and cormorants in their natural habitat. Open to the public and inviting to walkers, the course was host of the 1997 Canadian Amateur Golf Championship. There is quite a bit to do and see in Charlottetown from museums to theatre, as well as boating, fishing, and hiking.

The Prince Edward Island Department of Tourism and Parks, Visitor Services Division can provide you with more information about golf in this scenic part of Canada. Contact them at (800) 565-0267.

Quebec

Carling Lake $$$
Route 327
Pine Hill, Quebec J0V1A0
(514) 533-9211

About one hour from Montreal, Carling Lake is a year-round resort area nestled in the famous Laurentians mountains, boasting rock formations estimated to be over one billion years old. The course is mature, with wide, ambling fairways and undulating, elevated greens. Carts are mandatory. Water comes into play on four holes and bunkers abound. From the Lake Carling Hotel, you have just a short walk to the first tee. The delightful village restaurants offer outstanding après golf food and drink in a decidedly continental fashion. In cosmopolitan Montreal, there is something to do from sunup to sundown, including fine dining, antiquing, shopping, museums, and music.

There are dozens of fine courses and resorts in the Quebec Provence, many just minutes from Montreal. To learn more about this popular vacation destination, contact the Tourism Quebec Office at (800) 363-7777 or the Laurentians Tourism Office at (514) 436-8532.

Saskatchewan

Willows Golf and Country Club $$
303 21st Street East
Saskatoon, Saskatchewan 57K0C1
(306) 956-1100

Visitors to Willows Golf and Country Club, located just a short drive from Saskatoon, may choose among four 9-hole courses: Bridges, Island, Lakes, and Xena. The Lakes course is considered the most difficult of the four with narrow, protected greens, and a steady wind. The signature hole on the Island course is the eighth, which is over water to an island green, while the Bridges course presents players with a dogleg left heading toward a deep green with a bunker on one side and water on the other. Accuracy is rewarded on any hole played here and distance off the tee is a must to master the Xena course. The club house is modern and well-appointed and there is a spacious practice area. Music festivals, rodeos, horse shows, art galleries, and museums make for great entertainment when you aren't on the links.

The Saskatchewan Trade and Convention Centre at (800) 667-7538 will gladly recommend other courses in the area.

… Appendix II: Golf Courses and Resorts

MEXICO

Acapulco Princess Golf Club $$$$
Playa Revolchadero/AP1351
Acapulco
(800) 223-1818

This is a rather large resort with a hotel offering over 1,000 rooms, (including suites, condos, and villas), awash with flowers, manicured gardens, and places to find quiet retreat. Just minutes from the airport and situated on Acapulco Bay, it is arguably one of the world's most picturesque harbors. The Acapulco Princess Course is rather new, having been constructed in 1991, and is not one that will cause a high level of stress. It is flat and even-tempered; a solid short game should leave a novice golfer feeling quite exhilarated. On the other hand, the Pierre Marques Course, designed by Robert Trent Jones, is a longer and more difficult track owing to the wind, hills, and hazards. There is a great deal to enjoy at the Princess, known the world over for pampering guests, including fine food, health and fitness appointments, beaches, shopping, scuba diving, and an exciting night life.

Cabo del Sol Golf Club $$$$
Highway 1
Los Cabos
(800) 637-2226

Minutes from Los Cabos International Airport, Cabo del Sol is described as "a formidable Jack Nicklaus design" running along the Sea of Cortez and the Bay of Whales. Greens are Bermuda grass and run true; the layout is challenging and scenic. With an abundance of fine hotels and a reputation for superb cuisine, particularly local seafood, this section of the Baja Peninsula also offers snorkeling, boating, sport fishing, and night life. Cabo del Sol is open to the public and carts are required.

Isla Navidad Country Club $$$$
Manzanillo
011-52-364-1-8283

One half hour from the Manzanillo Playa de Oro International Airport, the landscape is quiet and somewhat undeveloped. Upon arriving at the Isla Navidad Country Club, the scenery changes rather dramatically. An impressive 20,000-square foot clubhouse looms before you and plans are well underway for the construction of a hotel, marina, spa and shops which will launch this destination as one of Mexico's best.

The course is lovingly constructed with brick cart paths, undulating, quick greens, ample water hazards, and an array of bunkers which demand some proficiency. The activities most likely to be of interest after golf are snorkeling, fishing, surfing, horseback riding, dining, and great shopping for local crafts.

Marina Ixtapa Golf Club $$$
Paseo Ixtapa
Ixtapa
011-52-753-3-1500

There are a number of fine hotels to stay at when you plan to play here, including the Sheraton Ixtapa, the Westin Ixtapa, and the Stouffer Presidente Ixtapa. The course itself lies within a multi-million dollar real estate development and has a promising future. Designed by Robert von Hagge, Marina Ixtapa Golf Club boasts eleven water holes, tricky greens, and unpredictable ocean winds.

Marina Vallarta Golf Club $$$
Paseo de la marina Norte, KM
7.5 Carretera Aeropuerto
Puerto Vallarta

If you love to walk and enjoy the assistance of a caddie, this is the course for you. If you love a little romantic history, this is where Richard Burton and Elizabeth Taylor fell in love while filming "The Night of the Iguana" back in the mid-sixties. Walk across the street from the beachfront Marriott Casa Magna and try this classic resort-style course on for size. The water views, ocean breezes, and helpful caddies all contribute to a memorable round on a course that won't beat you up if you have a few good shots in your bag. Be sure to spend some time at the beach, a bullfight, searching for local crafts and jewelry, exploring a jungle, or marveling at the local waterfalls.

Palmilla Golf Club $$$$
Hotel Palmilla
Highway 1
Apartado Postal 52
San Jose del Cabo
(800) 286-2465

With three 9-hole Nicklaus courses to play punctuated with arroyos and rocky terrain, a soak in the tub in your comfortable hotel room will be a welcome respite. There are no televisions or telephones in the hotel rooms. Rather, you are transported back in time as you sip on a margarita, gazing out the plantation window at the ocean view while an overhead fan keeps a quiet rhythm in the background. Stretching out over the Baja Peninsula, nearly every hole offers a water view. The Arroyo, Mountain, and Ocean Courses join to make for an unforgettable golfing experience by presenting you with wind, water, tight fairways, bunkers, and doglegs to and fro. As with the previously mentioned resort, there is an array of activities to enjoy before or after your round.

Mexico abounds with fine resorts and great golf courses. To find out more about planning a golf vacation to Mexico, contact the Mexican Government Tourism Office in New York at (212) 755-7261.

Appendix III

How Golf Arrived at its Current Level of Sophisticated Instruction

It seems there will always be a lively debate over the precise roots of the game of golf. There are some camps who credit the Celts, while others speak of the Dutch as founders of the game we love. Mention has been made, too, of the Romans and even the Visigoths. All of these countries had games, dating back to the 13th century, which involved striking a small, round object with a club or a stick, over ice or in open fields.

But we can accurately trace the origins of golf instruction to mid-1300s Scotland, when an agreement was struck among golfers to allow a second, successive shot to be hit. Prior to that agreement, the ball was hit back and forth across a field with the intention of passing a goal line or placing the ball in such a place that the opponent could not extricate it without some sort of penalty. Clearly golf was not played then as it is played today but, as in every game, a strategy was required. Allowing a second shot required players to develop new strategies in order to win, and the task of explaining how to accomplish those strategies fell on the shoulders of the better players.

Golf had become so popular in Scotland that archery skills were suffering, thus leaving the country at risk from aggressive neighbors. At one point, it was against the law to play golf and the punishment was death by hanging. (I readily admit I would have never wanted to play so badly as to risk a noose around my neck, although after some terrible rounds the noose doesn't sound like such a bad idea.) Eventually, peace was established with Scotland's neighbors and the country was able to turn its attention, once again, to golf. This is the point in time when every aspect of ball-striking began to be examined.

The invention of the gutta-percha ball (aka "guttie") in 1848 moved the game in a dramatic new direction. The gutta-percha, while crude by today's standards, was the first ball to be mass-produced. Prior to the arrival of the guttie on the golf scene, golf ball production was by and large a cottage industry, as each ball was made by hand, primarily in Scotland. They were very expensive, especially as an exported product. The guttie allowed the game of golf to be exported to other countries and the clever Scots followed, becoming teaching pros in places like England, Ireland, India, and the United States. (The first book of golf instruction, *A Keen Hand* by H. B. Farnie, can be traced to 1857.)

While the guttie ball was an economic success, it was, by the players' standards, a bit of a flop. Alas, the guttie was difficult to get into the air and much discourse followed on the usefulness of an open or closed stance to play with the guttie. Then, the Haskell ball hit the golf scene around 1900. More akin to the balls we use today, the Haskell ball was made with a center substance that was "wound," giving it strength and the ability to travel a greater distance when struck. Just about this time, the concept of "touring pros" was catching on and men like Harry Vardon, Bobby Jones, and Walter Hagen capitalized on the soaring popularity of golf around the globe.

By the 1950s, golf had hit its stride in the United States. The PGA was firmly ensconced, offering large purses, colleges had golf programs, and legends like Arnold Palmer and Jack Nicklaus became household names. At the same time, people wanted to learn more about golf and sought out teachers, subscribed to the new magazines called *Golf Digest* and *Golf,* and flocked to local golf schools seeking to perfect their game.

The first people to see the demand and potential for a national golf school in the late 1960s were Ben Sutton, Penny Zavichas, and Linda Craft. With technological advancements in club making (the appearance of metal woods and cavity backed irons) and in course management (better irrigation and turf conditions), golf was like a rocket on the launch pad.

By the 1980s, we saw video instruction and specialized instruction (putting, short game, mental aspect) added to the golf school menu. Today there are some forty national golf schools and a host of schools associated with great golf courses, resorts, and famous pros. We offer below the ones that specialize in instruction just for women.

Questions you'll want to ask before signing up for golf school:
- How long are the programs (one day, three days, five days, etc.)? How much do they charge for each one?
- Does the fee include accommodations, airport transfers, meals, and the like?
- Do they have a different rate for commuters?
- What is the student-teacher ratio? (It should not be more than 5:1.)
- What time of the day does instruction take place?
- Is videotape used to analyze swing mechanics?
- Is the instruction limited to the practice area or is there also on-course instruction?
- Is the hotel on-site or do you have to travel to get to the course?
- Do they have special rates for alumnae should you wish to return in the future?
- Ask them to describe the philosophy of the school. In other words, what is their teaching style?
- Will they take you as you are with a swing that basically works but needs some fine tuning, or will they want to rebuild your swing from top to bottom?
- Do they have seminars on rules and etiquette?

What to Expect in Terms of Game Improvement

Most instructors agree that a minimum goal is to take three strokes off your handicap (up to a 33% reduction in your handicap, especially for players with higher handicaps). If your handicap is currently 30, you should aim for lowering it to 21, but if your handicap is 9, dropping to a 6 is a more reasonable goal. The instructions in mechanics and course management you'll receive at golf school will do quite a bit to help you reach your goal, but learning to trust your swing and relax on the course will do as much, if not more, to improve your game.

What to Bring

You'll want to have a few extra pairs of gloves to keep in your bag. No doubt, your hands will get sweaty and a dry glove will make you more comfortable. Definitely use sunscreen, and perhaps a hat, if you like wearing one, or a least a visor. Sunglasses and a supply of water should round out the necessities. You'll also want to buy a small notebook to carry with you to make notes during the day. Remember, you'll be loaded with instruction, tips, and playing strategies at golf school. The notes you jot down will refresh your memory a few months after the program.

Golf Schools for Women

Craft-Zavichas Golf School
600 Dittmer
Pueblo, CO 81005
(800) 858-9633
In Colorado (719) 564-4449

Founded in 1968 by Linda Craft and Penny Zavichas (the niece of Babe Didrickson Zaharias), the emphasis here is on personalized attention. Students learn how to leverage body movement to develop a powerful swing and straight shots. Extra care is given to beginners and left-handed golfers. Choose from three locations: Pueblo, Colorado; Palm Beach, Florida; or Bellaire, Michigan.

Gillette LPGA Golf Clinics
c/o The Jane Blalock Company
Flagship Wharf
197 Eighth Street
Boston, MA 02129
(800) 262-7888

Not what one would call a traditional golf school, but more a great day of networking for business women, the Gillette LPGA Clinics are held in

Appendix III: Golf Schools

several U.S. cities throughout the year. The field is limited to about 150 women and there are 22 instructors, so the student teacher ratio is high (almost 8:1).

There is a morning scramble designed for advanced and intermediate players with instructors alongside to help identify areas needing improvement, a luncheon for all participants, and afternoon instruction on the range. For the novice, the day is reversed with instruction in the morning, lunch with all participants, and then an afternoon scramble to test new skills with instructors alongside.

Clinics take place in the following cities: Phoenix, Los Angeles, San Francisco, Washington DC, Atlanta, Chicago, Boston, Detroit, New York City, and Dallas.

John Jacobs' Golf Schools
7825 East Redfield Road
Scottsdale, AZ 85260
(800) 472-5007
In Arizona (602) 991-8587

The largest by far of all golf schools (it is three times as large as the number two school, Golf Digest*), John Jacobs' teaches some 10,000 students annually. Also referred to as John Jacobs' Practical School of Golf, the emphasis here is on the swing plane and learning to develop consistency. Select from the short game school or the standard school for overall instruction.*

John Jacobs offers instruction in the following cities: Point Clear, Alabama; Litchfield Park, Mesa, Scottsdale, and Tucson, Arizona; Napa, Palm Desert, and Rancho Las Palmas, California; Skyland, Colorado; Fort Lauderdale, Orlando, Marco Island, and Vero Beach, Florida; Traverse City, Michigan; Osage Beach, Missouri; Las Vegas, Nevada; Atlantic City, New Jersey; Margaretville and Hauppage, New York; Portland, Oregon; South Padre Island, Texas; Hever Valley, Utah; Delavan, Wisconsin; Jackson Hole, Wyoming; Graz, Austria; Cadiz-Gibraltar, Spain; Hamburg, Germany; and Zhongshan City, China.

Marlene Floyd's For Women Only Golf School
5350 Club House Lane
Hope Mills, NC 28348
(800) 637-2694
In North Carolina (919) 323-9606

If you want to tap into this talented woman's program, you had best plan ahead—they offer three two-day schools in October and two in April. By heavily emphasizing the fundamentals—grip, stance, and alignment—Marlene's goal is to get you to relax, so your swing will be relaxed.

Ms. Floyd is a former member of the LPGA, daughter of renowned instructor L. B. Floyd and sister of PGA Tour favorite, Raymond Floyd.

Pine Needles/Golfari
c/o Pine Needles Lodges and Country Club
600 Midland Road
Southern Pines, NC 28388
(910) 692-7111

In February, March, and April, students enjoy a three-day session. The program then switches to twice a month for May, June, September, October, and November. Four-day sessions are available January through April, then twice a month for May, June, and July.

Golfari is their "women-only" five-day program, started by Pine Needles owner Peggy Kirk Bell, one of the original founders of the LPGA Tour. Ms. Bell is considered one of the most influential women in golf in the United States, having won many honors from golf writers. She and her husband bought Pine Needles in 1953 and their golf programs have been going strong ever since. The Donald Ross course is a fine destination; the entire resort caters to guests only, so getting a round in is never a problem.

Golfari's focus is on the whole game: beginning with swing mechanics and placing heavy emphasis on the short game. Course management, equipment selection, and on-course instruction are also covered in depth.

THE School of Golf for Women
Singing Hills Resort
3007 Dehesa Road
El Cajon, CA 92019
(800) 457-5568
http://www.singinghills.com

Presently in their twentieth year of operation, THE School of Golf for Women offers both three- and five-day sessions during all seasons. Led by two-time, peer-elected Teacher of the Year, Shirley Spork, the school is staffed with both Master professionals and Class A members of the LPGA and best serves women who have some golfing experience under their belts. Classes are small (one instructor per every five students) and focus on improving the female golfer's skills while developing playing confidence. Students receive videotapes of their practice sessions as well as personalized notebooks to record their lessons.

In 1997, Singing Hills was rated as one of the most women friendly facilities in North America by Golf for Women magazine. Aside from 54 holes of golf, the 420-acre resort also offers a 102-room lodge, tennis courts, two heated pools, and two spas.

Additional Recommendations

There are hundreds of other golf schools across the country. Although the ones already listed pay almost exclusive attention to the needs of women golfers, here are some others that are considered top drawer as well.

Appendix III: Golf Schools

Academy of Golf Dynamics
The Hills of Lakeway
45 Club Estates Parkway
Austin, TX 78738
(512) 261-3300

With one location in Colorado Springs, Colorado, and the other in Austin, Texas, this program gets high marks from a number of pros. The philosophy here is that individuals learn in different ways, so programs are generally designed with this in mind. Instructors work with students to achieve improvement not only in skills but in course management as well.

The Austin location's practice center was designed by Jack Nicklaus and offers three playing holes so students get much needed on-course instruction. The Colorado school gets rave reviews for the food and breathtaking rock formations, as well as the quality of instruction.

America's Favorite Golf Schools
P.O. Box 3325
Fort Pierce, FL 34948
(800) 365-6640

With twenty locations across the country, as well as Canada and the Bahamas, the bedrock of America's Favorite Golf Schools is fundamental, practical instruction from a full-time staff of teachers. The student/teacher ratio is low and the program is affordable. They even have a junior golf program.

Choose a location from the following list and plan to have a great learning experience at a reasonable price: Bellrock Inn & Oakcreek Country Club, Sedona, Arizona; San Vincente Inn & Golf Club, San Diego, California; Quality Inn & Adobe Creek Golf Club, Santa Rosa, California; Lone Tree Resort, Littleton, Colorado; Westcliffe Inn and Saint Andrews Golf Club, Colorado Springs, Colorado; Mystic Ramada Inn and Stonington Country Club, Mystic, Connecticut; Stouffer Pine Isle Resort, Lake Lanier, Georgia; Balmoral Woods Country Club, Crete, Illinois; Eagle Creek Resort, Findlay, Illinois; Maxim Hotel and Sahara Country Club, Las Vegas, Nevada; Green Valley Driving Range, Las Vegas, Nevada; Penn National Golf Club & Inn, Gettysburg, Pennsylvania; Days Inn and the Golf Professional's Club, Beaufort, South Carolina; Quality Atlantik Beach Golf Resort and the Lucaya Golf and Country Club, Freeport, Bahamas; Holiday Inn and Annandale Golf and Country Club, Toronto, Ontario, Canada.

Dave Pelz Short Game School
1200 Lakeway Drive
Suite 21
Austin, TX 78734
(800) 833-7270

With 65% of our total shots on any given round coming from 100 yards in, Dave Pelz believes this is where the game is won. Emphasis is placed on wedge play, chipping, pitching, bunkers, and putting by using video analysis, laser alignment, practice aids, and a host of superb instructors. Not for those on a budget, but what would you pay to turn three strokes into two around each green?

Select from two locations: The Boca Raton Resort and Club, Boca Raton, Florida, and PGA West, La Quinta, California.

David Leadbetter Academy of Golf
Lake Nona Golf Club
9100 Chiltern Drive
Orlando, FL 32827
(407) 857-8276

The guru to Nick Price, Nick Faldo, Ernie Els, and many other pros, David Leadbetter is known around the world for his industrious study of swing theory. His book Faults and Fixes *has enjoyed a long shelf life. If you're in the jet set, you can sign on for a Leadbetter program in Austria, England, Spain, France, Ireland, or Thailand, in addition to his Orlando and Naples locations.*

The Golf Clinic
P.O. Box 1129
Pebble Beach, CA 93953
(800) 321-9401

Indulge your golf fantasies and stay at The Lodge at Pebble Beach while attending this school. The food is extraordinary, the course is legendary (normal greens fee: $250!), and mere words on paper fail to describe the scenery. Accommodations are included if you sign on for a three- or five-day program with Head Instructor John Geertsen, author of Your Turn for Success!*

If you've done the Pebble Beach scene and want something a bit more exotic, enroll at The Golf Clinic's Hawaiian location at Royal Waikoloan Hotel on the Kohala Coast. They have a junior program if you want to make this a family golf adventure.

Golf Digest Schools
5520 Park Avenue, Box 395
Trumbull, CT 06111
(800) 243-6121

Second only in size to the John Jacobs' Golf Schools, these schools are very reputable for their service. The classes are small and the focus is on fundamentals like grip, posture, and that ever-present malady, alignment. Their motto could easily be "individual solutions for individual golfers" which in this era of miracle clubs, gadgets, and abundant advice is quite refreshing.

To their credit, they have programs for women, couples, and even parent and child programs, which really underscores their philosophy about golf being a game for a lifetime.

Appendix III: Golf Schools

Golf Digest Schools are located in North Scottsdale, Arizona; Carmel, Fallbrook and La Quinta, California; Vail, Colorado; Tarpon Springs, Florida; Braselton and Sea Island, Georgia; Sun Valley, Idaho; Chicago, Illinois; Bend, Oregon; and Williamsburg, Virginia.

Grand Cypress Resort and Golf Club
Grand Cypress Academy of Golf
One North Jacaranda
Orlando, FL 32836
(800) 835-7377

With its 21-acre practice area and par 3, 4, and 5 holes designed by Jack Nicklaus for on-course instruction, the Academy is regarded as one of the finest schools in the country. Several of the instructors have earned high marks from Golf Magazine. *By using a computerized swing analysis method, students are able to view their videotaped swings with the goal of improving strengths and eliminating weaknesses. This unique form of instruction was designed by Dr. Ralph Mann, following his study of the swings of fifty of the top professional players.*

The resort has luxurious accommodations and two Nicklaus courses to enjoy. The Academy has a variety of golf school packages which are offered year round.

Nicklaus/Flick Golf Schools
11780 U.S. Highway 1
North Palm Beach, FL 33408
(800) 642-5528

This must be quite an experience, as all instructors are hand-picked by Messrs. Nicklaus and Flick; a master player and a master instructor. The program offers a sports psychologist, one-on-one swing instruction, short game tutelage, course management advice, video analysis, fitting clubs, and opportunities for play and competition. Choose from the Ibis Golf & Country Club (PGA National Resort and Spa), Palm Beach Gardens, Florida; Desert Mountain Golf Club or the Scottsdale Princess Resort, Scottsdale, Arizona; Pebble Beach Resort, Inn at Spanish Bay, Pebble Beach, California; and Boyne Highlands Resort, Heather Highland Inn, Harbor Springs, Michigan.

Professional Golf Schools of America
Winter: 4105 Luff Street #1
Panama City Beach, FL 32408
(800) 447-2744
Summer: P.O. Box 1543
Maggie Valley, NC 28751
(800) 447-2744

Boasting a teaching philosophy that in plain terms means "Keep it Simple," the credo at the Professional Golf Schools of America is to help students grasp the simplicities of the swing. Beginning on the course with short irons and putting instructions (they even have a section on helping you to read the greens and lag putting), it is not until later in the program that the long irons and driver come out of the bag.

The locations are in Mesa, Arizona; Hollywood and Fort Meyers, Florida; and Maggie Valley, North Carolina.

Roland Stafford Golf Schools
P.O. Box 81
Arkville, NY 12406
(800) 447-8894

It is easy to understand why this school is widely regarded as one of the most successful golf schools around, once you read the Roland Stafford theory on golf and simplicity. Students learn to develop a good grip, a level swing plane, and a steady tempo. In addition, rules and etiquette clinics are conducted and students are exposed to equipment demonstrations.

One of the really endearing aspects of the school is the discount given to repeat students, which increases with each year the student returns.

Sign up for a program at these locations: Grand Palms Resort, Pembroke Pines, Florida; Perdido Bay Resort, Pensacola, Florida; Tory Pines Resort, Francestown, New Hampshire; Peek'n Peak Resort, Clymer, New York; Christman's Wyndham House, Wyndham, New York; and Hotel L'Esterel, Quebec, Canada.

Swing's The Thing Golf Schools
Box 200, Rier Road
Shawnee-on-Delaware, PA 18356
(800) 221-6661

Low cost and low key are the watch words for this popular golf program. "Learning for a Lifetime" is the focus of Swing's instruction, with an agreement between student and instructor that an individual swing rather than reconstruction is the key to a long-term relationship with the golf game. Returning students are happily accommodated with refresher courses carved from personal profiles. The instructors are touted as among the best in the country and the phrase "user-friendly" seems to be foremost in the minds of the people who operate the locations at PGA West in La Quinta, California; Orange Lake Resort & Country Club in Orlando, Florida; Ocean Pines Golf & Country Club, Ocean City, Maryland; Shawnee Country Club in Shawnee, Pennsylvania, and Colonial Charters Country Club, Myrtle Beach, South Carolina.

Appendix III: Golf Schools

United States Golf Schools
1631 S. W. Anglico Lane
Port Saint Lucie, FL 34984
(800) 354-7415
With two, three, and five-day programs that place a good deal of emphasis on the short game and on-course instruction, each student is assigned to one instructor who remains with her/him throughout the length of the school. Several hours of practice area instruction are followed by on-course work. Finish the day with unlimited post-instruction golf and range balls. Plunge yourself into the "golf zone" at the following locations: Belleview Mido Resort Hotel, Clearwater, Florida; The Inverrary Resort, Fort Lauderdale, Florida; Cutter Sound Golf & Yacht Club/Holiday Inn, Palm City, Florida; Spring Lake Golf & Tennis Resort, Sebring, Florida; French Lick Springs Golf & Tennis Resort, French Lick, Indiana; Broadwater Beach Resort & President Casino, Biloxi, Mississippi; Huff House, Roscoe, New York; Grossinger Resort, Liberty, New York; Breezy Point Resort, Brainerd Lakes, Minnesota; and The Bahamas Princess, Freeport, Grand Bahamas Island.

For more information on golf schools, refer to First Person Press's *Golf Schools: The Complete Guide to Hundreds of Instruction Programs for Adults and Juniors* and James Lane's *Peterson's Golf Schools and Resorts.*

Appendix IV

Cyberspace has brought a wealth of information to our businesses and homes via the computer. Many businesses have designed web pages to promote products and services, and more consumers are feeling safe making purchases on-line. Surfing is a favorite pastime for many of us, and now with improved browsing capabilities, we can find just about anything at any time of the day or night.

Here are some sites—on everything golf-related—that you may want to visit over the coming months. New sites are being built every day, so let me know at BTGC CAL@aol.com, and we'll try to add them to future editions of *Breaking the Grass Ceiling*.

Arlington Women's Golf Association
www.startext.net/homes/awga/
An Arlington, Texas-based women's golf association.

Atlanta Golfer
www.AtlantaGolfer.com/
www.golfatlanta.com/
These sites provide information on golfing in the Atlanta area, with listings of courses, directions, etc.

Chipmunk Golf
www.chipmunk.com/
Helps you to make selections for junior equipment.

Coastal Golfaway
www.golflink.net/coastal/
Filled with information on golf vacations on the Carolina coast.

www.Golf.com
NBC and Golf Digest *have teamed up to create this site which has several sections of golf information: news from the golf industry, upcoming*

tournaments, travel ideas, and an area where you can talk on-line with the pros.

Golf Archives at Princeton
http://dunkin.princeton.edu/.golf
and
Golf Home Page at Dartmouth
http://coos.dartmouth.edu/~pete/golf
Both sites offer golf information, lessons, tips on club making, and tell you how to link up with other golf pages.

Golf Link
www.golflink.net
A useful, albeit somewhat limited site in that all the information provided is paid for by advertisers. Still, you can pick up some good ideas on hotels and resorts, merchandise, real estate, and golf schools.

Golf Travel On-Line
www.gto.com
Straightforward, easy to use. Do-it-yourself vacation planning at no charge. You can also call 1-888-GTO-Golf by phone.

Golf Web
www.golfweb.com/gwpp.htm
Just about the slickest web site on the net. Heralded as one of the "7 Best Web Sites of 1996" by Business Week *magazine, Golf Web offers a comprehensive source of information including trips, courses, merchandise, playing tips, investment information, classified ads, and lots of chat.*

Hale Irwin's Golfer's Passport Program
www.powerxgolf.com
Membership entitles you to a listing of hundreds of participating courses and resorts around the world, two free rounds of golf at each course, and a minimum of 10% discount on packages and room rates. Cost: $49.95.

igolf@aol.com
A comprehensive site loaded with graphics and information. Several icons offer specific areas such as Leaderboards, Stocks, Architecture, Pro Shop, Travel, Profiles on Players, and the like. There is a fun section called "greenside glossary" filled with new "golfisms" from players around the country who make up words to describe life on the course and around the clubhouse.

www.iquest/michigangolfer/
Provides a listing of courses in Michigan.

Appendix IV: Golf On Line

Ladies Professional Golf Association
www.LPGA.com
A fun, informative and interactive site with articles to read, playing tips, profiles of the tour players, and stories about what the LPGA is doing to continue its commitment to juniors and women players in general. Get tour dates, results, and plenty of women's golf history.

19th Hole
www.sport.net/golf
An unusual site that offers photographs of tour players, 800 numbers for golf equipment and products, a classified ad section, and tour schedules for the upcoming week.

NuGolf
www.sfadv.com/nugolf
A little off the beaten path to improved golf, NuGolf provides you with a personalized, interactive audio program that helps you to reprogram bad golf habits through affirmations and inductions. Costs about the same as a top-of-the-line driver.

Parker Golf
www.parkergolf.com
A very attractive site filled with travel advice and up-to-the-minute news about tournaments around the world and how you can get there. Parker Golf is particularly proud of their employees, all of whom know the golf industry from top to bottom. They have event planners who can make any and all arrangements for you, including something like an incentive trip to the Ryder Cup. This company is detail- and service-oriented.

Professional Golfer's Association
PGA.online.com
Same approach as the LPGA site, but covering the world of men's professional golf.

Southern California Preferred Tee Times
www.teevision.com/1-888-Join-PGA
For a small fee and a modest monthly charge (under $10), you can get great tee times at about thirty courses in the Orange County, San Diego, and San Bernadino area.

The United States Golf Association
www.usga.org/
Review the Rules of Golf, Decisions on the Rules of Golf, *and check out the* USGA Handicap System Manual. *Get dates for upcoming tournaments, buy golf gifts, books, videos, and apparel.*

The U.S. Golf Travel Home Page
www.golftravelplus.com/
Direct reservation system for golf packages around the world. One time $59.00 membership charge lets you load software into your PC so you can book directly. Monthly updates of new courses and resorts available at small additional charge.

WebGuide Golf
www.webguide.com.au/golf/
Lists public courses, resort courses, tips from the pros, golf news, equipment reviews, and other information pertaining to golf.

Women's Golf World
www.insync.net/~ldlent/
For women who love the game. Has the latest books, videos, software, gift items, golf fashions, and ideas for vacations. You can post upcoming golf events in your area, talk to other golfers, and share your views with WGW.

Women's South Carolina Golf Association
www.golfnet.com/wscga/wschome.htm
South Carolina golf association site offering information on activities and membership.

Women's Southern California Golf Association
www.womensgolf.org
Provides information on golf in southern California, along with membership details and events.

World Golf
www.worldgolf.com
This is a fun site to spend time in because there is quite a bit of information to browse through, like course reviews, club making, collectibles, golf jokes, golf tips, rules, schools, and tours. There is even a hole-in-one registry.

Yahoo
www.Yahoo.com
Index to the web with endless sources of information for those willing to spend some time surfing. You can find logo items, golf clubs, photos of great golf holes around the world, a hole-in-one club, and thousands of golf enthusiasts with whom you can chat.

Appendix V

You're dressed and ready to play a round. But do you have a partner or a foursome? Sometimes the most intimidating aspect of golf is heading for a new course on your own. It always helps to have a few colleagues to play with, especially when you're starting out and trying to gain confidence in your game. Women's golf groups often can give you information about amateur local tournaments, clinics, leagues, and other events that will help your golf game and expand your business contact list.

This appendix lists many of the women's golf groups around the country, including all chapters of the Executive Women's Golf Association, a national organization devoted to business women who want to make contacts through golf. Also included is a list of USGA regional and state women's golf organizations that have agreed to list their information in this book.

If you can't find a group in your area or are looking for even more choices, start calling the courses and clubs in your area for any information they might have on leagues, clinics, and outings. Your local Chamber of Commerce or business women's associations may also have information on area golf organizations, and some university alumni associations sponsor golf leagues for graduates.

EXECUTIVE WOMEN'S GOLF ASSOCIATION

Following is a list of the individual chapters of EWGA, featuring the 1997-1998 president or chapter contact and other relevant information listed alphabetically by state. For more information, call the national EWGA office or the individual chapters.

An asterisk (*) marks chapters currently organizing for 1998.

National Headquarters

Executive Women's Golf Association
Nancy Oliver, President
300 Avenue of the Champions
Palm Beach Gardens, FL 33418
(800) 407-1477 or (561) 691-0096
FAX: (561) 691-0012

Alabama

Birmingham

Lyndy Rogers
Account Director, NCR
5616 Afton Drive
Birmingham, AL 35242
(205) 993-5735 or (205) 991-2933
FAX: (205) 991-2975

Sylvia Sumners
Membership Vice President
(205) 620-8167

Dana Boehling
Events Vice President
(205) 991-2792

Arizona

Old Pueblo (Tuscon)

Susan Maxwell
President, Max Merchandising
7260 N Cathedral Rock Road
(520) 577-5266
FAX: (520) 577-1055

Joy Jennings
Events Chairperson
(520) 290-7627

Appendix V: Golf Groups and Organizations

Valley of the Sun

Kathy George
Consultant, Arizona Education Association
40 North Central, Suite 900
Phoenix, AZ 85004
(602) 955-5519 or (602) 264-1774 or (602)998-5187

Mary Byrd
Membership Chairperson
(602) 564-0517

Maria Crimi Speth
Events Chairperson
(602) 240-2916

California

Fresno

* **Vicky Childers**
Owner, Ladies World of Golf
2053 West Bullarel
Fresno, CA 93711
(209) 438-2323

Gold Country

Barbara Ford
CPA
7263 Hickory Avenue
Orangevale, CA 95662
(916) 863-9636 or (916) 989-8127 or (916) 989-1496
FAX: (916) 988-1802
E-mail: bford1.@aol.com

Lynn Schweig
Membership Secretary
(916) 394-4597

Ellen Burmester
Events Chairperson
(916) 967-6677

Los Angeles

Joanne Williams
P.O. Box 64737-491
Los Angeles, CA 90064
(310) 335-5446
FAX: (310) 393-3466
1998 Chapter President

Helene Landers, LPGA
8032 Loyola Boulevard
Los Angeles, CA 90045
(310) 335-5446 or (310) 645-9578
FAX: (310) 645-4271

Sue Smith
Membership Chairperson

Gina Uible
Events Chairperson

Orange County

Cindy Lorenzini
Sales Representative, VWR Scientific Products
P.O. Box 9654
Newport Beach, CA 92658
(714) 451-2002 or (714) 552-2952
FAX: (714) 552-2957

Colette Sosnowski
Membership Chairperson
(714) 969-1889
FAX: same

Bernette K. Cripe
Events/Tournaments
(714) 634-4922 or (714) 779-7559

San Diego

Donna Lafreniere
4774 Mount St. Helens Way
San Diego, CA 92117
(619) 683-9028 or (619) 495-9241
FAX: (619) 495-0528

Carolyn Elliott
Membership Secretary
(619) 583-8023

Donna Bechthold
Events Chairperson
(619) 436-7016

San Francisco Bay Area

Barbara Dominguez
78 Avenida Espana
San Jose, CA 95139
(408) 227-4601
FAX: (408) 227-0768

Jeannie Burke
Membership Secretary
(510) 793-5158

Allyson Kumataka
Events Chairperson
(800) 334-6368

Santa Barbara

Carolyn Fryer
5501 San Patricio Drive
Santa Barbara, CA 93111
(805) 961-2778 or (805) 964-1951
FAX: (805) 966-3622

Bobbie Kline
Membership Secretary
(805) 967-2843 (evenings)

Michol Colgan
Events Chairperson
(805) 684-9989 (evenings)

Sonoma-Marin County

P.O. Box 4494
Petaluma, CA 94955
(707) 522-8800

Pat Edelstein
Membership Secretary
(707) 538-0403

Kathy Essick
Events Chairperson
(415) 459-4514

Colorado

Denver

Joy Spring
P.O. Box 262097
Highlands Ranch, CO 80163-2097
(303) 938-5771
FAX: (303) 938-9232
E-mail: jspring@leisuretrends.com

Kristal Kraft
Membership Secretary

Nadine Lange
Events Chairperson

Northern Colorado

Marta L. Farrell
Attorney
518 Ramah
Ft. Collins, CO 80526
(970) 206-1582
FAX: (970) 350-5369

DeeDee Smidt
Events Chairperson
(970) 204-4772

Appendix V: Golf Groups and Organizations

Connecticut

Fairfield County

Janet Sia
Director of Office Administration, Durant, Nichols, Houston
68 York Road
Fairfield, CT 06430
(203) 451-9999 or (203) 366-3438
FAX: (203) 384-0317
E-mail: Jan@DurantNic.com

Trish Caruso
90 Sasco Hill Terrace
Fairfield, CT 06430
(203) 451-9999 or (203) 255-2029
FAX: (203) 255-2029
E-mail: Trishgolfr@worldnet.att.net

Linda Bruner
Membership Chairperson
(800) 541-4224

Cyndy Berry
Events Chairperson
(860) 513-7541

Central Connecticut

Maureen Morris
Manager Treasury Control, Advest Inc.
90 State House Square
Hartford, CT 06103
(860) 509-1000 Ext. 2250 or (860) 563-9905
FAX: (860) 509-2005

M. J. Petretto
Membership Chairperson
(203) 457-9522

Michelle Hackley
Events Chairperson
(203) 315-0135

District of Columbia

Washington Metro

Eileen Maguire
Director, Carrier Administration, Citicorp
P.O. Box 10516
Rockville, MD 20849
(202) 737-4653 or (703) 708-1046 or (703) 404-8536
http://www.ewgdc.org

Pat Whitehead
Membership Secretary
(202) 418-8802
E-mail: patwhitehd@aol.com

Jane Ribadeneyra
Events Chairperson
(202) 628-9374
E-mail: wesgjane@aol.com

Florida

Brevard County

* **Kristine H. Stewart, CFP ChFC**
Vice President, Wall St. Investment Managers
100 Rialto Place, Suite 530
Melbourne, FL 32901
(407) 951-8000 or (407) 253-9091
FAX: (407) 951-8911

Fran Hill
Membership Chairperson
(407) 722-1305

Jean Butcher
Events Chairperson
(407) 452-2235

Broward County

Patricia A. Slagor
P.O. Box 4228
Boca Raton, FL 33429-4228
(954) 969-0963
FAX: (954) 746-9874

Penny Chalich
Membership Chairperson

Gerry Cross
Events Chairperson

Jacksonville

Margaret Downey
P.O. Box 550795
Jacksonville, FL 32255-0795
(904) 279-4407
FAX: (904) 279-5257
E-mail: Margaret_Downey@CSX.Com

Diane Ciehoski
Events Chairperson
(904) 824-2821

Manatee County

Carol A. Miers
Administrative Coordinator, Manatee County Public Safety
P.O. Box 1614
Bradenton, FL 34206-1614
(941) 758-3396
FAX: (941) 748-0863
E-mail: SReim@aol.com

Gayle Gibbons
Membership Secretary
(941) 746-1903

Jen Harding
Events Chairperson

Martin County

Tina Luce
President, Florida's Competitive Edge
7886 SW Ellipse Way
Stuart, FL 34997
(561) 225-8860 or 561) 221-0234 or (561) 692-4776
FAX: (561)221-0214

Geneva Maines
Membership Chairperson

Linda Simbritz
Events Chairperson
(561) 781-0429

Miami

Gayle E. Coyle
P.O. Box 430434
Miami, FL 33175
(305) 663-2593
FAX: (305) 643-5700

Phyllis Salzman
Membership Chairperson

Jackie Cox
Nancy O'Brien
Co-Events Chairperson

Greater Orlando

Madeline Kinney
508 Bristol Drive
Altamonte Springs, FL 32714
(407) 841-8660 or (352) 383-8397
FAX: (352) 383-9795
E-mail: MADKAY@aol.com

Denise Autorino
Membership Secretary
(407) 292-2550

Sandra Chaskauich
Events Chairperson

Palm Beach County

Joan Swinson
President, Return Plus, Inc.
12932 Calais Circle
Palm Beach Gardens, FL 33410
(561) 775-4674 or (561) 622-3397 or (561) 622-3065
FAX: (561) 622-7273
E-mail: SCHWANEE1@aol.com

Appendix V: Golf Groups and Organizations

Polk County

Debbie Noel
Supervisor, Sterile Processing, Lakeland Regional Hospital
1148 Ashboro Court
Lakeland, FL 33801
(941) 666-5695 or (941) 687-1224 or (941) 666-5695
FAX: (941) 967-9273

Peggy G. Cook
Membership Secretary
(941) 291-6633

Jo Duncan
Events Chairperson
(941) 421-5007

Tampa Bay

Nancy J. Karnavicius
Vice President, Bayprint
1101 First Ave. S.
St. Petersburg, FL 33705
(813) 854-8174 or (813) 823-1965
FAX: (813) 822-2252
E-mail: Bayprint@aol.com

Donna Smith
Membership Secretary
(813) 289-2020

Joanne Smith
Events Chairperson
(813) 785-2028

Georgia

Atlanta

Anita Denney
Secretary/Treasurer, Aerospace Aviation
1579 F Monroe Drive, Suite 815
Atlanta, GA 30324
(770) 984-7617
FAX: (770) 594-1319

Diane London
Membership Secretary
(404) 817-4515

Julie Tauber
Events Chairperson
(770) 995-5280 Ext. 4011

Augusta

Becca Phelan
814 Barrett Lane
Augusta, GA 30909
(803) 510-3253 or (800) 241-2401 or (706) 724-2601 or (706) 733-5749
FAX: (706) 722-2410

Michelle Sizemore
Membership Secretary
(706) 724-4443

Victoria Byrd
Events Chairperson
(706) 823-6600

Savannah

* **Nancy Eschette**
P.O. Box 1300
Tybee Island, GA 31328
(912) 352-2921 or (912) 786-9374
1998 Network Coordinator

Hawaii

Hawaii

Emily Gail
Emily Gail Public Relations and Marketing
P. O. Box 4164
Kailua-Kona, Hawaii 96745
(808) 329-7683
FAX: same

Colleen Cochlin
EWG Volunteer Contact
(808) 873-7882

Illinois

Chicago

Bev Rzewski
804 West Higgins Road
Park Ridge, IL 60068
(847) 329-4125
FAX: (773) 693-8781
E-mail: Act T Bev@aol.com

Michele Feinberg
Membership Secretary
(847) 578-6606

Quad Cities

Victoria Kauzlarich
Director of Human Resources, Litton Life Support
P.O. Box 64
Cordova, IL 61242
(319) 388-5328
FAX: (319) 383-6106

Marcilene McCabe
Membership Secretary
(319) 787-4041 Ext. 421

Lyn Lear
Events Chairperson
(319) 333-4661

Indiana

Indianapolis Host Club

* **Cynthia Lamb**
General Manager, Sugar Ridge Golf Club
21010 State Line Road
Lawrenceburg, IN 47025
(812) 537-9300
FAX: (812) 537-0386

Iowa

Greater Des Moines

Jan Gillum
Corporate Assistant Secretary, The Ruan Companies
P.O. Box 93222
Des Moines, IA 50393-3222
(515) 245-5305 or (515) 245-2561 or (515) 288-7762
FAX: (515) 245-2684

Diane Franco
Membership Secretary
(515) 248-7157

Kelli Johnson
Events Chairperson
(515) 283-9174

Iowa City

Lori J. Ellingson
World Marketing Alliance, Inc.
2101 ACT Circle, Suite 200
Iowa City, IA 52245
(319) 388-5328 or (319) 351-2280 or (319) 354-5764
FAX: (319) 358-0976
E-mail: ellingson,lori@mcleod.net
1998 Co-President

Yvonne Wernimont
1521 1st Avenue #202D
Coralville, IA 52241
(319) 364-0259 or (319) 351-4801
FAX: (319) 397-9509
E-mail: TednVon@aol.com
1998 Co-President

Sally Cline
Membership Secretary

Appendix V: Golf Groups and Organizations

Kentucky

Louisville

Robin Craddock
Attorney, Stites & Harbison
P.O. Box 70081
Louisville, KY 40270
(502) 583-6937

Carrie Raymond
Membership Chairperson
(502) 897-0202

Louisiana

Metropolitan New Orleans

Nanette Alba
Senior Vice President, Evangeline Health Care
3505 Lake Trail Drive
Kenner, LA 70065
(504) 456-0143
FAX: (504) 871-7950
E-mail: NALBA@aol.com

Jan Hersey
Membership Chairperson

Cheryl Young
Events Chairperson

Maryland

Annapolis/Chesapeake Bay

Jane Ramsay
Specialized Leasing Agent, Annapolis Accommodations
P.O. Box 1482
Annapolis, MD 21404
(800) 995-7128
FAX: (410) 263-1703

Jane Murray
Membership Chairperson
(301) 567-0100

Linda Demmler
Events Chairperson
(410) 280-2585

Baltimore

Judy Herman
Secretary/Treasurer, Baltimore Orthotics, Inc.
P.O. Box 196
Riderwood, MD 21137-0196
(410) 624-4653 or (410) 828-0818 or (410) 821-1166
FAX: (410) 828-0831

Katherine T. Sanzone
Membership Chairperson
(410) 539-5936

Virginia M. Sacilotto
Events Chairperson
(410) 388-5205

Eastern Shore

Nancy Dofflemyer
Sales Manager
P.O. Box 381
Showell, MD 21862
(410) 208-1021
FAX: (410) 641-8565

Judy Johnson
Membership Secretary
(410) 524-9460

Janet Reed
Events Chairperson
(410) 208-0648

Massachusetts

Boston

Emily Strawn
Zeitech Inc.
P.O. Box 1154
Boston, MA 02103
(617) 438-9099 or (617) 891-7668
FAX: (617) 438-7465

Appendix V: Golf Groups and Organizations

Susan Ryan
Membership Secretary
(617) 928-0752

Pandora Picciano
Events Chairperson
(617) 527-4980 Ext. 1148

Hamden County

Jean Deliso
New York Life Insurance
P.O. Box 274
Agawam, MA 01001
(413) 785-1100 Ext. 3009 or (413) 534-6630
FAX: (413) 746-4626

Christine Tazzini
Membership Secretary
(413) 732-8200

Susan Major
Events Chairperson
(800) 554-5420 Ext. 9135

Michigan

Metro Detroit

Shirley Wold
Owner, Tournament Productions
P.O. Box 1329
Royal Oak, MI 48068
(810) 988-0108 or (734) 459-7833
FAX: (734) 459-7678

Roseanne Dolega
Membership Secretary

Ann Mikols
Events Chairperson

Minnesota

Minneapolis Metro

Mary Jo Burke
5408 Pompano
Minnetonka, MN 55343
(612) 362-5940 or (612) 938-3901
FAX: (612) 938-0867

Jodie Skolnick
Membership Secretary
(612) 773-8589

Jeri Meola
Events Chairperson
(612) 939-4310

Missouri

Heart of America

Lori Cook North
Director of Marketing, Blackwell Sanders
11184 Antioch #162
Overland Park, KS 66210
(913) 338-9400 or (816) 893-8781 or (913) 782-9355
FAX: (816) 983-9781
E-mail: lnorth@bsmat.com

Lisa Grosdidier
Membership Chairperson
(816) 854-5622

ReNae L. Allen
Events Chairperson
(913) 381-5211

St. Louis

* **Karen Burkhart**
34 North Meramac
St. Louis, MO 63105
(314) 512-9414
1998 Membership Chairperson

Nevada

Las Vegas

Lori Clayton
Clayton Insurance Services
2001 South Jones Blvd. #E
Las Vegas, NV 89102
(702) 260-0929 or (702) 873-4505 or (702) 876-7540
FAX: (702) 873-4884

Eileen Franklin
Membership Chairperson
(702) 361-2425.

Reno/Lake Tahoe, Host Club

* **Ted Jackson**
Lake Tahoe Golf Course
2500 Emerald Bay Road
South Lake Tahoe, CA 96150
(530) 577-0788 or 0802
FAX: (530) 577-4469

New Hampshire

Southern New Hampshire

Karen Furtado
32 Berkeley Street
Nashua, NH 03060
(603) 437-2497
FAX: (978) 686-0130
E-mail: KFurtado@ISISYS.com

Eleanor Russell
Membership Chairperson
(603) 622-0967

New Jersey

Central New Jersey

Mary Humecke
District Manager, Lucent Technologies
P.O. Box 76
Pluckemin, NJ 07978
(908) 828-4653 or (908) 953-3417 or (908) 864-8431
FAX: (908) 864-8451

Kirsten Rose
Membership Chairperson

Linda Keene
Events Chairperson

Northern New Jersey

Cece Peabody
P.O. Box 732
Pine Brook, NJ 07058
(973) 442-4653
FAX: (973) 812-6529
E-mail: info@ewgnnj.org

Barbara Bailey
Membership Secretary
(973) 227-1173 Ext. 11

Barbara Mauer
Events Chairperson
(201) 437-3763

New Mexico

New Mexico Host Club

* **Debbie Zamprelli**
Paradise Hills Golf Course
10035 Country Club Lane NW
Albuquerque, NM 87114
(505) 898-7001

New York

Capital Region (Albany)

Elaine Neiss
Manager, Discus Inc.
24 Esopus Drive
Clifton Park, NY 12065
(518) 453-3866 or (518) 371-2238

Lisa Roberts
Membership Chairperson

Jan Simoneau
Events Chairperson

Buffalo

* **Lisa Boynton**
  Senior Special Product Representative, M & T Mortgage
  4619-F Chestnut Ridge Road
  Amherst, NY 14228
  (716) 691-3018

New York City

Marian Hausman
110-64 Queens Boulevard, Suite 362
Forest Hills, NY 11375-6347
(212) 603-9753

Pat Gericke
Vice President

Adeline Ellis
Events Chairperson

Rochester

* **Clair Catillaz**
  Drake Beam Morrin, Inc.
  135 Corporate Woods, Suite 100
  Rochester, NY 14623
  (716) 273-8690

North Carolina

Capital Area

Woody Dicus (Mary)
1213 Filmore Street
Raleigh, NC 27605
(919) 870-6549 or (919) 546-6880 or (919) 833-6858

Pat Everhart
Membership Secretary
(919) 380-7715

Meg Guile
Vice-President Events
(919) 785-9009

Charlotte-Mecklenburg

Missy Carlson
Rehab Quality Advisor, Living Centers of America
12601 Moores Mill Road
Huntersville, NC 28078
(704) 948-1868 or (704) 948-4650
FAX: (704) 948-1971

Lorraine Bonura
Events Chairperson
(704) 386-3292

Piedmont-Triad

Mary Lytton
Sales Associate, First Tee Pro Shop
P.O. Box 11604
Winston-Salem, NC 27106-1604
(336) 760-2799 or (336) 659-9280 or (336) 760-2799

Deborah K. Shetterly
Events Chairperson
(336) 945-4201

Sandhills (Pinehurst)

Betty O. Sapp
P.O. Box 512
Pinehurst, NC 28374
(910) 295-3180 or (910) 235-0734 or (910) 295-9686
FAX: (910) 295-4056

Denise Bennett
Membership Secretary
(910) 295-0838

Faith Morrison
Events Chairperson
(910) 695-1886

Appendix V: Golf Groups and Organizations

Ohio

Akron

Lynn Greathouse
Owner, Ladies Choice Hair Fashions
P.O. Box 2484
Akron, OH 44309-2484
(330) 628-1443 or (330) 784-4225

Linda Hastings
Membership Secretary
(330) 297-3850

Chris Jones
Events Chairperson
(330) 376-3572

Canton

Linda Smith
Sirak Financial Services
P.O. Box 20441
Canton, OH 44701
(330) 492-3361
FAX: (330) 493-5939

Gerry Radcliffe
Membership Secretary
(330) 494-6820

Sheila Klenner
Events Chairperson
(330) 493-3211

Cincinnati

Cynthia Lamb
General Manager, Sugar Ridge Golf Club
21010 State Line Rd.
Lawrenceburg, IN 47025
(513) 231-3705
FAX: (812) 537-0386

Jean McConnaughey
Membership Chairperson
(513) 489-7007

Linda Kramer/Cindy Kobman
Events Co-Chairperson
(513) 752-0922

Cleveland

Cindy J. Darwal
P.O. Box 31704
Independence, OH 44131
(216) 999-9664
FAX: (440) 729-7132

Gloria Leight
Events Chairperson
(216) 999-9664

Columbus

Susan Schneiter
2640 Westmont Boulevard
Columbus, OH 43221-3333

Elisabeth Roush
Membership Secretary

Faye Gibson
Events Chairperson

Cross Country OHPA

Kadie Bowen
P.O. Box 5062
Niles, OH 44446
(330) 544-0199
FAX: (330) 544-7763
E-mail: moe-san@ix.netcom.com

Debbie Budd
Membership Secretary
(330) 373-1010 Ext. 13 or (330) 856-9712
FAX: (330) 393-6483
E-mail: djbudds@ibm.net

Appendix V: Golf Groups and Organizations

Dayton

* **Deborah Gross**
  142 Chartley Court
  Beavercreek, OH 45440-3600
  (513) 748-5210 or (937) 426-7940
  FAX: (513) 748-5215
  E-mail: grossdeb144@worldnet.att.net

Toledo

Nancy Wilson
Regional Administrator, Director of Marketing & Communication
Mercy Health Partners
P.O. Box 14683
Toledo, OH 43608
(419) 381-7555
FAX: (419) 472-7282 or (419) 251-2104

Oklahoma

Oklahoma City

* **Todis McDonald**
  4016 Ripple
  Norman, OK 73072
  (405) 447-2685
  FAX: (405) 447-2768
  E-mail: todis@aol.com

Oregon

Portland

Shirley Clay
9220 SW Barbur Boulevard, Suite 119-225
Portland, OR 97219
(503) 297-3304
E-mail: Sclay@hevanet.com

Rogue Valley

* Jean Hull
Jafra
625-B East Jackson Street, Suite 334
Medford, OR 97504
(541) 779-8579
FAX: (541) 779-1900

Sue Parelius
Membership Secretary
(541) 779-2215

Jan Madsen
Events Chairperson
(541) 857-4121

Pennsylvania

Lehigh Valley

Dottie Swafford
P.O. Box 21560
Lehigh Valley, PA 18002
(610) 965-6937
FAX: (610) 965-4595

Kimberly Ike
Events Chairperson
(610) 820-3679

Greater Philadelphia Area

Lori Hoppmann
Principal, Aon Consulting
P.O. Box 767
Conshohocken, PA 19428-0767
(610) 668-3866
FAX: (610) 834-2297

Polly Hook
Membership Secretary
(215) 619-4850

Dyan Mashman
Events Chairperson
(610) 687-9400 Ext. 1165

Pittsburgh

Marilyn Ross
Co-Director Intramurals/Recreation, University of Pittsburgh
P.O. Box 44262
Pittsburgh, PA 15205
(412) 366-6775 or (412) 648-8277 or (412) 788-1604
FAX: (412) 648-7092

Pat Wickersham
Membership Secretary
(412) 234-0956

Lee Ann Briggs
Events Chairperson
(412) 227-2892

Stroudsburg

Carole McGarry
Real Estate Sales Agent, Park Avenue Realtors
P.O. Box 190
Stroudsburg, PA 18360
(717) 992-3684
FAX: (717) 424-2416
1998 Network Coordinator

South Carolina

Charleston

Holly Wilson
Advertising & Marketing Manager, MBM Corporation
P.O. Box 40249
Charleston, SC 29423
(803) 552-2700 or (803) 763-6847 or (800) 223-2508 Ext. 235
FAX: (803) 760-3813

Greater Columbia

Joyce McDonald
The Principal Financial Group
1331 Elmwood Avenue, Suite 315
Columbia, SC 29201
(803) 750-8767 or (803) 540-7600 or (803) 765-9332
FAX: (803) 540-7606

Rosa Diaz
Membership Secretary
(803) 343-8063

Johnette Jeffcoat
Events Chairperson
(803) 356-1730

Myrtle Beach

Betty Ballou
Director of Finance, Myrtle Beach Air Base Redevelopment Authority
421 Persimmon Lane
Myrtle Beach, SC 29579
(803) 477-6575 or (803) 238-0681 or (803) 236-1891
FAX: (803) 238-0579
E-mail: bettyb@sccoast.net or bballou@sccoast.net

Linda W. Parks
Membership Secretary
(803) 626-6611

Carol Bernier
Social Events Chairperson

Sue Jones
Golf Events Chairperson

Tennessee

Memphis

* Tobi Travis
8660 Cedar Trails Drive
Cordova, TN 38018
(901) 757-2392
FAX: (901) 757-2011
1998 Network Coordinator

Middle Tennessee

Deb Schlofman
General Manager, Cue Paging Network & Mid South Paging
P.O. Box 680095
Franklin, TN 37068
(615) 831-GOLF or (615) 321-7121 or (615) 791-9213

Appendix V: Golf Groups and Organizations

Jolene McKenzie
Membership Secretary
(615) 835-PUTT

Melissa K. Collins
Events Chairperson
(615) 831-GOLF

Texas

Beaumont

* **Patricia Lager**
6275 Park West Drive
Beaumont, Texas 77706
(409) 860-3295
1998 Co-Chapter Contact

* **Julie Harris**
Vice President, First Bank & Trust
10607 Highway 69 South
Port Arthur, TX 77642
(409) 724-2002
FAX: (409) 721-6444
1998 Co-Chapter Contact

Corpus Christi

Christine Wisian
District Manager, CSC Credit Service
4113 Harry
Corpus Christi, TX 78411
(512) 985-6007 or (512) 852-1098
FAX: (512) 985-2174

Fran Williams
Membership Chairperson

Kitty Donohue
Events Chairperson
(512) 884-6366

Denton Host Club

Kyle Farley
Golf Pro, Denton Golf Center
1710 South Loop 288
Denton, TX 76205
(817) 387-4653

Fort Worth Metroplex

Cindy Orchard
P.O. Box 101794
Fort Worth, TX 76185
(817) 731-8841 or (817) 731-8701
FAX: (817) 377-9101

Debbie Shepherd
Membership Chairperson
(817) 731-8841

Kathy Felix
Events Chairperson
(817) 731-0101

Houston

Cynthia DeGabrielle
P.O. Box 842261
Houston, TX 77284-2261
(713) 267-7430
http://www.ewga.org

San Antonio

Cyndi Baldwin
Internal Audit, Valero Energy Corp.
7990 IH 10 West
San Antonio, TX 78230-4715
(210) 231-5718 or (210) 370-2623 or (830) 985-3071
FAX: (210) 370-2234
E-mail: baldwinc@valero.com

Barbara Plovsky
Membership Chairperson
(210) 684-8350

Patty Yarbrough
Events Chairperson
(210) 340-9600

Utah

Salt Lake City

Veda Barrie
Veda Barrie Real Estate
7231 South 900 East
Midvale, UT 84047
(801) 561-7200 or (801) 278-8838
FAX: (801) 561-5055
E-mail: Veda VBRE@aol.com

Virginia

Norfolk Host Club

* **Molly Flanagan**
Asst. General Manager, Chesapeake Golf Club
1201 Club House Drive
Chesapeake, VA 23320
(757) 547-1122
FAX: (757) 547-8546

Washington

Seattle

Shelia Sampolesi
(206) 781-5813
E-mail: ssamploesi@aol.com

Tri-Cities Host Club

* **Wendy Rash**
Teaching Professional, Canyon Lakes Golf Club
West 3700 Canyon Lakes Dr.
Kennewick, WA 99337
(509) 582-3736
Founder

Wisconsin

Madison

* **Andrea Barbera**
MEG Communications
4902 Hammersley Road
Madison, WI 53711
(608) 282-9003 or (608) 277-3220
E-mail: abarbera@megcom.com

Following are the USGA State and Regional groups who have agreed to be listed for this book, listed alphabetically by state.

USGA NATIONAL HEADQUARTERS

Golf House
P.O. Box 2000
Far Hills, NJ 07931
(908) 234-2300
FAX: (908) 234-9687

USGA REGIONAL ASSOCIATIONS

Alabama

Alabama Gulf Coast Ladies Golf Association
812 High Point Circle
Mobile, AL 36693
Jo Ann Miller, President
(334) 661-3415

Ladies Birmingham Golf Association
405 Sunset Drive
Birmingham, AL 35216
Peggy Kelley, President
(205) 979-9047

Women's Alabama Golf Association
403 North Cherokee
Dothan, AL 36303
Mrs. Janie Solomon
(334) 794-6491
FAX: same

Appendix V: Golf Groups and Organizations

Alaska

Anchorage Women's Golf Association
3374 Mt. Vernon Court
Anchorage, AK 99503
Dannelle R. Gransbury, Jr. Golf Chairman
(907) 562-7769

Arizona

Central Arizona Golf District
15395 West Pinchot Court
Goodyear, AZ 85338
Jinny Pearson, President
(602) 935-7901

National Club Championship for Women
6444 North 77th Place
Scottsdale, AZ 85250
Dale Danenberg, Executive Director
(602) 596-0483
FAX: (602) 596-1248

Northern Arizona Women's Golf Association
3653 North Stonecrest Street
Flagstaff, AZ 86004
Linda Dalsin, President
(520) 526-6168
E-mail: pterodalsn@aol.com

Women's Southwestern Golf Association
P.O. Box 3842
Carefree, AZ 85377
Cindy Carroll, President
(602) 488-2114

Arkansas

Arkansas State Golf Association
#3 Eagle Hill Court, Suite B
Little Rock, AR 72209
Bev Hargraves, Director
(501) 455-2742
FAX: (501) 455-2742
E-mail: asga@aristotle.net

Arkansas Women's Golf Association
P.O. Box 17321
Monticello, AR 71655
Jeanie L. Prewitt, President
(501) 513-2900
FAX: (870) 367-9548
E-mail: cutoff@seark.net

California

California Women's Amateur Championship
P.O. Box S-3555
Carmel, CA 93921
Beverly Lewis, Chairman
(408) 624-4923
FAX: (408) 624-5591
E-mail: Bevcarmel@aol.com

Northern California Niner's Association
3730 Cowell Road
Concord, CA 94518
Bernice English, President
(510) 798-6381

Pacific Women's Golf Association
2542 South Bascom Avenue, Suite 117
Campbell, CA 95008
Caroline O'Brien, Office Manager
(408) 377-2430
FAX: (408) 377-0735
E-mail: pacwomensga@usga.org

San Diego County Women's Golf Association
9933 Meadow Glen Way East
Escondido, CA 92026
Ellen Koury, President
(760) 749-1190
FAX: (760) 749-0375
E-mail: sdiegocwga@usga.org

Western American Golf Association
929 East Foothill Boulevard #150
Upland, CA 91786
Nancy Pluss, Office Manager
(909) 920-0056
FAX: (909) 931-3988
E-mail: westernga@usga.org
www.womensgolf.org

Appendix V: Golf Groups and Organizations

Women's Golf Association of Northern California
5776 Stoneridge Mall Road, Suite 160
Arnold, CA 95223
Kaytee Lively, President
(510) 737-0963
FAX: (510) 737-0964

Women's Public Links Golf Association of Southern California, Inc.
437 Eucalyptus Drive
Redlands, CA 92373
Janet Millar, President
(909) 793-0402
FAX: (909) 793-0402

Colorado

Colorado Women's Golf Association
5655 South Yosemite, Suite 101
Englewood, CO 80111
Kathy Roady, President
(303) 220-5456
FAX: (303) 290-0593
E-mail: cowga@usga.org

Florida

Coral Ridge Country Club
3801 Bayview Drive
Fort Lauderdale, FL 33308
Robert Trent Jones, Director
(954) 564-1271
FAX: (954) 563-8628

Florida Women's State Golf Association
10,000 North US Highway 98 #107
Lakeland, FL 33809
Judy Comella, Executive Director
(941) 815-1646
E-mail: fwsga@usga.org

Fore County Women's Golf Association
5733 S.E. Doubleton Drive
Stuart, FL 34997
Shirley Szczepanik
(561) 220-4394
FAX: same
E-mail: shcrlock39@aol.com

253

Sunshine State Senior Women's Golf Association
545 Solitaire Palm Drive
North Indialantic, FL 32903
Nancy Butcher, President
(407) 724-2225
FAX: (407) 723-8868
E-mail: Nbutcher@aol..com

Women's International 4-Ball
Orangebrook Golf & Country Club
400 Entrada Drive
Hollywood, FL 33021
Jane W. Read, President
(954) 967-4653 Ext. 23
FAX: (954) 967-4652

Women's South Atlantic Amateur Championship
Oceanside Country Club
P.O. Box 367
Ormond Beach, FL 32175-0367
Connie Foley, President
(904) 673-7896 or (904) 672-7200
FAX: (904) 672-1926

Women's Southern Golf Association
400 Durrell Road
Winter Haven, FL 33884
Peggy Spillane, President
(941) 967-2874 or (941) 324-3444
FAX: (941) 967-2864

Georgia

Georgia Women's Golf Association
Contact Georgia PGA for current information

Hawaii

Hawaii State Women's Golf Association
1025 Wilder Avenue, Apartment 8B
Honolulu, HI 96822
Sally Harper, President
(808) 536-0157
FAX: same

Idaho

Idaho Golf Association
P.O. Box 3025
Boise, ID 83703
Vicki Davis, Administrative Director
(208) 342-4442
FAX: (208) 345-5959
E-mail: idahoga@usga.org

Illinois

Illinois Women's Golf Association (IWGA)
31 Wildwood Drive
Rock Island, IL 61201
Sue Boeye, President
(309) 797-1372
FAX: (309) 797-1375

Women's Western Golf Association
P.O. Box 85
Golf, IL 60029
Susan Wagner, President
(800) 753-WWGA or (630) 512-0922
FAX: (630) 512-0920

Iowa

Iowa Women's Golf Association
3418-48th Street
Des Moines, IA 50310
Trudie Higgs, President
(515) 334-9087
FAX: (515) 334-9087
E-mail: iawga@usga.org

Kansas

Kansas Women's Golf Association
5701 E. 19th Street N.
Wichita, KS 67208
Natasha Fife, President
(316) 687-2255 or (316) 684-5824
E-mail: kswga@usga.org

Women's Greater Kansas City Public Links Association
9819 Wedd Drive
Overland Park, KS 66212
June Arthur, President
(913) 888-9567

Women's Tri-State Golf Association
P.O. Box 794
Calvert City, KY 42029
Karen Puckett, President
(502) 395-1992
E-mail: SANDSTONESTREET@Prodigy.Net

Kentucky

Central Kentucky Ladies' Golf Association
312 West Maple Avenue
Lancaster, KY 40444
Brenda R. Hammons, President
(606) 792-4381
E-mail: bhammons@iclub.org

Louisiana

Baton Rouge Women's Interclub Golf Association
13546 Greencastle Avenue
Baton Rouge, LA 70816
Vicki Lea-Dees, President
(504) 752-0752

Maine

Southern Maine Women's Golf Association
128 Warren Avenue
Portland, ME 04103
Lyn Mann, Executive Director
(207) 797-2268

Appendix V: Golf Groups and Organizations

Maryland

Maryland State Golf Association - Women's Division
P.O. Box 16289
Baltimore, MD 21210
Pat Kaufman, President
(301) 292-2345
FAX: (301) 292-3289
E-mail: PatKaufman@aol.com

Women's District of Columbia Golf Association
6424 Wiscasset Road
Bethesda, MD 20816
Rose Marie Vargo, President
(301) 229-7056
FAX: (301) 229-7043

Massachusetts

Massachusetts Golf Association
175 Highland Avenue
Needham, MA 02192
Thomas Landry, Executive Director
(781) 449-3000
FAX: (781) 449-4020
www. MGA.links.org
FAX: (410) 641-8565

Women's Golf Association of Massachusetts
175 Highland Avenue
Needham, MA 02192
Janice Vance, Executive Director
(781) 453-0555
FAX: (781) 453-0827
E-mail: wgamass@usga.org

Michigan

Capital Area Women's Golf Association
P.O. Box 20055
Lansing, MI 48901-0655
Mary Pollock
(577) 351-7292

Huron Valley Women's Golf Club
1831 Stonebridge Drive N.
Ann Arbor, MI 48108
Geraldine Holmes, President
(734) 668-7346

Michigan Senior Women's Golf Association
1205 Ripley Road
Linden, MI 48451
Evelyn Cherba, President
(810) 735-4274
FAX: (810) 750-1822

Michigan Women's Publinx Golf Association (MWPGA)
8798 Forest Court
Warren, MI 48093
Sue Treciak, President
(810) 264-9881
FAX: (810) 268-7929
E-mail: michwopub@usga.org

Mississippi

Jackson Women's Golf Association
160 St. Andrew's Drive
Jackson, MS 39211
Mary Brown, President
(601) 956-2048

Mississippi Women's Golf Association
434 Forest Lake Place
Madison, MS 39110
Jerrie White, President
(601) 856-4573

Missouri

St. Louis Women's Golf Association
8752 A Santa Bella
Hazelwood, MO 63042
Peg Lampert, President
(314) 524-1528

Nebraska

Nebraska Junior Girls' Golf Association
1806 Brent Boulevard
Lincoln, NE 68506
Pat Sim, Executive Secretary
(402) 488-7276

Nebraska Women's Amateur Golf Association
707 East 4th Street
McCook, NE 69001
Theresa Wanek, President
(308) 345-7395
E-mail: NEBWAGA@USGA.ORG

Nevada

Nevada State Women's Golf Association
1840 Cedar Bluffs Way
Las Vegas, NV 89128
Brenda Knott, President
(702) 256-0826
E-mail: miszner@vegas.infi.net

New Hampshire

New Hampshire Women's Golf Association
15 Lisa Beth Circle
Dover, NH 03820
Pat Jewell, President
(603) 742-5540
FAX: same
E-mail: nhwga@usga.org

New Jersey

Garden State Women's Golf Association
60 Kean Road
Short Hills, NJ 07078
Honey Miller, President
(973)376-0488

New Mexico

New Mexico Women's State Golf Association
Debbie Midger, President

New York

Central New York Women's District Golf Association
467 Pennsylvania Avenue
Waverly, NY 14892
Jane Klinko, President
(607) 565-4985

***Golf for Women* magazine**
125 Park Avenue
New York, NY 10017
Leslie Day, Editor in Chief
(212) 551-6958
FAX: (212) 455-1246
E-mail: gfwmag@mdp.com

Northeastern Women's Golf Association
18 Deer Run
Gansevoort, NY 12831
Susan Charbonneau, President
(518) 587-2547
E-mail: TheDode@aol.com

Syracuse Women's District Golf Association
5864 Highcrest Circle
East Syracuse, NY 13057
Toni Ann Tropea, President
(315) 656-8632
FAX: (315) 432-0887

Western New York Women's Public Links Golf Association (WNYWPLGA)
212 Ashford Avenue
Tonawanda, NY 14150
Lindley S. Bowen, President
(716) 834-2507

Women's Metropolitan Golf Association
49 Knollwood Road
Elmsford, NY 10523
Bernadette Bleichert, Office Administrator
(914) 592-7888
FAX: (914) 592-7936
E-mail: WMETGA@USGA.ORG

North Carolina

Carolinas Golf Association
P.O. Box 319
West End, NC 27376
Paula Brzostowski, Director of Women's Golf
(910) 673-1000
FAX: (910) 673-1001
E-mail: CGA@Thecga.org

North Carolina Women's Golf Association
1600 Morganton Road, N-6
Pinehurst, NC 28374
Vicki DiSantis, President
(910) 692-8020

Old North State Golf Association
Nettie McKenney, President
(910) 799-6012

Piedmont Women's Golf Association
1119 West Cornwallis Drive
Greensboro, NC 27408
Sue Ireland, President
(910) 274-5354
E-mail: msuei@aol.com

Ohio

Ohio Women's Golf Association
12204 Girdled Road
Concord Township, OH 44077
Sharon Adams, President
(440) 354-0038

Tri County Women's Golf Association
P.O. Box 39453
Solon, OH 44139-0453
Sandra L. Cohen (Sandy), President
(440) 248-4228
Email: slc32563@aol.com

Women's Akron District Golf Association
2232 Lancaster Road
Akron, OH 44313
Renee Josof, President
(330) 867-6498
E-mail: RRSN80A@PROD.COM

Women's Ohio State Golf Association/
USGA Public Links (Women) Committee
4966 North Burgundy Bay
Medina, OH 44256
Jeanne Pritchard, Executive Director
(330) 725-8612
FAX: same

Oklahoma

Central Oklahoma Women's Golf Association
3141 Thornridge Road
Oklahoma City, OK 73120
Judy Greider, President
(405) 755-2621

Southwestern Oklahoma Golf Association
417 Chimney Creek
Lawton, OK 73505
Barbara Bullock, President
(580) 355-2929

Women's Oklahoma Golf Association
10215 South Knoxville
Tulsa, OK 74137
Pat McKamey, President
(918) 299-3328
E-mail: oklawga@usga.org

Oregon

Oregon Golf Association
8364 SW Nimbus Avenue
Beaverton, OR 97008
Sally Bolliger, Chairman, Women's Advisory Committee
(503) 644-9311

Willamette Valley Southern Oregon Golf Association
2040 Terrace Avenue
Klamath Falls, OR 97601
Linda Forosee, President
(541) 882-0633

Pennsylvania

Northeastern Pennsylvania Women's Golf Association
411A Country Club Road
Dallas, PA 18612
Carole S. Ertley, President
(717) 675-0202
E-mail: sisgolf@aol.com

Pennsylvania State Women's Golf Association
830 Lepland Road
York, PA 17403
Maisie Barlow, President
(717) 843-0533
FAX: (717) 843-3432

Women's Central Pennsylvania Golf Association (WCPGA)
2130 North 17th Street
Reading, PA 19604
Pat Wallace, President
(610) 921-0124
FAX: (610) 921-0123

Rhode Island

Ocean State Women's Golf Association
P.O. Box 9231
Providence, RI 02940
Trudy Dufault, President/Executive Director
(401) 353-8205
FAX: same

Rhode Island Women's Golf Association
284 Pleasant Street
Rumford, RI 02916
Susan Musche, President
(401) 434-8757
FAX: (401) 438-4058

South Carolina

Women's South Carolina Golf Association
P.O. Box 1745
Bluffton, SC 29910
Inez Long, Director
(803) 757-4653
FAX: (803) 757-4652
E-mail: wscarolinaga@usga.org

Tennessee

Nashville Women's Golf Association
127 Southern Trace
Hendersonville, TN 37075
Gen F. Williams, President
(615) 822-6037

Women's Tennessee Golf Association
Golf House Tennessee
400 Franklin Road
Franklin, TN 37069
Tina Sanders, President
(615) 790-7600
FAX: (615) 790-8600
E-mail: wtennga@usga.org

Texas

Dallas Women's Golf Association (DWGA)
5703 Preston Fairways Drive
Dallas, TX 75252
Linda Thrash, President
(972) 250-1290
FAX: (972) 250-4170

Women's Texas Golf Association
619 Hillsong
San Antonio, TX 78258
Rebecca Spears, President
(210) 545-7933
FAX: same

Utah

Utah Golf Association
1110 East Englewood Drive
North Salt Lake, UT 84054
Joe Watts, Executive Director
(801) 299-8421
FAX: (801) 299-9409
E-mail: UGA.ORG

Vermont

Vermont State Women's Golf Association (VSWGA)
33 Mountainview Boulevard
South Burlington, VT 05403
Sally Guerette, President
(802) 862-7161
FAX: (802) 656-0949
E-mail: squerette@zoo.uvm.edu

Virginia

Virginia State Golf Association Women's Division
6215 Thornwood Drive
Alexandria, VA 22310
Dr. Ruth Ann Verell, President
(703) 971-6068
E-mail: RAVGolf@aol.com

Women's Eastern Golf Association
4615 Archduke Road
Glen Allen, VA 23060
Joan A. Darden

West Virginia

Women's West Virginia Golf Association
Cindy Davis, President
(304) 842-5947
FAX: same

Wisconsin

Wisconsin Women's Golf Association
2306 Lakeland Avenue
Madison, WI 53704
Martha Brusegar, President
(608) 244-4955
E-mail: deanmops@aol.com

Canada

Ontario Ladies' Golf Association
1185 Eglinton Avenue E.
North York, Ontario M3C3C6
Norma Roberts, President
Honey Crossley, Executive Director
(416) 426-7090
E-mail: olga@osrc.com

Mexico

**Associacion Mexicana de Golf Femenil
(Mexican Golf Ladies Association)**
Ave. Lomas de Sotelo #1112 Desp. 103
col. Lomas de Sotelo C.P. 11200
Mexico D.F.
Silvia Torrescano de Torres, President
52-5-395-02-94
FAX: 52-5-395-32-45

Puerto Rico

Puerto Rico Golf Association
58 Caribe Street
San Juan, PR 00907
Sidney Wolf, President
(787) 721-7742
FAX: (787) 723-5760

GLOSSARY

Ace
A hole in one.

Addressing the ball
The position taken just before you hit.

Adjusted score
Your gross score minus your handicap.

Albatross
Another name for a double eagle.

All square
Tied match between two opposing sides.

Apron
The short grass around the green, also called the collar or fringe.

Away
The golfer who is farthest from the hole is considered to be away.

Back door
A putt that is holed by going into the cup on the far side.

Baseball grip
Holding the club without interlocking the fingers.

Best ball
A tournament format in which the best score from two balls or the best score from four balls is recorded for each hole; might also be the best two balls of four.

Birdie
A score of one under par on a hole.

Bite
Putting backspin on a ball, particularly on a lofted shot, which makes it stop sharply, often rolling backward rather than forward. Also a phrase used by a player who wishes her ball would stop once it has reached the green and is travelling past the hole.

Blast
A bunker shot used when the ball is buried in the sand.

Blind hole
A hole where you cannot see the landing area either from the tee or from the hitting area.

Bogey
A score of one over par.

Brain cramp
When all of your previous golf learning, including lessons, books and tapes, abandons your cerebral area to the point where you have no idea how you just botched that shot.

Break
The curves or slopes on the greens that are studied to "read" the break in order to determine how best to stroke the putt.

Bump and run
An approach shot that is hit firmly and runs up to the cup.

Bunker
A hazard.

Caddie
A person who carries a player's bag (or carries for two players) and gives advice about the course, club selection, and strategy.

Carry
The distance a ball travels between the place where you hit it and where it lands. For example, someone might say, "This hole is all carry."

Casual water
Any body of water that is not a part of the course 365 days a year. Take penalty-free relief. Note that dew and frost are not considered to be casual water.

Chili-dip
To hit the ball fat, usually with a wedge.

Chip
A low approach shot made with a lofted iron around the green.

Choke down
Could also be called grip down. It means holding your club lower on the grip.

Cleek
An old term for a 4-wood.

Closed face
For right-handed players, having the clubface aiming left of the target at impact.

Closed stance
At address, a right-handed player will have her right foot moved slightly back from a line parallel with the target, while her left foot will be on the line. Often used to solve a slicing problem.

Glossary

Cup
The hole.

Dance floor
The green.

Divot
A piece of the course (turf) dug out when the clubhead hits behind the ball during the swing. Be sure to replace them or fill the hole with sand/seed mixture.

Dogleg
A name given to an "L-shaped" hole that bends to the right or left.

Dormie
The term given to the situation in match play when a competitor is ahead by the number of holes left to play. For example, she is three up with three to play. Borrowed from Latin and French words meaning asleep or to sleep, dormie implies she can relax because she cannot lose that match. However, her competitor could win the next three to tie and they could go into a playoff, returning to the first hole. The better score would be four up with three to play. Then victory would be assured.

Double bogey
A score of two over par.

Double eagle
Hole score three strokes less than par.

Double par
Twice the par for the hole. Time to pick up.

Down
A term used by the side or player losing the match. Such as, "We are down by four."

Draw
A skillful, controlled shot that curves slightly from right to left for right-handed players.

Eagle
A score of two under par on a hole.

Executive course
A course designed to be a bit shorter, and therefore plays faster, than traditional courses.

Fade
A skillful, controlled shot that curves from left to right for right handed players.
Fairway
The closely mown part of the golf course that runs from the teeing area to the green.
Fat
An expression used when you hit well behind the ball. You might say you hit the big ball (planet earth) before you hit the little white ball.
Fellow competitor
In stroke play, it is the relationship between players.
Flagstick
A pole with a flag on it which tells players where the hole is on the green. Often color-coded to tell players exactly where the hole is (red: forward, white: middle, and blue: back), the flagstick is also called the pin.
Flight
Term used to group players by ability in a league or tournament. I.e., Flight A has scratch through 9-handicaps, Flight B has 10 through 19-handicaps, etc. Also the term used when a ball is in the air; it is considered to be in flight.
Follow-through
Finishing your swing after impact.
Fore
A verbal warning you must yell to other golfers if you are in danger of hitting them with your ball. Beware whenever you hear it yourself!
Four-Ball
Competition in which two golfers play their best ball against the best ball of the two other players.
Free lift
Moving your ball without penalty. See rules.
Fried egg
A ball partially buried in a bunker.
Fringe
The short grass around the green, same as the apron or collar.

Glossary

Get up and down
Making par from off the green with an approach shot and a one putt.

Gimme
A putt so close to the hole it does not have to be played, but the stroke must be counted. Gimmes are not recognized by the Rules of Golf, but are quite common in casual rounds.

Grain
The direction grass grows on a green. For example, if there is a pond nearby, it will grow toward the water.

Green fee
The price set by a club and charged for a round of golf. Does not necessarily include cart cost.

Grip
How you place your hands on the club.

Gross score
Your score without subtracting handicap.

Ground the club
Touching the ground behind your ball with your clubhead; a "no-no" in hazards.

Ground under repair
An area on the course that is off limits to players because it is unfit for play. Usually marked by white paint or roped off with a sign. It's a free lift.

Half/halved
In match play, a hole or match that was tied. The term "no blood" is often used in this instance.

Handicap
A number assigned to a player based on scores turned in which numerically categorizes playing ability. The game's equalizer in that the handicap gives strokes to players so that they can compete on even terms with better players.

Hard pan
Ground without grass.

Hazard
There are three kinds of hazards: water, lateral water, and bunkers. See Rules.

Heeled shot
A shot hit off the heel of your club.
Hit a house
A term used when a chip shot or putt is hit too firmly and the ball goes speeding by the hole.
Honor
The right to tee off first because you have won the previous hole.
Hook
A wild shot that goes from right to left for right-handed players.
Hosel
The spot where the shaft is attached to the clubhead.

Index
The number on your GHIN card you use to compute your handicap when playing various courses.
Inside the leather
A term used when on the green, referring to the distance between the ball and the cup being the same as or less than the length of the leather grip on the putter. It's a hint for a gimme.

Knee knocker
A short putt, usually from three to five feet.

Lag
A long putt that is hit to within a few inches of the cup.
Lay up shot
Playing a shot short to stay out of trouble, especially around hazards. Shows good course management skills.
Lie
1) Where your ball comes to rest. 2) The current number of strokes taken on a hole, e.g. "I lie four." 3) Also, what you might do on the 19th hole to describe your game!
Line
The direction the ball must travel to reach the hole. Often, someone will say of a putt, "You had the line, but not the distance."
Links
A course that is built without making significant changes to the lay of the land. Tee boxes are constructed as are the greens, but just about everything else is in a natural state. Pete Dye is famous for his links designs, and many courses in Europe are links style.

Glossary

In the United States, the Ocean Course at Kiawah is a good example of a links course.

Lip
Edge of the hole or bunker.

Lip out
A putt that dances around the rim of the hole but does not go in.

Local Rules
Rules a club will set to govern play on its course in addition to the Rules of Golf.

Loft
The number of degrees the clubface is angled. A driver may have a 10° loft while a wedge can be as high as 60°.

Long irons
The 1-, 2-, and 3-irons.

LPGA
Ladies Professional Golf Association.

Marker
Small round disk or coin used to identify the location of your ball on the green.

Match play
A type of play in which the number of holes won determines the winner.

Medal play
Count all strokes; lowest gross score wins. Also called stroke play.

Middle irons
The 4-, 5-, and 6-irons.

Mulligan
Not recognized by the USGA, and never used in real competition. It is a shot replayed (without counting the previous stroke) when a player's first shot is a disaster. The group has to agree at the first hole that mulligans are OK. Mulligans are often sold at charity golf events to raise money.

Nassau
A match play format whereby players wager on three things: winning the front nine, winning the back nine, and winning overall.

Net score
Final score after deducting handicap from gross score.

273

Nineteenth hole
After the round, players head for the bar for refreshments and conversation. Scores are added, bets are settled, and stories are exchanged—usually about the day's rounds.

Ninety degree rule
The way a cart must enter and exit the fairway from the rough or the cart path.

OB
Out-of-bounds; defined by white markers.

Open face
For right-handed players, having the clubface aiming to the right of the target at impact.

Open stance
For a right-handed player at address, the left foot is set slightly in back of the line running parallel to the target, with the right foot on the line.

Par
The number of strokes required to finish a hole in regulation. Holes have a par of 3, 4 or 5.

Penalty stroke
When you break a rule, you have to take a penalty stroke—or two—depending on the seriousness of your infraction. See Rules.

PGA
Professional Golfer's Association.

Pin
A commonly used misnomer for the flagstick.

Pitch
A short approach shot that is lofted and stops quickly.

Pitch and putt course
Shorter than an executive course, usually 9 holes with a par of 27. A great place for beginners or to work on the short game.

Pitch and run
A low approach shot that runs to the hole.

Play it down
You must play the ball where it lies.

Play it up
Also known as winter rules. You may roll the ball over for a better lie. Not recognized by the USGA.

Play through
If the group ahead of you is playing slowly, and the hole ahead of them is open, they should invite you to play through. They will step aside, let you tee off and resume their play after you are out of range. Do not hesitate to ask to play through under these circumstances.

Plugged lie
A common occurrence whenever the ground is very wet and your ball is embedded in the ground. You have some options: Play it where it lies, no penalty. Move it if it's in casual water, no penalty. If the course is using winter rules, lift, clean, and place it, no closer to the hole penalty free. If none of the above situations exist, you can declare it unplayable, drop, and take one penalty stroke.

Pot bunker
A sand trap that is small and deep.

Preferred lie
When winter rules are in effect, usually following a severe storm which has caused muddy conditions, a player may move her ball (she may not lift, clean, and place) to improve her lie. Up to six inches, no closer to the hole, is allowed. Preferred lies are not recognized by the Rules of Golf.

Pre-shot routine
Any procedure which mentally and physically prepares you to hit your ball.

Pro-Am
A tournament, usually for charity, in which professional golfers (Pro) play with amateur golfers (Am).

Pull
A wild shot that travels sharply left for right-handed players.

Punch
Under some low trees? Try a punch shot to get back into play. Use a 3- or a 4-iron, close the clubhead a bit and hit the ball firmly off your right foot (rather than from the center of your stance), keeping it low and long enough to get you out of trouble.

Push
A bad shot that travels sharp right for right-handed players.

Putt line
The course your ball must follow to go from where it lies on the green into the cup.

Rain maker
> A popped up shot off the tee that goes high into the sky instead of long and low.

Ranger
> An employee of a golf course who patrols the course to keep the pace of play moving smoothly. The ranger has the authority to revoke the privileges of individuals who are intentionally hitting into other players or being a nuisance on the course.

Ready golf
> An agreement among players that speeds play because players hit when ready, assuming it is safe to do so.

Recovery shot
> A difficult or risky shot made from a trouble area, such as heavy rough or a stand of trees.

Relief
> If your ball rolls into casual water or ends up on a cart path, you are entitled to relief. See Rules.

Rider
> Term coined by my friend, Terry Hansberry, when she was taking up the game and would hit the ball far enough to warrant actually getting into the cart and "riding" to the next shot!

Rough
> The long grass on the golf course on either side of the fairway.

Rub of the green
> Term used to define a ball in flight accidentally stopped or deflected by an outside agency such as an observer, a forecaddie, or marker.

Sand trap
> A hazard filled with sand.

Sandbagger
> Not a flattering term. Implies one is a skilled player who keeps her handicap artificially inflated to gain the competitive advantage by getting extra strokes.

Scotch foursome
> A form of competition for males and females. They are a team of either two or four, playing the same ball but alternating shots into the cup. Can be completed over 9 or 18 holes.

Glossary

Scramble
An outing format and a term used when someone gets out of trouble to make par. As an outing format teams of two or four continuously pick the best shot. Then all players hit from that location until the ball is holed.

Scratch player
A person with a zero handicap, shooting even par on average.

Scuff
A shot hit thin or a mark on the cover of your ball.

Set up
Your posture and ball position at address.

Shank
When the ball is hit by the hosel instead of the clubface and ricochets right.

Short game
Usually described as beginning about 100 yards from the green. This is when the skillful use of wedges and accurate chipping and putting are critical to a good score.

Short irons
The 7-, 8-, and 9-irons and all wedges.

Shotgun start
A competition format which allows all contenders to start at different holes on the course at the same time, thus allowing everyone to finish at about the same time.

Skins
A wager which moves from hole to hole with the lowest score winning. In the event of a tie on a given hole, the skin just rolls over until a player wins the next hole outright.

Skulled
Hitting the top of the ball with the club. Also called a topped or thin shot. Result: a dribbled shot.

Slice
An out-of-control shot that goes off to the right for a right handed player. A slice is the most common ailment for amateur golfers and is often associated with improper grip, clubhead position at impact, and weight transfer.

Spoon
An old term for a 3-wood.

Square
A term for a match that is all even, or a term regarding a stance which has feet, shoulders, elbows, and knees parallel to the target line.
Square face
The correct position for the clubhead at impact.
Stance
The position of your feet with regard to the target line at address.
Starter
The person at the golf course responsible for signaling players towards the first tee.
Stroke and distance
A way to get back into play. See Rules.
Stroke hole
The hole(s) where you receive a handicap stroke.
Stroke play
See medal play.
Sweet spot
A small area on every clubface which, when proper contact is made with the ball, results in the best shot in terms of aim, control, and distance.
Swing speed
Measured in miles per hour, it reveals how fast the clubhead is moving at impact.

Take away
Refers to the beginning of your backswing.
Tee
The implement, usually wood, on which you place your ball for a tee shot. Also refers to the tee box.
Tee box
The area in which a player may tee up.
Tempo
Refers to the pace or speed at which you swing.
Texas wedge
The term used when a putter is used for a shot off the green. For example, hitting a ball out of a sand trap that has no lip.
Thin shot
A ball hit just slightly on the top, rather than getting under it. They never travel very far.

Glossary

Through the green
The whole area of the golf course, except the teeing ground and the putting green of the hole being played and any hazards.

Toed shot
A shot hit on the outer area of the clubface. If a shot is sliced, it's often because the player hit the ball "off the toe," which will push the clubface open.

Topped it
Hitting the top of the ball. Similar to a skulled or thin shot.

Trajectory
A ball's height and flight pattern after being hit.

Trap
A bunker.

Triple bogey
Three strokes over par.

Underclub
Another common ailment among amateurs. It means a player has not selected the right club from the bag to hit the ball the distance it needs to get to the green. In other words, someone used a 7-iron instead of a 6 to allow for the wind or the fact that the green was elevated, so the ball didn't quite get there.

Unplayable lie
A ball that can not be hit due to interference from a tree, fence, or other unmovable obstruction. Take a one stroke penalty.

Vardon grip
The most widely used golf grip whereby, for right-handed players, the pinkie finger of the right hand is inserted between the index and middle finger of the left hand, which is supposed to offer the most comfort and control.

Waggle
A little back and forth motion a player makes at address with the clubhead, just before the take away, to keep the body and mind in motion. We waggle to keep our hands relaxed.

Water hazard
Defined by red stakes or paint. See Rules.

Whiff
　　Every golfer's nightmare. It means to miss the ball completely when you are trying to hit it. It counts as a stroke and is one of golf's most humbling experiences.

Wind cheater
　　A solidly hit shot that stays low to avoid trouble from the wind.

Winter rules
　　See preferred lie.

Worm burner
　　A poorly hit shot that rolls along the ground.

Wrist cock
　　During the backswing, the wrists hinge.

Yips
　　An ailment among nervous putters. Nervousness causes the hands and arms to move erratically while putting, producing less than satisfactory results. Also known as a brain cramp among my golfing friends.

BIBLIOGRAPHY

Chapter One

Driscoll, Dawn-Marie and Carol Goldberg. *Members of the Club: The Coming of Age of Executive Women.* New York: Free Press, 1993.

Hyatt Hotels. A report researched and published by Hyatt Hotels on the travel habits and lifestyles of their customers revealed that executive women who are accomplished golfers tend to earn more money than their male counterparts with similar backgrounds and responsibilities.

Ladies Professional Golf Association. "Businesswomen's Golf Council Survey Report." Daytona Beach, FL: 1993. Prepared for The Women in Golf Summit 1993 Steering Committee by the National Golf Foundation.

National Foundation for Women Busienss Owners. "National Study Finds Women in Business Growing Demand for SBA Mentoring Program Reaches Record High." U.S. Small Business Administration, 1995. Report published on status of women and business based on research conducted by the National Foundation for Women Business Owners.

Peters, Tom. *The Pursuit of Wow! Every Person's Guide to Topsy-Turvy Times.* New York: Vintage Press, 1994.

Chapter Two

Penick, Harvey with Bud Shrake. *Harvey Penick's Little Red Book: Lessons and Teachings from a Lifetime in Golf.* New York: Simon and Schuster, 1992.

Chapter Three

Dennis, Larry. *A Beginner's Guide to Golf: How to Get Started and Have Fun Doing It.* Jupiter, FL: National Golf Foundation, 1994.

Gould, David. *The Golfer's Code: A Guide to Customs, Manners and Gamesmanship On and Off the Golf Course.* New York: Fairchild Publications, 1993. Distributed by Triumph Books, Chicago.

The Rules of Golf: The Heart of the Game. Videotape. Features PGA Pro Tom Watson, LPGA Pro Juli Inkster, and ABC/BBC TV Commentator Peter Allis. USGA, 1994. 24 min. Available through the USGA catalog.

Schrook, Chris. *Spalding Women's Golf Handbook.* Indianapolis: Masters Press, 1995.

United States Golf Association. *The Official Rules of Golf.* Chicago: Triumph Books, 1998. The rules of golf are revised every four years by the USGA.

Women in Business and Golf: How Women Can Use Golf in the Business World. Videotape. Bergdorf Productions, Inc., 1992. 28 min. Available by calling (216) 668-2009.

The Women's Golf Guide: Understanding the Game, Its Rules and Etiquette. Videotape. Features LPGA teaching professional Helene Landers. 60 min. Available by calling (800) 637-3557.

Chapter Four

United States Golf Association. *USGA Handicap Systems Manual.* USGA. To order, write to USGA Order Department, P.O. Box 708, Far Hills, NJ 07931.

Chapter Five

Dennis, Larry. *A Beginner's Guide to Golf: How to Get Started and Have Fun Doing It.*

Chapter Eight

Chambers, Marcia. *The Unplayable Lie: The Untold Story of Women and Discrimination in American Golf.* New York: Golf Digest and Pocket Books, 1995.

Fornoff, Susan. "Equal Time." *Golf Magazine* June 1995: 162-63.

Appendices Sources

Balliett, William and F. Stop Fitzgerald. *USA Today Golf Atlas: The Traveling Golfer's Road Companion.* New York: H. M. Gousha, 1993.

Golf Digest. *Places to Play.* Trumbull, CT: Golf Digest, 1995.

Golf Digest. "The 65 Golfiest Places in America." *Golf Digest* January 1995.

Lane, James M. *Peterson's Golf Schools and Resorts.* Princeton, NJ: Peterson's, 1995.

McCord, Robert. *The Best Public Golf Courses in the United States, Canada, the Caribbean, and Mexico: A Complete Guide to 617 Courses.* New York: Random House, 1993.

Pedroli, Hubert and Mary Tiegreen. *The American Golfer's Guide.* Atlanta: Turner Publishing, Inc., 1992.

Executive Golfer's Guide. Atlanta: Turner Publishing, Inc., 1995.

Penick, Harvey with Bud Shrake. *For All Who Play the Game: Lessons and Teaching for Women.* New York: Simon and Schuster, 1995.

INDEX

A
Academy of Golf Dynamics, 205
ace, 267
addressing the ball, 17, 47, 267
adjusted score, 267
Alabama
  golf courses and resorts, 162
  golf school, 203
  women's golf groups, 220, 250
Alaska
  golf course, 180
  women's golf group, 251
albatross, 267
alumni associations, 219
"A" membership, 111
America's Favorite Golf Schools, 205
apron, 267
Arizona
  female friendly courses, 139
  golf courses and resorts, 175-76
  golf schools and clinics, 202, 205, 206, 207
  women's golf groups, 220-21, 251
Arizona Department of Tourism, 175
Arkansas
  golf courses, 162
  women's golf groups, 251-52
Arlington Women's Golf Association, 213
Arnies, 70
Atlanta
  golf clinic, 203
  golf courses, 130, 168
  golf website, 213
  women's golf group, 229-30

B
backspin, 267
Bahamas
  golf courses and resorts, 186-87
  golf schools, 205, 209
balata ball, 28
ball markers, 50-51, 52, 273
ball mark repair tool, 51
ball marks, repairing, 51, 52
balls. *See* golf balls
Baltimore
  female friendly courses, 130-31
  women's golf group, 234
barkies, 70
baseball grip, 99-100, 267
beginners, 9
  hosting guests, 77
  golf courses for, 11, 275
  and lessons, 17-19, 22
  mentoring, 99
  purchasing equipment, 24-25
  schools and clinics for, 202, 204
  tees for, 35
  tips for, 11, 27, 28, 36, 99-100

Bell, Peggy Kirk, 204
Berg, Patty, 123
Bermuda courses and resorts, 187-88
best ball, 267
bets, 35, 67, 68-72
better ball, 69
bingle bangle bungle, 69
bingo bango bungo, 69
birdie, 267
bite, 267
blind hole, 267
"B" membership, 110, 111
bogey, 267
Bond, Susan, 34, 84-85
Boston
  female friendly courses, 131
  golf clinic, 202
  women's golf group, 234-35
bunkers, 42-43, 44, 268
Business and Professional Women's Golf Association (BPWGA), ix, 117
business associations, 97
business discussions during golf outing, 81, 86, 92
business leaders, 3-4, 77, 109, 112
business women. *See* executive women

C
caddies, 79-80, 151, 268
Cahill, Christine, 77-78
California
  female friendly courses, 136, 140-42
  golf courses and resorts, 181-83
  golf schools and clinics, 202, 203-204, 205, 206, 207, 208
  golf website, 215, 216
  women's golf groups, 221-24, 252-53
Canada
  golf courses and resorts, 190-94
  golf schools, 205, 208
  women's golf groups, 266
career goals, 4, 6, 13, 76, 97
Caribbean courses and resorts, 186-87, 188-89
carry, 268
casual water, 43, 44, 268
Cedar Brook Golf and Tennis Club, 107-109
Chambers, Marcia, 107, 112
Chapman, 71-72
charity outings, 28, 71, 75, 89-90, 276
  what to expect at, 91-93
Chicago
  female friendly courses, 131
  golf courses, 171
  golf school and clinics, 203
  women's golf group, 231
Chipmunk Golf, 213
chip shots, 20, 21, 268

283

Cincinnati
  female friendly courses, 132
  women's golf group, 241-42
Cleveland
  female friendly courses, 132
  women's golf group, 242
clients
  golf outings with, 4, 5-6, 90
  hosting for round, 77, 78-79, 81-86
  identifying golfers among, 7, 75
  and personalized attention, 4-6, 76
closed face, 268
closed stance, 268
club. See private clubs
clubface, 24, 25, 269, 274, 279
club grips, 24, 26-27
clubhead, 24, 40, 279
clubhead speed, 25, 28
clubs
  and caddies, 80
  construction of, 23-24, 200
  distance from, 20, 47
  grounding, 41, 42
  insurance for, 25
  maintenance of, 26-27
  number allowed, 34-35
  purchasing first set of, 24-25
  traveling with, 25
club selection, 45, 47, 280
Colorado
  female friendly courses, 133-34
  golf courses and resorts, 178
  golf schools, 203, 205
  women's golf groups, 224, 253
Columbus
  female friendly courses, 132-33
  golf courses, 174
  women's golf group, 242
comfort zone, pushing, 99
community involvement, 76-77
company-sponsored golf events, 89-91, 98-99
compression, 28
Connecticut
  golf courses, 153
  golf school, 205
  women's golf groups, 225
corporate culture, 3-4, 76, 98, 112
corporate outings, 90, 98. See also company-sponsored golf events
country club. See private clubs
course architecture, 8, 14
Course Handicap Table, 61
course rating and slope, 11, 59, 61, 63, 129
course management, 122, 273
course rules. See local rules
Craft, Linda, 200, 202
Craft-Zavichas Golf School, 202
cup lip, 52, 53, 273
customers. See clients
cycling, 119

D
Dallas
  female friendly courses, 133
  golf clinics, 203
  golf courses, 177
  women's golf group, 264
Dave Pelz Short Game School, 205
David Leadbetter Academy of Golf, 206
Decisions on the Rules of Golf, 55
deep breathing exercises, 118
Delaware golf courses, 153
Denver
  female friendly courses, 133-34
  women's golf group, 224
Detroit
  female friendly courses, 134
  golf clinics, 203
  women's golf group, 235
discrimination at private clubs, 14, 104, 105, 106-109, 113
  handling, 107, 111-12
disqualification, rules about, 35, 46
distance balls, 27
District of Columbia. See Washington, DC
"Divorce Open," 72
divots, 10, 37-38, 269
dogleg, 269
dormie, 269
double bogey, 269
double eagle, 267, 269
double par, 269
draw, 269
dress codes, 28
Driscoll, Dawn-Marie, 4
driver, 20
driving range, tips for using, 19-20, 21
dropping a ball
  how to, 41
  situations for, 42, 43, 44-45, 48
Duval, Betsy Ann, 10-11

E
eagle, 269
equipment. See golf equipment
Equitable Stroke Control, 48, 60-61
etiquette of golf
  for caddies, 79-80
  for cart driver, 48-50
  and cell phones and beepers, 82
  and divots, 37-38
  for fairways, 45-46
  and foursome behind yours, 54, 69, 72
  on green, 50, 51-53, 54
  importance of, 34, 77
  at ninth hole, 82
  for tee box, 38, 39-40
  for wagers, 72
executive course, 269
executive women, 3, 4, 97-99, 219. See also golf and women
Executive Women's Golf Association (EWGA), 129, 219-50

Index

F

fade, 270
fairway, 45-46, 49, 270
fat, hitting the ball, 268, 270
flagstick, 51, 52, 53, 270, 274
flight, 270
Florida
   female friendly courses, 136, 143-44
   golf courses and resorts, 163-67
   golf schools, 202-203, 205, 206, 207-209
   women's golf groups, 226-29, 253-54
Florida Division of Tourism, 163
Floyd, Marlene, 203
follow-through, 17, 270
fore, 39, 270
Forman, Ronald, 108
Fort Worth
   female friendly courses, 134-35
   women's golf group, 248
four-ball, 69, 270
free lift, 270
Freeman, Stephanie, 106-107
fringe, 270
full membership in private club, 104, 110, 111

G

Garbage, 70
Georgia
   female friendly courses, 130
   golf courses and resorts, 167-68
   golf schools and clinics, 203, 205, 207
   women's golf groups, 229-30, 254
Gillette LPGA Golf Clinics, 202
gimme putt, 33, 52, 271, 272
Goldberg, Carol R., 4
golf
   and advice, 84, 99
   and alcohol, 85-86, 92
   and anger, 83, 123
   for beginners (*see* beginners)
   as business tool, 4-8, 12, 13, 75-77, 89-90, 93 (*see also* business discussions during golf outing)
   and career goals, 4, 6, 13, 76, 97
   cheaters at, 83
   committing to, 12-13
   costs of, 13, 59, 79, 151, 271 (*see also* charity outings)
   dealing with difficult people during, 83-84
   dressing for, 28-29
   equalizing nature of, 8 (*see also* handicaps)
   focusing on, 19, 67, 122, 123
   as fun, 11, 124
   as game of honor, 8, 33
   inviting business associates to play, 75, 77-78
   hosting a round of, 77, 78-79, 81-86
   and keeping your head down, 17
   letting others win at, 84-85
   mechanics of, 17, 23
   and meditation, 118
   mental skills for, 84, 117, 118-19, 122-23
   as mentoring tool, 98-99, 100
   origins of, 199-200
   playing within yourself, 123-24
   and poor play, 48, 60, 84, 122-23
   popularity of, 103, 104-105, 112-13
   and positive thinking, 117, 118-19, 122-23
   practice routines for, 19-21
   record book for, 12-13
   as revealing character, 8, 76, 84
   rules of (*see* rules of golf)
   and self-control, 8, 83, 84, 122, 123
   snacks and hydration during round of, 83
   speeding play of (*see* speeding play of golf)
   stretching for, 29, 119-21
   strength building for, 119
   time management for, 12-13
   wagering on round of, 35, 67, 68-72
   and the weather, 28-29, 54-55
   and women, 3, 9-14 (*see also* executive women)
   See also golf balls; golf clubs; golf courses; golf instruction; golf lessons; golf outings; golf schools; golf vacations
Golf, 200
golf bag, 30, 50
golf balls
   buckets of, 19
   construction of, 27-28, 200
   damaged during play, 46
   dropping, 41, 42, 43, 44-45, 48
   finding during round, 38, 45, 47
   hitting another player's, 46-47
   marking on green, 50-51
   picking up during hole, 46, 48, 53, 60-61
   playing a second, 38-39
   special marks on, 36, 46, 47
   teeing, 36
   tips on using, 36, 38, 39
   types of, 27-28
golf camp. *See* golf schools
golf carts, 45, 48-50, 91
golf clinics, 22, 98, 202
Golf Clinic, The, 206
golf club. *See* private clubs
golf clubs. *See* clubs
golf competition forms, 67-68
golf courses, 149
   conduct on (*see* etiquette of golf)
   damage and repair of, 37-38, 51, 52-53
   female friendly, 103, 106, 129-145
   improvements to, 200-201
   listings of, 130-45, 153-96
   public, 103
   skill level ratings of, 11, 59, 61, 129
   types of, 269, 272, 274
   vacations and, 149, 150
   websites on, 213, 214, 215, 216

285

Golf Digest, 200, 213
Golf Digest Schools, 206-207
golf equipment, 14, 23-28, 213. *See also* golf balls; golf clubs
golf etiquette. *See* etiquette of golf
golf exercises, 119-21
Golf for Women magazine, ix, 260
Golf Games: The Side Games We Play and Wager, 72
Golf Games Within the Game, 72
golf gloves, 30
golf grip. *See* grip
golfing interviews, 76
golf instruction
  early, 199, 200-201
  video tape, 205, 207
  See also golf lessons; golf schools
golf lessons, 17-20, 22-23, 214, 215. *See also* golf instruction; golf schools
Golf Link, 214
golf news websites, 213-214, 215, 216
golf organizations and groups, 219-66
golf outing management companies, 90-91
golf outings
  company sponsorship, 89-91
  hosting guests, 75, 77, 78-79, 81-86, 98
  See also charity outings
golf packages, 149-50
golf pros, 17-19, 20, 22, 24, 200
golf resorts
  listing of, 153-96
  vacations at, 149-51
golf scholarships, 100
golf schools, 22-23
  listing of, 202-209
  questions to ask about, 201
  resources on, 209
  what to expect, 201-202
golf shoes, 25-26, 27, 51, 52, 85
Golf Travel On-line, 214
golf vacations, 149-51
  websites for, 213-14, 215, 216
Golf Web, 214
golf widows and orphans, 11
grain, 271
green fee, 271
greenies, 70
greens, 49, 50-54, 268
grip, 30, 99-100, 271
gross birdies, 70
gross score, 63, 68, 267, 271
grounding the club, 41, 42, 271
ground under repair, 44, 271
gurglies, 70
gutta-percha ball, 200

H
Hale Irwin's Golfer's Passport Program, 214
Handicap Index, 59-60, 61
handicaps, 59-63, 68, 69, 271
  improving, 201-202

hard pan, 271
Haskell ball, 200
Hawaii
  golf courses and resorts, 183-84
  golf schools, 206
  women's golf groups, 230, 254
hawk, pig, or wolf, 71
hazards, 47, 48, 271. *See also* bunkers; water hazards
head covers, 26
heel, 24
heeled shot, 272
Hilton Head courses and resorts, 160
historic areas for golf, 154, 161, 169
Hogans, 70
holing out, 52
honor, 35-36, 272
hook, 272
hosel, 24, 272
hosting a round of golf, 77, 78-79, 81-86
Houston
  female friendly courses, 135
  women's golf group, 248
hydration, 80, 83, 85

I
Idaho
  golf courses and resorts, 179
  golf school, 207
  women's golf group, 255
Illinois
  female friendly courses, 131
  golf courses, 171
  golf schools and clinics, 204, 205, 207
  women's golf groups, 231, 255
Index, 272. *See also* Handicap Index
Indiana
  golf courses, 171
  golf school, 209
  women's golf group, 231
instruction. *See* golf instruction; golf lessons; golf schools
instructors, choosing, 17-19
interlocking grip, 99-100
international golf courses, 186-96
international golf schools, 203, 205, 206, 208, 209
Internet, 149, 213-16
Iowa
  golf courses, 172
  women's golf groups, 232, 255
irons, 24, 273, 278
  working with, 19-20, 21

J
Jamaica golf courses, 188
John Jacobs' Golf School, 203
junior equipment, 213
junior golfers, 100
junior golf programs, 205, 206

Index

K

Kansas
  golf courses and resorts, 172
  women's golf groups, 255
Kansas City
  female friendly courses, 135
  women's golf group, 255
Kentucky
  golf courses and resorts, 169
  women's golf groups, 233, 256

L

Ladies Professional Golf Association (LPGA), 18, 215. *See also* LPGA events
lag putt, 272
Las Vegas
  golf courses, 185
  golf schools, 203, 205
  women's golf groups, 237, 259
lateral water hazards, 42
Leadbetter, David, 206
lie, 272. *See also* preferred lie, unplayable lie
lift, clean, and place, 46
lightning, what to do in, 54-55
line, 272
links, 272
lip, 52, 53, 273
Little Red Book, 17
local rules, 46, 48-49, 50, 273
loft, 24, 273
long irons, 273
loose impediments, 41, 42, 47, 53
Los Angeles
  golf clinics, 203
  female friendly courses, 136
  women's golf group, 222
Louisiana
  golf courses and resorts, 169
  women's golf groups, 233, 256
low-ball, 71
Lowell, Lee, 107-109
LPGA events, 156, 163, 165, 183, 185
  sponsoring, 90-91

M

Maine
  golf courses and resorts, 153
  women's golf group, 256
male golfers, 9-10, 84
Mann, Ralph, 207
marker. *See* ball marker
Marlene Floyd's for Women Only Golf School, 203
Maryland
  female friendly courses, 130-31
  golf courses, 157
  golf school, 208
  women's golf groups, 233-34, 257

Massachusetts
  female friendly course, 131
  golf clinics, 203
  golf courses and resorts, 154
  women's golf groups, 234-35
match play, 67-69, 70-71, 269, 274
McQuillan, Leslie, 75-76
medal play, 61, 67, 68, 71, 273
meditation, 118
membership associations, 97
Members of the Club: The Coming of Age of Executive Women, 4
mentoring, 97, 98-99, 100
Mexico
  golf courses and resorts, 195-96
  women's golf group, 266
Mexican Government Tourism Office, 196
Miami
  female friendly course, 136
  golf courses, 164, 167
  women's golf group, 228
Michaels, Susan, 99
Michigan
  female friendly course, 134
  golf courses and resorts, 172
  golf schools and clinics, 202-203, 207
  golf website, 214
  women's golf groups, 235, 257-58
Mid-Atlantic region courses and resorts, 157-61
middle irons, 273
Midwest region courses and resorts, 171-75
Milwaukee golf courses, 137
Minneapolis/St. Paul
  female friendly courses, 137
  golf courses and resorts, 173
  women's golf group, 236
Minnesota
  female friendly courses, 137
  golf courses, 173
  golf school, 209
  women's golf group, 236
Mississippi
  golf courses, 170
  golf school, 209
  women's golf groups, 258
Missouri
  female friendly courses, 135, 143
  golf courses and resorts, 173
  golf school, 203
  women's golf groups, 236, 258
Montana golf courses, 179
mulligans, 33, 71, 273
muscle memory, 20, 23
Myrtle Beach
  golf courses and resorts, 158-59
  women's golf group, 246
Myrtle Beach Golf Holiday, 158
My Usual Game, 158

287

N

Nassau, 68, 273
National Golf Foundation, 72
Nebraska
　golf courses, 173-74
　women's golf group, 259
net score, 63, 68, 273
networking, 6, 75, 77, 92, 97, 202
Nevada
　golf courses and resorts, 185
　golf schools, 203, 205
　women's golf groups, 237, 259
New Hampshire
　golf courses and resorts, 154
　golf school, 208
　women's golf groups, 237, 259
New Jersey
　golf courses and resorts, 155
　golf school, 203
　women's golf groups, 237-38, 259
New Mexico
　golf courses and resorts, 176
　women's golf groups, 238, 260
Newport News. *See* Virginia
　Beach/Norfolk/Newport News
New York City
　female friendly courses, 138
　golf clinic, 203
　women's golf group, 239
New York State
　female friendly course, 138
　golf courses and resorts, 155
　golf schools and clinics, 202, 203, 208, 209
　women's golf groups, 238-39, 260-61
Nicklaus/Flick Golf Schools, 207
nineteenth hole, 85-86, 274
19th Hole (website), 215
ninety degree rule, 49, 274
Norfolk. *See* Virginia Beach/Norfolk/Newport News
North Carolina
　golf courses and resorts, 157-58
　golf schools, 204, 207
　golf website, 213
　women's golf groups, 239-40, 261
North Dakota golf course, 174
Northeast region courses and resorts, 153-157
NuGolf, 215
nutrition, 82, 83

O

OB, 38-39, 48
obstructions, 43, 47-48
offie, 70
O'Hara, Nancy, 13
Ohio
　female friendly courses, 132-33
　golf course, 174
　women's golf groups, 241-43, 261-62

Oklahoma
　golf courses, 176-77
　women's golf groups, 243, 262
O'Neill, Paul H., 112
open face, 274
open stance, 274
Oregon
　female friendly courses, 140
　golf courses and resorts, 185-86
　golf schools, 203, 207
　women's golf groups, 243-44, 263
out-of-bounds, 38-39, 48
Owens, David, 158

P

par, 274
Parker Golf, 215
penalties, 46-47
　and equipment, 49, 54
　on greens, 52, 53-54
　for grounding club, 41, 42
　with hazards, 41, 42, 43
　for loose impediments, 42, 47
　for out-of-bounds shots, 38, 39
　situations without, 36-37, 39, 43, 46, 54
　for tee shots, 36
　for unplayable lies, 43, 48
penalty-free relief, 43, 44-45
penalty stroke, 274. *See also* penalties
Penick, Harvey, 17
Pennsylvania
　female friendly courses, 138, 139-40
　golf courses and resorts, 156
　golf schools, 205, 208
　women's golf groups, 244-45, 263
Peters, Tom, 4
PGA. *See* Professional Golfer's Association
PGA events, 70, 161, 163, 165, 166, 185
　sponsoring, 90-91
PGA Skins Games, 70
Philadelphia
　female friendly courses, 138
　women's golf group, 244
Phoenix
　female friendly courses, 139
　golf courses, 175
　golf schools and clinics, 202, 205, 207
　women's golf group, 221
pin. *See* flagstick
Pine Needles/Golfari (golf school), 204
pitch, 274
pitch and putt course, 274
Pittsburgh
　female friendly courses, 139-40
　women's golf group, 245
planning committees, 89-90
playing it down, 38, 46, 274
playing through, 82, 275
playing within yourself, 123-24
plugged lie, 275

Index

Portland
  female friendly courses, 140
  women's golf group, 243
positive thinking, 117, 118-19, 122-23
pot bunker, 275
practice, need for, 20-21, 22
practice putting green, 20, 21
practice swings, 37, 40, 42, 118-19
preferred lie, 46, 275
pre-shot routine, 275
press (wager), 68-69
private clubs
  advantages of, 18, 113
  culture of, 104-105, 106-107, 111
  discrimination at, 14, 104, 105, 106-109, 111-12, 113
  joining, 103-104, 109-111
  lessons from, 18
  and non-members, 18, 113
Pro-Am outings, 92-93, 275
probation period, 110-11
Professional Golfer's Association (PGA), 18, 200, 215. *See also* PGA events
Professional Golf Schools of America, 207-08
prospects and golf, 4, 5-6, 76. *See also* clients
provisional ball, using, 38, 39
Puerto Rico
  golf courses and resorts, 188-89
  women's golf group, 266
pull, 275
pull cart, 50
punch shot, 275
Pursuit of Wow, The, 4
push, 275
putting, 20-21, 52-54, 267, 280. *See also* gimme putt
putt line, 51, 52, 53, 275

Q

Quiet Corner, A, 13

R

Rafuse, Bonnie, 34
rain suit, 29
ranger, 11, 276
rating
  defined, 59
  using, 11, 61, 63, 129
ready golf, 35, 45, 276
record book, keeping, 12-13
recovery shot, 276
red lines and stakes, 41, 42
relief, 38, 43, 48, 276
  penalty-free, 43, 44-45
Rhode Island
  golf courses, 156
  women's golf groups, 263-64
Robert Trent Jones Trail, 162
Rocky Mountain Region courses, 178-80
Roland Stafford Golf Schools, 208
rough, 47, 276

rowing, 119
Royal and Ancient Golf Club of St. Andrews, 33
Royko, Mike, 84
rules of golf, 34-37, 38-39, 40-49, 51, 52-54
  bending, 33-34
  cheaters, 83
  importance, 34, 77
  learning, 33, 34, 55

S

Sacramento golf courses, 140-41
San Antonio
  female friendly courses, 141
  women's golf group, 248
San Diego
  female friendly courses, 141-42
  golf courses, 183
  women's golf groups, 222-23, 252
sandies, 70
sand trap, 276. *See also* hazards
San Francisco
  female friendly courses, 142
  golf clinics, 203
  women's golf group, 223
School of Golf, 204
score cards
  and handicaps, 59, 61
  marking, 50
  stroking, 35, 61-63
Scotch foursome, 276
Scotland, golf history of, 199-200
scramble, 47, 69, 71, 77, 277
scratch, playing at, 62
scratch player, 59, 277
Seattle
  female friendly courses, 142-43
  women's golf group, 249
self-control, 8, 83, 84, 122, 123
set-up routines, 37, 277
shaft, 24, 25
shag bags, 19
shank, 277
short game, 20-21, 277
  schools for, 203, 204, 206, 207
short irons, 19, 277
shotgun start, 277
side bets, 68-69, 70
Six Six Six, 69
skins game, 70-71, 277
slice, 269, 277
slope, 11, 59, 61, 129
slow play. *See* speeding play of golf
Smith, John F., Jr., 112
snacks, 82, 83
social member of private club, 111
soft spikes, 26
sole, 24
South Carolina
  golf courses and resorts, 150, 159-60
  golf schools, 205, 208

289

golf websites, 213, 216
women's golf groups, 245-46, 264
South Dakota golf courses, 174
Southern region courses and resorts, 162-70
Southwest region courses and resorts, 175-77
speeding play of golf, 39, 45, 49, 82
  bending rules, 33-34
  greens, 50
  picking up ball, 48
  ready golf, 35, 45
spikes, 26, 27, 51, 52, 85
Spork, Shirley, 204
spouse member, 110, 111
square face, 278
Stableford, 72
stance, 278
starter, 81, 278
St. Croix courses and resorts, 189
St. Louis
  female friendly courses, 143
  women's golf group, 236
St. Paul. *See* Minneapolis/St. Paul
stroke and distance, 38, 39, 41, 42, 43
stroke hole, 278
stroke play, 61, 67, 68, 71, 274
stroking a scorecard, 61-63
summer rules, 38
Sutton, Ben, 200
sweet spot, 24, 25, 278
swimming, 119
swing mechanics, 17, 23
Swing's The Thing Golf Schools, 208

T

take away, 17, 278
Tampa
  female friendly courses, 143-44
  golf courses and resort, 166
  women's golf group, 229
teaching methods, 17-19
team play formats, 68-68, 71-72
tee, 36, 278
tees, 35-37, 278
  design of, 8, 14, 35
  etiquette for, 39-40
  handicaps and, 63
tees times, 104, 105, 106, 107
tempo, 278
Tennessee
  golf courses and resorts, 170
  women's golf groups, 246-47, 264
tennis, 119
Texas
  female friendly courses, 133, 134-35, 141
  golf courses and resorts, 177
  golf schools and clinics, 203, 205
  golf website, 213
  women's golf groups, 247-48, 264-65
tipping, 79, 151
Titleist, 27
Title IX of the Education Amendments, 105

Title VII of the Civil Rights Act of 1964, 105, 106
touring pros, 200
tournament play, 61, 63, 68
trap. *See* bunkers
Trash, 70
triple bogey, 279
twilight league, 12, 60

U

underclub, 279
United States Golf Association (USGA)
  listing of women's groups, 250-66
  website, 215
United States Golf Schools, 209
unplayable lies, 41, 42, 43-44, 48, 279
Unplayable Lie: The Untold Story of Women and Discrimination in American Golf, The, 107-109, 112
USGA Handicap System, 59
USGA Handicap System Manual, 63
USGA Official Rules Book, 33, 46, 55, 83
Utah
  golf courses, 179-80
  golf school, 203
  women's golf groups, 249, 265

V

valuables, taking care of, 80
Vardon grip, 99-100, 279
Vermont
  golf courses and resorts, 156-57
  women's golf group, 265
Virginia
  female friendly courses, 144
  golf courses and resorts, 160-61
  golf school, 205
  women's golf groups, 249, 265
Virginia Beach/Norfolk/Newport News
  female friendly course, 144
  women's golf group, 249
Von Klemperer, Cathy, 12-13, 117, 123

W

wagers during round, 35, 67, 68-72
waggle, 279
waiting lists at private clubs, 110
walking, 119
warm-up before round, 19-20, 81
Washington, DC
  female friendly courses, 144-45
  golf clinic, 203
  women's golf group, 226
Washington State
  female friendly courses, 142-43
  golf courses, 186
  women's golf groups, 249
water, casual, 43, 44
water hazards, 40-42, 279
WebGuide Golf, 216

Index

weight training, 119
Western region courses and resorts, 180-86
West Virginia
   golf courses and resorts, 161
   women's golf group, 266
whiffs, 37, 280
white lines or stakes, 38-39, 44, 50
wind shirt, 29
winter rules, 33, 46, 275
Wisconsin
   female friendly courses, 137
   golf courses and resorts, 174-75
   golf school, 203
   women's golf group, 250, 266
women
   in business, 3, 4 (*see also* executive women)
   discrimination against, 104, 105-109, 111-12, 113
   and golf, 3, 9-14
   and golf clubs, 25
   golf courses for, 82-83, 129-45
   golf groups for, 219-63
   golf schools for, 202-204
   and private club memberships, 104, 106-107, 109-110, 111-12, 113-14
   tees for, 8, 14, 35

women executives. *See* executive women
women-friendly courses, 82-83, 129-45
women-only business groups, 97
women's golf groups, 219-66
women's golf schools, 202-204
women's golf websites, 213, 215, 216
woods, 20, 21, 24
World Golf, 216
World Wide Web, 213-16
worm burner, 280
wrist cock, 280
Wyoming
   golf courses and resorts, 180
   golf school, 203

Y

Yahoo, 216
yardage markers, 20, 45
yellow lines or stakes, 40, 41
yips, 280

Z

Zavichas, Penny, 200, 202

GOLF COURSES AND RESORTS

See also under state and city names in main index.

A
Acapulco Princess Golf Club, 195
Algonquin Resort, 191
Amana Colonies Golf Course, 172
Amelia Island Plantation, 163
Anchorage Golf Course, 180
Ancil Hoffman Park Golf Course, 140
Angus Glen Golf Club, 192
Arrowhead Golf Club, 178
Ashbourne Country Club, 138
Astorhurst Country Club, 132
Atlantis, Paradise Island, 186
Aviara, 141

B
Baker National Golf Course, 137
Banff Springs, 190
Bardmoor North Golf Club, 163
Bay Hills Golf Club, 130
Bayshore Golf Course, 136
Bear Creek (Texas), 135
Bear Creek Golf Club (Maryland), 130
Belle Terre Country Club, 169
Belmont Hotel and Golf Club, 187
Bent Creek Golf Resort, 170
Bent Oak Golf Club, 135
Bent Tree Golf Club, 174
Big Sky Golf Club, 179
Bing Maloney Golf Course, 140
Black Hawk Golf Course, 139
Blackledge Country Club, 153
Blackwolf Run, 175
Bluffs on Thompson Creek, 169
Boca Raton Resort and Club, 163
Bodega Harbour Golf Links, 181
Bonaventure Country Club, 164
Breckenridge Golf Club, 178
Brigantine Golf Links, 138
Broadmoor, 178
Buffalo Run Golf Course, 133
Bunker Hills Golf Course, 137

C
Cabo del Sol Golf Club, 195
Camelback Golf Club, 139
Canaan Valley Resort, 161
Carambola Beach Resort and Golf Club, 189
Carling Lake, 194
Castle Harbour Golf Club, 187
Cedar Creek, 141
Champions Club, 130
Chardonnay Club, 181
Chateau Elan Golf Club, 167
Cherokee Village South Golf Course, 162
Clifton Park Golf Course, 130
Coeur d'Alene Resort, 179
Cog Hill Golf and Country Club, 171

Colonial, 131
Cooks Creek Golf Club, 132
Copper Creek, 134
Coronado Golf Course, 141
Cotton Bay Club, 187
Country Club of Wisconsin, 137
Crandon Park Golf Course, 136
Crooked Tree, 132
Crumpin-Fox Club, 154

D
Deer Run Golf Club, 139
Del Webb's Sun City Roseville, 141
Desert Inn Golf Club, 185
Divi Bahamas Beach Resort and Country Club, 187
Doral Golf Resort and Spa, 164
Dub's Dread Golf Club, 135

E
Eagle Lodge Country Club, 138
Eagles Golf Course, 143
Eastmoreland, 140
Eastwood Golf Course, 164
Edgewood Golf Course, 174
Edinburgh USA, 137
Elkhorn Resort, 179
Emerald River Resort and Country Club, 185

F
Forest Park Golf Course, 143
Forest Ridge Golf Club, 177
Fossil Creek, 134
Four Seasons Resort and Club (Texas), 177
Fox Creek Golf Club, 130
Foxfire Golf Club, 133
Fox Hills Golf and Convention Center, 134
Fox Hollow, 134

G
Garland, 172
Geneva Farm Golf Club, 131
Ghost Creek at Pumpkin Ridge, 140
Glen Abbey Golf Club, 193
Golden Ocala Golf Course, 164
Golf Center at King's Island, 132
Golf Club of Illinois, 171
Golf Club of Indiana, 171
Golf Resort at Indian Wells, 181
Goose Creek Golf Club, 144
Grand Cypress Golf Club, 164, 205
Grand Traverse Resort, 172
Greenbrier, 161

Golf Course and Resort Index

H
Half Moon Bay Golf Links, 142
Half Moon Golf Club, 188
Heritage Hills Golf Course, 173
Heron Lakes, 140
High Hampton Inn, 157
Homestead, 160
Hominy Hill Golf Course, 155
Horseshoe Bay Resort, 177
Hyatt Bear Creek Golf and Racquet Club, 133
Hyatt Dorado Beach, 188
Hyatt Regency Cerromar Beach, 188-89

I
Incline Village Golf Resort, 185
Indian Canyon Golf Course, 186
Innisbrook Hilton Resort, 165
Inn of the Mountain Gods, 176
Isla Navidad Country Club, 195
Izatys Golf and Yacht Club, 173

J
Jackson Hole Golf and Tennis Club, 180
Jackson Park Golf Club, 142
Jefferson Park, 143
Jeremy Ranch Golf Club, 179
Juniper Hill Golf Club, 131

K
Kaluakoi Golf Course, 183
Kapalua Golf Club, 183
Karsten Creek Golf Course, 176
Kearney Hill Golf Links, 169
Keltic Lodge, 192
Kiawah Island Inn and Villa, 159
Kiln Creek Golf and Country Club, 144
Kingsmill Resort, 161
Ko Olina Golf Club, 183

L
La Costa Resort and Spa, 181
Lake Valley Golf Club, 134
Latourette Park Golf Course, 138
Leatherstocking Golf Course, 155
Lindenwood Golf Course, 140
Links at Crowbush Cove, 193
Links at Key Biscayne, 165
Links at Spanish Bay, 181-82
Little Bennett Golf Course, 145
Lodge of the Four Seasons (Missouri), 173

M
Madden's on Gull Lake, 173
Mahogany Run Golf Course, 189
Malibu Country Club, 136
Mallard Creek Golf Club, 132
Manakiki, 132
Marina Ixtapa Golf Club, 196

Marina Vallarta Golf Club, 196
Marriott's Grand Hotel at Lakewood Golf Club, 162
Marriott's Griffin Gate Resort, 169
Marriott's Lincolnshire Golf Course, 131
Marriott's Seaview Resort, 155
Mauna Lani Resort, 184
Meadowbrook Golf Course, 174
Miami National Golf Club, 136
Mountain Ranch Golf Course, 162
Mt. Washington Resort Golf Club, 154
Muskego Lakes Country Club, 137

N
Needwood, 145
Northstar-at-Tahoe, 182

O
Ocean Edge Resort, 154
Ocean View Golf Course, 144
Olde Atlanta Golf Club, 130
Old Orchard Golf Club, 135
Oyster Bay Golf Links, 158

P
Palmas del Mar, 189
Palm Beach Polo and Country Club, 165
Palmilla Golf Club, 196
Park Meadows Golf Club, 180
Pebble Beach Golf Links, 182
Pecan Hollow Golf Course, 133
Pelican's Nest Golf Club, 165
PGA National Golf Club, 165-66
PGA West, 182
Pinehurst Resort and Country Club, 157
Pine Island Golf Club, 170
Pine Meadows, 131
Pit Golf Links, 158
Pointe Golf Club on Lookout Mountain, 139
Port Armor Club, 168
Port Royal Golf Course, 187-88
Port Royal Resort, 160
Presidio Golf Course, 142
Princeville Resort, 184

Q
Quail Creek Golf Club, 143

R
Rancho Park Golf Course, 136
Rancocas Golf Club, 138
Ravines, 166
Raymond Memorial Golf Course, 133
Recreation Park Golf Course, 136
Red Mountain Ranch, 139
Red Wing Lake Golf Course, 144
Resort at Long Boat Key Club, 166
Ridgeview Ranch, 133
Riverchase Golf Club, 135

293

Ron Jaworsky's Garrison's Lake Golf Club, 153
Royal Colwood Golf Club, 190

S

Saddlebrook Resort, 144
Saddlebrook Resort, Tampa, 166
Sagamore Resort, 155
Samoset Resort Golf Club, 153
Sand Hills Golf Club, 173-74
Sandpiper Golf Course, 183
Sandy Burr, 131
San Juan Oaks Golf Club, 142
Sea Island Golf Club, 168
Sea Pines Resort, 160
Sedona Golf Resort, 175
Semiahmoo Golf and Country Club, 186
Sentry World Golf Course, 174
Shamrock, 133
Sheraton Savannah Resort and Country Club, 168
Shipyard Golf Club, 160
Sky Meadow Country Club, 154
Southwick, 135
Spencer T. Olin Community Golf Course, 143
Squaw Valley, 135
St. Christopher's Resort, 191
Steele Canyon Golf and Country Club, 142
Steeple Chase, 131
Stonehenge Golf Club at Fairfield Glade Resort, 170
Stouffer Renaissance PineIsle Resort, 168
Stratton Mountain Country Club, 156
Sugarbush Inn, 157
Sugarloaf Golf Club, 153
Sugar Ridge Golf Club, 132
Sunriver Lodge and Resort, 185
Swan Point, 157
Sycamore Hills, 134

T

Tamarron Resort at Durango, 178
Tamiment Resort, 156
Tapatio Springs Resort, 141
Terradyne Resort Hotel and Country Club, 172
Teton Pines Resort and Country Club, 180
Tidewater Golf Club, 159
Tiger Point Golf and Country Club, 166
Timberton Golf Club, 170
Toftrees Resort, 156
Tokatee Golf Club, 186
Torrey Pines Golf Courses, 183
Tournament Players Club at Sawgrass, 167
Tournament Players Club at Scottsdale, 175
Triggs Memorial Golf Course, 156
Troon North Golf Club, 175
Tryall Golf, Tennis and Beach Club, 188
Turnberry Isle Resort and Club, 167

U

University of New Mexico Golf Course, 176

V

Van Cortlandt Golf Course, 138
Ventana Canyon Golf and Racquet Club, 176
Volcano Golf and Country Club, 184

W

Wailea Golf Club, 184
Walt Disney World Resort, 167
Wasagaming Golf Course, 191
Waterwood National Resort and Country Club, 177
Westchase, 144
Western Lakes Country Club, 137
Whistler, 190
Willow Run Golf Club, 143
Willows Golf and Country Club, 194
Willow Springs, 141
Windbrook Country Club, 135
Wyncote Golf Club, 138